4th Edition Guide to Good Speech

JAMES H. McBURNEY

Northwestern University

ERNEST J. WRAGE

Northwestern University

PRENTICE-HALL, INC., ENGLEWOOD CLIFFS, NEW JERSEY

Library of Congress Cataloging in Publication Data

McBURNEY, JAMES HOWARD, 1905–
    Guide to good speech.

    Includes bibliographical references and index.
    1. Speech.   2. Oratory.   I. Wrage, Ernest J.,
joint author.   II. Title.
PN4121.M173 1975   808.5   74–32427
ISBN 0-13-367938-1

JUN 19 '75

Some of the material in this book appeared, in modified form,
in The Art of Good Speech, published by Prentice-Hall, Inc., in 1953.

Printed in the United States of America

10   9   8   7   6   5   4   3   2   1

PRENTICE-HALL INTERNATIONAL, INC., *London*
PRENTICE-HALL OF AUSTRALIA, PTY. LTD., *Sydney*
PRENTICE-HALL OF CANADA, LTD., *Toronto*
PRENTICE-HALL OF INDIA PRIVATE LIMITED, *New Delhi*
PRENTICE-HALL OF JAPAN, INC., *Tokyo*

Contents

24 Microphone and Camera, *256*

25 Sample Speeches, *261*

Preface

This fourth edition of *Guide to Good Speech,* like its predecessors, is designed to accomplish exactly what the title claims—a book that will guide the readers to good speech in all their personal and public relations.

In this edition we take more direct notice of the contemporary scene in which people speak and listen, the urgencies which this imposes on all communication, and the resulting responsibilities and opportunities for both speakers and listeners. This has led us to a more operational definition of speech in terms of communication and the settings in which it takes place, more explicit explanations of basic philosophical assumptions, and a refined statement of the principles of good speech. It has also led us to reconsider certain pedagogical recommendations.

As a result, the book has been revised to accommodate the doctrine of earlier editions to these new insights. And throughout we have tried to keep in view what we believe to be a growing maturity in today's students —in social awareness, in seriousness of purpose, and in the desire and capacity to communicate.

Each chapter concludes with searching questions addressed to students. These replace the brief chapter summaries, and are designed to invite discussion of critical issues. Hopefully, these will provide a basis for personal philosophies of speech and sound commitments to speech improvement, whether or not they agree with the authors. As before, we also suggest exercises for classroom use.

Guide to Good Speech is an enterprise developed over two decades in the School of Speech at Northwestern University. The book has certainly profited by the observations and use of many teachers and students here and elsewhere. The authors have remained the same throughout the project, in a close partnership, including Dr. Naomi Wrage, a remarkably able student and teacher of speech in her own right.

This revision is the work of the senior author and he assumes responsibility for it. But Dr. Ernest Wrage's substantial contributions to earlier editions continue to give us the benefit of his insights. Knowing him as I did for many years as a close personal friend, student, and colleague, I am sure he would wish to treat charitably what has been done to the book. This edition is dedicated to his memory.

James H. McBurney

1. Speech Communication: The Contemporary Scene

There have been substantial changes in American life and customs in the last few decades—changes in our life styles, in social conventions and behavior, and in our attitudes and goals. To be sure the history of the human race records constant change. We never stand still. But the changes we have seen have been far reaching and at times explosive and cataclysmic. Few institutions in America have escaped the pressures of vigorous dissent. Some have resisted and others have yielded, but the scars remain. We appear to be in uneasy transition with signs of tension all around us.

As a preface to our study, we think it useful to explore the relations of the communicative processes to this contemporary scene. There are two important questions: Are breakdowns in communication a significant factor in this social unrest? And what is the impact of social change on communication?

We face a population explosion that has brought people closer together. We are living longer with wider generation gaps. There are racial, cultural, and economic gaps that breed misunderstanding and cynicism. There is increasing concern that our scientific advances have been achieved at the expense of moral and social stability. We are aware of the erosion of our physical environment. Our natural resources face depletion. New attitudes toward sex and marriage threaten the family. Machines are displacing workers. Economic controls are proving to be less sensitive than we thought them to be. Government has become bigger and more impersonal. Law and order is an omnipresent concern. And the perennial problems of war and peace have reasserted themselves with new dimensions.

It is true that many of these problems peaked in the late 1960s. The violence in the streets and on college campuses has subsided, and ameliorating forces are now at work in other areas. But difficulties and uncertainties remain that challenge our faith and our engagement. Here is where communication has a role to play.

Daniel P. Moynihan, writing in the *Saturday Review World,* points out "the danger of dwelling only, or mainly, on the nation's troubles. . . . To recognize and acknowledge success, however modest, is fundamental to the practice of government. It is a first principle of leadership in a democracy, where loyalty must be directed more to institutions than to individuals."[1] If Mr. Moynihan is right, this counsel most certainly should be heeded by all involved in communication. Too often, however, this has not been the case. There are significant evidences of an adulteration of the quality of communication: the polarization of positions on critical questions; the personalization of social criticism; the politicized style of addressing social problems; and the withdrawal of vast numbers from participation in constructive dialogue dealing with these problems. When opposition becomes inflexible, verbal attack against individuals becomes epidemic and rhetoric becomes inflammatory; the result is a noisy stalemate that weakens morale and institutional stability. Such is the fate of any institution, be it the family, church or synagogue, school or college, community, state, or nation.

This kind of irrationality and withdrawal runs counter to the major thesis of this book. We believe that human problems approached in the spirit of moderation, cooperation, and fair play are amenable to solution. We believe that whenever and wherever we engage in common causes, our successes and failures will be determined in no small part by our capacity to communicate with each other in ways that utilize our best reflective and creative efforts. The need was never greater. When people are thrown closer together, they are going to have to learn to talk together; when people of different ages, races, cultures, and economic resources mistrust each other, they are going to have to learn to talk out their differences; and when emotionally charged issues divide us, we must learn to participate effectively in decision-making deliberations that provide the best hope for their resolution.

People speak to many purposes, and we shall try to consider all worthy purposes, but none is more worthy or more critical in our times than the communication that seeks understanding and mutuality as a basis for constructive action. Speaking to this end imposes high demands on speakers and listeners alike. You have engaged in such deliberation all your lives. Our first purpose here is to develop attitudes, knowledge, and skills that will help you do a better job of it.

Is this asking too much? It shouldn't be! We invite you to read on and draw your own conclusions. Our position is developed more fully in the next chapter.

There is a further question, related but different: What is the impact of social change on communication? To put it more specifically, this is the fourth edition of the *Guide to Good Speech:* Is it reasonable to expect that

[1]September 9, 1973, p. 20.

the principles and methods set out here will be any different from those developed earlier? In other words, does the social, political, and technological milieu in which communication takes place condition the nature and character of this communication?

In his *Rhetoric,* written some 300 years before Christ, Aristotle alleges that speech is an art whose principles are determined by an examination of the methods and practices of successful speakers. If this be the case, since all speech communication involves speakers, media of communication, messages, and listeners, it appears reasonable to conclude that circumstances affecting any of these factors necessarily affect the nature and character of communication. Let's look at this more carefully.

Changes in social mores and in personal attitudes and beliefs have significant impact on both speakers and listeners. The people who talk and listen today are not the same as those who talked and listened a decade ago. They have been conditioned by both their social and physical environment and can be expected to respond differently in communicating.

One of the most dramatic changes in the nature and character of communication has come with television. Here our participation is largely limited to watching and listening. In this passive role we take what is given to us with our choices limited to the numbers on the dial. Most of the forces operate to give us what we want to see and hear, or what is thought we want to see and hear. But the predilections of reporters and commentators inevitably show through. Public opinion polls now "pigeon-hole the network newscasters as to political leanings—at least as the viewers see them—liberal, conservative, or in the ideological middle."[2] It would appear that advocacy journalism creeps into television as it frequently does in the press.

Apart from television, most speech now takes place in relatively informal face-to-face settings where there are opportunities for speakers and listeners to shift roles. Even radio and television present panel discussions and forums. The image of the speaker mounting the platform before a vast audience assembled to hear him is no longer typical. And in any setting, large or small, near or remote, most audiences are more perceptive than ingenuous; eloquence for its own sake is not highly regarded; they want speakers to talk sense.

A whole array of new concerns and divisive issues has changed the prevailing mood and character of the message—the things we talk about and listen to. Often we are breaking new ground without benefit of old precedents. There is a new seriousness in communication; many subjects that were relevant a few decades ago are now dismissed as frivolous and mundane.

Persons of greater and lesser distinction have been studying and

[2]The Doan Report, *T.V. Guide,* Vol. 21, No. 37, Sept. 15, 1973, p. 27.

writing about the principles and methods of speech communication for centuries. These treatments usually mirror the audience and settings for which they are intended. This probably is as it should be. We have tried to accommodate the received principles and methods to the contemporary scene. The result has been shifts in emphasis, what we believe to be new insights (at least for us), and it is hoped, more felicitous statements of old precepts.

Many who read this book may not apply its principles in any professional capacity, but all can share the rewards of responsible communication in our kind of society. These rewards are both personal and social. The chapter that follows sets out the conditions and circumstances under which these rewards can best be realized.

QUESTIONS FOR DISCUSSION

1. Grayson Kirk, President of Columbia University, delivered the commencement address at the University on June 5, 1962; the full text of the speech, *The Malaise of our Times,* appears on pp. 261–65. The seeds of unrest were evident on American college and university campuses in 1962, but few would have predicted the violent eruptions that occurred on many of these campuses a few years later, Columbia included. Read this speech and discuss the questions that follow.

    a. Does President Kirk's analysis of the *causes* of social troubles and cynicism apply today as it did in 1962? Are these same causes operating today? Have times changed significantly?

    b. How would you amend this analysis now, more than a decade later, in the light of subsequent events and the contemporary scene?

    c. What do you see as the role and impact of the mass media (the press, radio, television, and film) in reporting social and political ills?

    d. How do you see the role and impact of the individual communicator (yourself, for example) in confronting potentially explosive issues at home, on the campus, or in the political arena?

2. Theodore H. White, author of *The Making of the President—1972,* draws some conclusion about the impact of Vice President Spiro T. Agnew's downfall. Read these excerpts and discuss the questions that follow.

> He (Agnew) had a gift of rhetoric, an authentic cadence to his speech which no other American conservative ever approached. He had courage. He seemed, above all, intelligent and perceptive. . . . Agnew understood and spoke for the emotions of the homeowners, strivers, Middle Americans. His

assault on the press, the most self-important power system in American life, was the most vivid public examination of its functioning by a political figure in recent years.

Had Spiro Agnew—the publicly perceived Agnew of a few months ago —run in 1976, the country would have been the better for it. The political system would have been refreshed by real outspoken debate between an intelligent conservative force and an intelligent liberal resistance.

Spiro Agnew, as the ablest spokesman of the conservative cause, has now and for some time to come deprived the country of this choice. No one else in our time who again used the honorable words that Agnew so slickly mastered can speak them without arousing instant suspicion. No one who challenges the institutions he made his enemies—the press, the television networks, the great foundations, the universities—will be able to examine reasonably their power and their manner of using it. (*Newsweek,* October 22, 1973, p. 29)

a. How clearly are publicly perceived personalities identified with the issues and institutions they espouse or attack?

b. To what extent can you—should you—separate the merits of a spokesman's case from the personal strengths or frailties of the spokesman?

c. To what extent is public discussion and debate a clash between personalities or a confrontation between reasoned differences of opinion based on the available evidence? What should it be? What are the potentials of these alternatives. What are realistic expectations?

d. Does an unfortunate denouement of a public spokesman foreclose further reasoned discussion of the causes he espoused?

e. In a democracy should our loyalties (affections and disaffections) be directed more to institutions than individuals?

3. Read this description of President Lincoln as a speaker. To what extent does this characterize public discussion today? Does it specify worthy goals for speakers?

No higher compliment was ever paid to a nation than the simple confidence, the fireside plainness, with which Mr. Lincoln addressed himself to the reason of the American people. This was, indeed, a true democrat, who grounded himself on the assumption that a democracy can think. "Come let us reason together about this matter," was the tone of all his addresses to the people. We have never had a chief executive who so won to himself the love and at the same time the judgment of his countrymen. To us, the simple confidence of his in the right mindedness of his fellow men is very touching, and its success is as strong an argument as we have ever seen in favor of the theory that men can govern themselves. He never appealed to vulgar sentiment, he never alluded to the humbleness of his origin; it probably never occurred to him, indeed, that there was anything higher to start from than manhood; and he put himself on the level with those addressed, not by going down to them, but only by taking it for granted that they had brains and would come up to a common ground of reason. (James Russell Lowell)

EXERCISES

1. Be prepared to present two or three general topics or areas of discussion that meet these specifications: (1) of interest to you; (2) involve differences of opinion; (3) can be investigated in the library; and (4) lend themselves to class speeches and discussion. Present each subject, indicate some of the issues involved, and tell why you recommend it to the class. Make this an orderly report, present it carefully, then follow with class discussion.

Here are some general topics that might be considered; the national power crisis; consumer protection; the powers of Congress, the president, and the courts; conservation of natural resources; the role of the national government in the arts; censorship of the media; directions for higher education; public support of private education; ecological problems.

Other general topics: television programming; college degree requirements; the drug problem; the Olympic games; summer theater; vocations; travel abroad; women's liberation; vacations; military service.

2. Select *one* of the general topics discussed in class (see Exercise 1). Prepare a paper on this topic including the following: (1) two or three specific topics suitable for short speeches; (2) two or three questions suitable for class discussion; (3) a short bibliography listing four or five references that provide background reading on the general topic. Discuss these papers in class.

3. Select a prose passage from a competent source on one of the general topics discussed in class (see Exercises 1 and 2), and be prepared to read it aloud in class. Observe the following instructions: (1) Select a passage that is largely self-contained; (2) provide necessary context in opening your presentation; (3) read aloud with extemporaneous interpolations if they will help; (4) conclude with your own interpretations.

2. Speech Communication: A Point of View

WHAT IS SPEECH

Speech may be defined as the communication of ideas and feelings through visible and audible symbols originating in speakers, listeners, and observers, and in the settings in which communication takes place. A conventional conception of speech limits it to the spoken word, but this ignores the many nonverbal factors inherent in oral communication. These nonverbal factors include the perceived character, personality, action, and appearance of the speaker; they also include stimuli developing from the immediate physical and psychological environment in which the communication takes place.

Speech is a dynamic process based on stimulus and response, on unfolding interactions between speaker and audience in a given setting. A skillful speaker consciously strives for a specific response from his audience through symbolic representation of information, ideas, and feelings. He is continuously guided by the developing reactions of his listeners and observers, and, if he is wise, he is also sensitive to the setting and mood of the occasion. As we shall see, effective speaking is far more complex, subtle, and demanding than simply delivering messages in the manner of transporting freight from one point to another.

Speech follows a pattern of its own that is best described as circular rather than linear. It originates as an idea in the mind of a person. His brain, acting much like a radar system, scans his available store of symbols and then speedily converts the idea into its verbal equivalents. The speaker's nervous system activates appropriate muscle groups to express these symbols overtly. Sounds and gestures are then transmitted by air and light waves which impinge upon the sensory systems of the audience. Their nervous systems relay these symbols to their brains for decoding and interpretation, resulting in a determination of the meaning and the implications of what they heard. Having evaluated the message, listeners tend to react in some way, with signs of approval or disapproval, encouragement or discouragement, indifference or excitement; and sometimes they respond verbally. Whether covert or overt, response is inevitable in some degree and guides the speaker. If he is equal to his task, he will accept the flow of incoming cues and adapt to them in a manner that enhances his prospects for winning the desired response.

This interaction between speaker and audience takes place in situations that range from the commonplace to unique and carefully planned settings; moods that run the gamut of human emotions may be encountered. Here again, if the speaker is equal to his task, he will make the necessary accommodations.

It should be added, however, that the audience or the listeners, few or many, are as much a part of communication as the speakers; ideally the responsibility for rewarding communication is shared by speakers and listeners alike.

WHAT IS GOOD SPEECH?

The purpose of all speech is response, and the quality of the speech can be judged by the quality of the response and the methods used to elicit this response. In other words, speech is good in the degree it achieves a desirable response through methods best designed to secure this response.

This quick answer leaves us with two questions. What is a desirable response? And what are the best methods? The answers to both of the questions turn upon certain reasoned assumptions, and upon observation of the successes and failures of speakers employing different methods in different settings.

In this chapter we make four basic assumptions concerning speech, and then set out what we believe to be the basic principles that serve as reliable guides to good speech. If you accept these assumptions and are prepared to guide your speech by these principles, we can proceed on this common ground. If you do not, you may be reading the wrong book. In any case, all of these matters will profit by close study.

FOUR BASIC ASSUMPTIONS

These assumptions underlie what we regard as good speech and are essential to full appreciation of the principles that serve as guides to practice and criticism.

1. DELIBERATIVE SPEECH IS THE BEST MODEL FOR GOOD SPEECH

Deliberative speech is decision-making speech typically applied to the analysis and solution of personal and public problems. In this capacity it is concerned with the formulation of policy affecting future conduct and action. Such deliberation may be public or private, addressed to one or more persons, and take place in settings where there are one or more participants as speakers.

In our analysis, explained later, speech may be addressed to four purposes, each served by its own methods. These are inquiry, reporting, advocacy, and evocation. In any given speech one of these purposes is primary, and the others secondary. Deliberative speech usually takes as its primary purpose either inquiry or advocacy, but the aims and methods of reporting and evocative speech usually appear in secondary roles.

Deliberative speech serves a vital function in a free society. It is the principal means by which free people make choices, because properly conducted, it brings their best reflective and creative effort to bear on these decisions. It thrives in a democratic setting. And when freedom is usurped or abdicated, it is first to be censored and curtailed.

We take deliberative speech, then, to be the best model for good speech because it serves the most vital personal and social functions, it embraces all of the purposes of speech in its execution, and it makes the highest demands on both speakers and listeners. It should be made completely clear, however, that this does not preclude respect for other types of speech where they serve worthy purposes.

2. GOOD SPEECH IS AN ART GOVERNED BY AESTHETIC AND UTILITARIAN PRINCIPLES

An art, in the sense in which we are using the term, may be defined as "the principles or methods governing any craft, skill, or branch of learning." These principles and methods, in the case of speech, are derived by investigating the ways in which successful speakers have achieved their objectives and, correlatively, the factors causing unsuccessful speakers to fail in their objectives. The universal purpose of all speech is to win response, but since speech always takes place under conditions where other factors also affect the outcome, any adequate investigation must take these other factors into account. Failure to do this results in attributing effect to a single cause where many causes are operating. Such investigations have been going on for centuries, and if they are properly controlled to isolate the stimuli provided by speech from the stimuli coming from other factors, they may be relied upon to give us the principles of good speech. Such a body of principles and methods qualify speech as an art.

Some examples will help to clarify this important matter. We ask, did the student persuade his professor to give him an "Incomplete," rather than flunk him? Did the salesman sell his product? Was the campaigner elected? Did the lawyer win the case? Did the father persuade his daughter to finish school before marriage? Since we always speak to win response, it might seem logical to judge a speech by success or failure in getting the desired reponse. This plausible theory, however, suffers from one fatal defect: It ignores the fact that in every speaking situation there are many factors that influence the outcome. Some of these factors may be so stacked against the speaker that they will prevail despite his own brilliant performance. The professor may be moved by the student's appeal for a revised grade in a course, but he cannot ignore university standards. The salesman cannot sell to a customer who has neither money nor credit.

Outside factors may also work *for* the speaker. Listeners committed to a fixed belief, their minds tightly locked to hold that belief, will not only accept a speaker who tells them what they want to hear; they may even endow him with eloquence he does not demonstrate and "hear" arguments he did not advance.

Thus, a good speaker, through no fault of his own, may fail to get results, and a poor speaker may win approval in spite of his weaknesses. To generalize principles of speech on these specious grounds leads to false evaluation of speech and misleading advice to students.

We are discussing the assumption that "good speech is an art governed by aesthetic and utilitarian principles." There is a time worn distinction between the "fine arts" and the "applied arts" that will help us here. The fine arts are exemplified in such fields as music, dance, poetry, sculpture, and painting. Many of the skills of the theater such as acting and design are also regarded as fine arts. Sometimes the term "performing arts," conceived as fine arts, is stretched to include the kind of speech we are dealing with here. The fine arts, so it is said, are governed by *aesthetic* principles. Here "a high degree of sensitivity toward the beautiful" and "pure emotion and sensation as opposed to pure intellectuality" are primary considerations.

The applied arts, on the other hand, are governed by *utilitarian* principles, "having regard to usefulness rather than beauty or ornamentation." Examples would be the art of politics, the healing arts, the technological arts, and perhaps such practical skills as cookery, plumbing, and horse shoeing.

Theorists and practitioners of the art of speech often have strong preferences about the company they keep. Some prefer to be classified with the musicians, the poets, and the sculptors—in the fine arts; others are more comfortable with the politicians, the economists, and the social scientists, to say nothing of the worthy cooks, plumbers, and horseshoers. Some of our colleges and universities have even yielded to these predilections in establishing and housing the department of speech.

The problem is real because properly conceived, speech, like most arts, is governed by *both* aesthetic and utilitarian principles. There may be *pure* fine arts and *pure* utilitarian arts, but speech certainly is not one of them.

It is true that most speech has utilitarian purposes and should be judged primarily by utilitarian standards. Does it get the job done? But there is no reason whatsoever why such speech need be dull, stodgy, sloppy in voice and diction, and enervated in style. Aesthetic qualities generally enhance utility. Deliberative speech, for example, is certainly utilitarian in conception, but it will just as surely profit by aesthetic distinction. As a matter of fact, we can think of no speech where this is not the case unless it be such cryptic remarks as "pass the butter" or "get out of my way," and even these might be handled a bit more elegantly. There are, of course, occasions for speech in which a speaker is under aesthetic obligations which would be boorish to ignore—ceremonial speeches, after-dinner speeches, many speeches to entertain or inspire, occasional addresses to luncheon clubs and other groups who may have no immediate problems at stake. But even here, if the speaker can be admired for nothing more than his eloquence, he will be written off by most of his potential listeners and will probably not be given a return engagement.

It is our second basic assumption, then, that aesthetic and utilitarian standards play complementary roles in the guidance and appraisal of speech. The principles of good speech embrace both, and their application to practice and criticism will be guided by the purposes in view and the nature of the occasion.

3. ETHICAL INVOLVEMENT IS INHERENT IN GOOD SPEECH

The Roman rhetorician, Quintilian, defines the orator as "the good man skilled in speaking." There are at least two ways in which the moral integrity of persons engaged in communication are relevant considerations. It is a factor in the quality of interaction between speaker and listener; and it is often a critical factor in the constructive resolution of the matters under discussion.

Certainly in any case in which the issues are of personal and social significance, the interaction between speaker and listener will be strengthened if the listener perceives the speaker as an honest, forthright, trustworthy person, and the speaker perceives the listener to be similarly motivated. Furthermore, unless these perceptions are warranted, it is unlikely that the deliberations will yield dependable conclusions.

It is a third major assumption of this book, then that ethical principles are inevitably involved in speech, and that students of speech demean their field of study unless they accept the responsibilities imposed by this involvement. The degree of involvement obviously varies with the nature and purpose of the speech, but its relevance to our study is inescapable.

4. GOOD SPEECH IS SUBJECT TO BOTH FORMAL AND SUBSTANTIVE CRITICISM

The content of speech is the message, the substance of *what* is being said and reacted to. The form of the speech is *how* it is said. Substantive criticism deals with the content of the speech: How well informed is the speaker? Does he know what he is talking about? Formal criticism deals with all matters affecting the composition and delivery of the speech.

These formal matters are clearly within the province of the student of speech. They are traditionally his stock-in-trade. Unfortunately, even these formal considerations have been severely limited in some cases to such matters as voice and diction, to posture, movement, and gesture, or to style and literary competence. Important as these matters are, formal criticism also includes such things as analysis, sound reasoning, adequate evidence, and organization. All of these matters, and more, are legitimate and necessary considerations.

The more difficult questions arise in determining the speaker's *substantive* responsibilities, and the degree to which students of speech can and should lay claim to this area of criticism. In Plato's *Gorgias,* Socrates maneuvers Gorgias, the speaker and rhetorician, into the untenable position of laying claim to all knowledge by virtue of his rhetorical competence. None of us would like to be backed into this corner, and it is apparent that some interpretation and qualification is necessary if our position is to hold.

As in the case of ethical considerations, the speaker's grasp of his subject is a factor in the quality of the interaction between the speaker and listener; and it most certainly is a critical factor in determining the wisdom and merit of the conclusions. Ideally, speakers and listeners alike should be well informed participants. And the more significant the matter is under discussion, the more urgent and pressing such substantive competence is. Realistically, however, we all know we often fall short of this ideal in many situations in which speech occurs.

In our complex society, we cannot possibly attain the kind of expert knowledge required to make independent decisions in many of the areas that touch our lives. Nor are we always equipped to appraise the reports and recommendations of experts unless their field of expertise coincides with ours. These considerations have led some, mistakenly we think, to limit us to purely formal matters—how speech is constructed and delivered. Let's examine this more carefully.

Experts and specialists obviously play an important role in communication. Seminars, conferences, and consultations in which findings are reported and views exchanged are commonplace. Here informed, qualified persons speak, listen, and discuss issues in their own areas of competence. This kind of deliberation provides its own checks and correctives. The problem arises when these specialists attempt to communicate with persons who do not share their knowledge and experience.

There is a real need for communication between the scientific community, the professions, and the public. And if such communication is to be meaningful, every effort should be made to engage all participants thoughtfully and critically. Nothing is gained by surrounding expertise with an aura of mysticism.

In the first place, any speaker, expert or otherwise, has the responsibility to make himself understood. If he fails in this, he has chosen the wrong subject or the wrong audience, or what is more likely, his own competence as a speaker leaves something to be desired. If the last is the case, remedies are usually at hand.

In the second place, the content of speech, no matter how erudite, consists in facts, opinions, and interpretation of facts and opinions. There are tests which even laymen can apply to check these allegations. They are discussed in chapter 12.

There are, moreover, various practical expedients for introducing expert counsel into deliberations that can profit by it. Special resource persons can be included; legal and technical advice can be provided; committees can be appointed to investigate matters that do not yield to general discussion; and decisions can be deferred to give participants an opportunity to conduct their own investigations.

What is said in any speech, then, is a responsibility of the speaker and a concern of the listeners. Unless understanding is achieved, any communication is truncated and largely futile. In our judgment, any other view of speech reduces it, in Plato's term, to an "empiric knack," or an art of ornamentation akin to cosmetology and cookery.

THIRTEEN BASIC PRINCIPLES

The four assumptions we have just discussed are admittedly controversial. They are fundamental questions and merit serious discussion. We have stated our positions and argued them briefly. Taken together these positions are a philosophy of speech which we recommend to you. In our judgment, they justify the hopes and goals held for speech in chapter 1, and warrant the kind of study proposed in chapters 3 and 4.

The basic principles that follow are grounded in and flow from these assumptions. These are the principles you can apply in learning how to speak better and in evaluating speech—your own and that of others.

1. GOOD SPEECH IS SOCIALLY RESPONSIBLE

A socially responsible speaker comprehends the social context of his remarks and is aware of his potential influence on attitudes, values, traditions, and institutions. He is sensitive to possible consequences and appropriately circumspect and disciplined. Irresponsible speech can be as dangerous as shouting fire in a crowded theater. If speech is to serve constructive social purposes, it must be in the hands of socially responsible people.

2. GOOD SPEECH ENGAGES THE BEST RESOURCES OF BOTH SPEAKERS AND LISTENERS

Good speech makes heavy demands on the intellectual and emotional resources of all who are engaged. The speaker is perceived as informed and competent, emotionally sensitive, and reliable. The listeners' responses give evidence of this perception. The result is mutual respect and understanding.

3. GOOD SPEECH IS DIALOGUE BETWEEN SPEAKERS AND LISTENERS

Communication is served best by participating and sharing in the communicative act. I talk and you listen, then you talk and I listen. Shared interaction through overt and covert responses makes dialogue a helpful model, even though circumstances do not always permit verbal response.

4. GOOD SPEECH IS ANALYTICAL

Speech always takes place in a context—a setting. This setting is created by the subject, the audience, the occasion, and the speaker himself. *Analytical speech is speech that takes these factors into account.*

A good speaker is sensitive to every element in the setting. He sizes up the situation. If the speaker has made a poor analysis of his *subject,* he may deceive both himself and his audience. If he makes a poor analysis of his *audience,* his speech may miss its mark completely. If he makes a poor analysis of the *occasion,* he may stumble into improprieties of the worst kind. And if he makes a poor analysis of *himself* in relation to all the other factors, he may display attitudes that will block communication.

Analysis is involved at every step along the way, from the moment of choice of subject until delivery of the last word.

5. GOOD SPEECH IS CREATIVE

Originality, imaginative insight, inventiveness, resourcefulness, and integrative capacity are all signs of creative power. Creative speech is often characterized by new ideas and novel interpretations of old ideas. It has the quality of freshness in conception, thrust, and style. It is lively and often spontaneous. It avoids "the smell of ink" and risks the unconventional.

6. GOOD SPEECH IS GUIDED BY A SPECIFIC PURPOSE

The specific purpose is simply the response that the speaker is seeking, the objective toward which he directs all his efforts. Without purpose, speech is random and aimless. And if the speaker without a purpose gets any response at all from his audience, it is not likely to be one that he values.

7. GOOD SPEECH DEALS WITH WORTHWHILE SUBJECTS

We talk about countless things—experiences, events, problems, hopes, aspirations, joys, sorrows, and fears. Some of these subjects are so urgent that they cannot be denied. They *must* be talked about. Others are tempting simply because they seem to be worth exploring. The *subjects* people talk about affect the level and quality of speech. Good subjects tap the best resources of both speaker and listener.

8. GOOD SPEECH HAS WORTHWHILE CONTENT

Effective speech reflects the best supporting facts, arguments, illustrations, and other material that a speaker is capable of bringing to his subject. Form is important in speech, but form without substance degrades speech. Silence is preferable to uninformed speech.

9. GOOD SPEECH IS BASED ON SOUND METHOD

The speaker's method is his plan of attack, dictated largely by his purpose and by his analysis of the situation. Four primary purposes of speech are served by four basic methods: inquiry, reporting, advocacy, and evocation. We shall explain these purposes and methods in later chapters. Suffice it to say here that a good speaker knows *when* and *how* to use the appropriate method. It is a fair test of any speech to ask: Has the speaker used the method best designed to accomplish his purpose?

10. GOOD SPEECH CLAIMS THE ATTENTION AND INTEREST OF THE LISTENER

Communication stops when attention is lost. And attention will not persist very long unless the audience's interest is engaged. The best speech is rewarding to both speaker and listener, for then the speaker is motivated to give his best, and the audience is motivated to get the most out of what he says. This kind of motivated speech is realized only when the speaker analyzes and adapts to his audience and when the listeners analyze and adapt to the speaker.

11. GOOD SPEECH MAKES EFFECTIVE USE OF VOICE AND BODILY ACTION

Without voice and bodily action there can be no speech, for they carry the symbols out of which all speech is fashioned and the symbols to which listeners respond. The human voice and body are flexible instruments with enormous potentialities for sensitive communication far beyond the relatively simple demands of making oneself heard and seen.

Good speakers exercise artistic control over these means of communication.

12. GOOD SPEECH EXPRESSES ITSELF IN ACCEPTABLE LANGUAGE, STYLE, AND DICTION

The ideas of a speech are invigorated, clarified, and enhanced by appropriate words, accurately selected and arranged, and correctly pronounced. Standards of good taste and usage are always changing, but the speaker ignores them at his peril. Diction, language, and style are not ends in themselves. Rather, they facilitate communication by giving it precision, vigor, and beauty.

13. GOOD SPEECH IS TIMELY

We should know when to talk and when to keep still. Untimely speech, no matter how good it is otherwise, is an intrusion, usually in poor taste and poorly received. Silence has its own rewards, and speech that serves only to break silence does so at the sufferance of others. Unless the silence is unwanted, the speech is better left unsaid.

A SUMMARY OF OUR POINT OF VIEW

Speech that is conceived as we have defined it and circumscribed by the assumptions we have made will be judged good speech in the degree it meets the tests imposed by the basic principles we have set out. As we have said before, these assumptions and these principles constitute a philosophy of speech and a guide to sound instruction and practice. For the most part, they are time-tested and sanctioned by the best tradition in our field. But there is no reason whatsoever for you to accept them at face value. You will find them far more meaningful if you test them for yourself. The chapters that follow are designed to help you make this test, both in your speech class and in all the years of speaking that lie ahead of you.

QUESTIONS FOR DISCUSSION

1. "Deliberative speech serves a vital function in a free society." Why and how is this the case, if indeed it is the case? What are the typical settings in which deliberative speech takes place?

2. Moody Prior discussed the role of scientists in public affairs in his book *Science and the Humanities.* Read the quotation below and discuss the questions that follow.

> President Truman made the decision to approve the project which produced the fusion, or hydrogen, bomb in the face of strongly divided opinion among

distinguished scientists who apparently could not agree on either the feasibility of such a weapon or the desirability of giving it priority over others. This conspicuously non-scientific man was able to make this decision under difficult circumstances because it involved his judgment as to how probable a successful outcome might be in view of the strong conviction of some distinguished experts, and how much of a gamble the circumstances allowed him to take on this one possibility. The decision, in short, was a common-sense decision and did not involve him as a scientist. As things turned out, it was, scientifically at least, a correct gamble. Was it the right decision other than scientifically? This question still arouses differences of opinion among scientists, politicians, military men, and the interested public. Could Truman have arrived at a decision more expeditiously or correctly if he had had a greater degree of scientific knowledge? He could never be expected to know as much nuclear physics as the scientists who disagreed with one another, yet he might have known just enough to incline him toward one group rather than the other on scientific grounds—not necessarily a better state of affairs.[1]

a. Was President Truman, or any other nonscientific man, qualified to make this decision?

b. Should such decisions be made by scientists? What do you do when the scientists disagree?

c. Did the president make the right decision, other than scientifically? What decisions were involved other than a scientific decision? What qualifications are needed to make the "other decisions" involved?

d. What recommendations would you make to guide the formulation of public policy decisions involving scientific expertise?

e. Do these recommendations apply to such policy decisions involving experts in nonscientific fields?

EXERCISES

1. Read aloud the quotation from Mr. Prior cited above. Read it "thoughtfully" with attention to pauses, emphasis on words or phrases, and variations in the pitch of your voice; in short, in ways that best bring out the meaning.

2. Read the quotation again to yourself and prepare a short speech on the question: did President Truman make the *right* decision in approving the project which produced the hydrogen bomb? Answer the question "yes" or "no" in the light of subsequent events and possible future events. Write this out, if you wish, and read it to the class; or outline your views and speak extemporaneously. In either case practice it "out loud" a few times.

[1]Moody Prior, *Science and Humanities* (Evanston, Ill.: Northwestern University Press, 1962),
p. 78–79.

3. Prepare a short speech in which you pose a value judgment as a question; then, answer your own question and give your reasons. Write it out and read it, or speak extemporaneously. Here are sample topics:

    a. Should ecological considerations give way to the demands of industry when acute human needs are at stake?

    b. Is the family a viable institution in our society today?

    c. Do we have a moral obligation to aid underprivileged and underdeveloped foreign countries?

    d. Is the slogan "love America or leave it" sound advice?

    e. Should government attempt to regulate personal habits when they do not affect the lives of others?

    f. Should the public be denied access to televised events if such broadcasts reduce paid attendance at such events?

3. Guidelines for Speaking

Understanding the basic principles of speech is the first step toward speech improvement. Practice in the application of these principles is the second step, and criticism or evaluation of these applications is the third step. In your course in speech, these three activities will go on concurrently. The first four chapters of this book will help you get started: chapter 1 relates your speech to the contemporary scene; chapter 2 gives you an introduction to the principles of good speech; this chapter gives you preliminary advice on speaking; and chapter 4 gives you similar advice on listening to understand and appreciate, and listening to provide suggestions for speech improvement.

MODELS FOR PRACTICE

This book is primarily designed for courses in speech communication in which opportunities are given for practice in speech. In our analysis, the basic purposes of speech are classified as *inquiry, reporting, advocacy,* and *evocation,* and separate chapters are devoted to the methods best suited to each of these purposes. Depending on time, place, subject, and participants, these purposes can be achieved best through conversation, public speech, discussion, debate, and reading aloud. All of these provide models for practice exercises.

The best models for practice (1) require investigation beyond immediate personal resources; (2) invite questions, discussion, and other participancy; (3) can profitably be pursued in some depth; (4) have significant contemporary relevance; and (5) lend themselves to extemporaneous development.

We have already said that deliberative speech is the best model for understanding and deriving the basic principles of speech. In most cases, we think it is also the best model for practice. As we have seen, it may proceed through group discussion or one or more public speeches, and all the purposes and methods of speech may be involved in primary or secondary roles. But most important, it deals with questions of policy that yield to creative and analytical skills, and profits by full participancy of all concerned. Persons who have acquired the ability to handle themselves effectively in lively give and take deliberation (where what they say is subject to close scrutiny, and where questions are asked and adaptations to developing situations are required) are likely to communicate with greater ease, assurance, and resourcefulness no matter what the occasion may be. In short, they have developed skills and insights of general utility in all communication.

EXTEMPORANEOUS SPEAKING

It is helpful to distinguish among impromptu speech, extemporaneous speech, memorized speech, and reading aloud. There are occasions in which all are useful, but extemporaneous speech serves most situations best. Moreover, as circumstances may demand, the accomplished extemporaneous speaker will be better prepared to speak impromptu or speak from memory or read from manuscript with greater impact.

The essence of extemporaneous speech is the composition of language as you speak. You prepare in advance by investigating and analyzing your subject, arranging your ideas, selecting materials for the development of these ideas, and preparing a suitable outline. In the case of a public speech, you may even rehearse it out loud, but you do *not* freeze the speech into a language mold. You rely upon your own resources to supply the appropriate words at the moment of delivery. The best extemporaneous speech, then, develops from a solid foundation of rigorous preparation. On this assured ground, you will find the freedom, flexibility, and spontaneity needed to adapt to the shifting reactions of your listeners.

THE IDEA-ORIENTED CLASSROOM

Extemporaneous public speeches and group discussions provide the typical, and probably the best, speech exercises. In any case, the models for practice should meet the five specifications we have set out—worthy subjects, participancy, depth, contemporary relevance, and extemporaneous development. These specifications can hardly be met, however, unless the speech class is one in which significant ideas are dealt with responsibly and critically. All speeches and every discussion should represent the best effort of fully prepared speakers. There should be opportunities for questions, disagreement, and constructive comments dealing with the *content* of the speech. The speech engaged in this kind of questioning and reply can be fully as vital and fully as instructive as the presentation invoking it.

This kind of idea-oriented class differs dramatically from one in which you listen apathetically to a series of short speeches on trivial subjects while you nervously wait your turn to bore the class.

A class atmosphere in which speakers and listeners are idea conscious also provides the best opportunities for formal criticism—for constructive suggestions for speech improvement. This is no place for the poorly prepared speaker, and he will soon find this out; moreover, the situation encourages the speaker to concentrate on what he is saying—to do his best for the ideas he is presenting. The result is likely to be the best speaking of which he is capable. Suggestions for speech improvement applied to such best efforts yield maximum results. If these conditions do not exist, if the speaker is poorly prepared, with attention divided between his ideas and his manner of presentation, he will almost surely perform below his present level of competence. Under these circumstances, criticism of his effort is like carrying coals to Newcastle. He already knows better.

COMMON SOURCES FOR SPEECH EXERCISES

Students can sometimes gain by consulting the same sources for speech assignments—the same book, article, essay, lecture, play, or poem. In this way the preparation and background of each speaker is more nearly comparable, and the speeches themselves, rather than the selection and availability of sources, are under scrutiny. If the source or sources agreed upon are worthy of serious study, if they are provocative, and invite analysis and interpretation, then originality, variety, and adaptation to other speakers are a reasonable expectation.

This is one way of stimulating discussion and providing a closer link between substance and form, between knowledge and expression. Since all have a critical acquaintance with the *matter* under discussion, all are better qualified to judge the *manner* of discussion.

Many of the exercises suggested here are planned to take advantage of common sources that can be made readily available.

A PRELIMINARY SPEAKER'S MANUAL FOR EXTEMPORANEOUS SPEECH

Here is a short "How to Do It" manual that will help you with speech assignments.

This section takes you through the stages of preparation to the delivery of the extemporaneous speech. Most of what is said here is applicable to all speaking, however, extemporaneous or otherwise. Specific suggestions for other methods of presentation are given later.

SUBJECT AND PURPOSE

First, decide on what you should talk about and the specific response you hope to achieve. You will find your best subjects at those junctures where your liveliest interests and concerns overlap those of your listeners. Once you have made your decision, then state your specific purpose as concisely as possible in a single sentence.

Usually you will come to this purpose sentence by stages. The topic "Our changing educational scene," although too broad and indeterminate, suggests other possibilities of narrower scope, such as "The new admission policies now being applied by State University" or "Making higher education available to all who can benefit from it." But these somewhat narrower topics still lack the limitation, specificity, and direction that characterize the following purpose sentences: "Intense grade consciousness among students in my dormitory has killed extracurricular activities," or "I intend to show that excessive grade consciousness is killing intellectual life on campus." A worthwhile subject and a carefully devised purpose sentence provide a solid foundation on which to build your talk.

DEVELOPING YOUR TALK

Having formulated your purpose sentence, presumably you are already in possession of some information and ideas for developing your talk. Make the most of what you already know and have thought, for every good speech bears the authentic stamp of a speaker's individuality. Effective speeches are never mere collections of items taken from something that others have said or written. This does not mean, of course, that good speeches can be fabricated from thin air. When talking about matters of consequence, responsible people exercise utmost care to be sure that the information they have on hand is both accurate and sufficient; whenever necessary, they take pains to supplement it with additional facts, statistics, examples, and other materials that will help to give credence to their views. Experienced speakers draw upon their own resources, but they also verify and augment their knowledge of a subject through additional observations, interviews, and reading.

Your purpose sentence will not only guide your investigations, but it will help you to formulate key points in your talk. In one way or another, you have come to a conclusion now formulated as a purpose sentence; but if you hope to convince others, you must speak to the basic questions that are likely to arise in their minds. If your purpose sentence is well considered and sharply stated, it will offer strong indications of the points you must take up.

Suppose your purpose sentence were this one: "I intend to show that excessive grade consciousness is killing intellectual life on campus." Analyze this statement thoughtfully, and you will quickly see that your listeners must be satisfied on various basic points before you can reasonably expect to gain their assent. You would need to show that (1) because of many pressures, the pursuit of grades seems to be foremost in the minds of students today; (2) although good grades are not incompatible with the intellectual life, excessive grade consciousness—grades for their own sake —stifles curiosity and joy of learning; (3) we ought to and can nourish a spirit of learning that relegates grade acquisition to a by-product.

A careful analysis of a well-conceived purpose sentence, you can see, virtually prescribes steps to take in developing your talk.

OUTLINING YOUR SPEECH

An outline organizes the results of your analysis and investigation. It charts the main points and subpoints along the course that your speech will follow. Main points support or explain your purpose sentence; subpoints support or explain either your main points or still other subpoints to which they are subordinate.

Visualizing the form of an outline helps to fix in mind these relationships among the points.

I. Main point that supports or explains purpose sentence.
   A. Subpoint that supports or explains main point I.
      1. Subpoint that supports or explains subpoint A.
      2. Subpoint that supports or explains subpoint A.
   B. Subpoint that supports or explains main point I.
II. Main point that supports or explains purpose sentence.

With this form before us, we can begin to develop an outline that supports our specific purpose.

Purpose sentence: I intend to show that excessive grade consciousness is killing intellectual life on campus.

I. Emphasis upon grades overshadows other motivations for learning.
   A. High schools seem less interested in inculcating the spirit of learning for its own satisfaction than in getting students admitted to prestige colleges and universities.
      1. Counselors are forever reminding students of requirements for admission to Ivy League schools.

    2. Teachers are driven to "lay on" the work in order to qualify students for these colleges and universities.

B. In college it is the same thing all over again.

    1. Outside pressure to qualify for admission into college is exceeded only by pressure from the inside to get the grades required to stay in college.

    2. Students with scholarships must make consistently high grades to hang onto their stipends.

    3. Students with ambitions for graduate or professional schools become greasy grinds instead of intellectual questers.

II. Widespread grade consciousness today actually fosters anti-intellectualism on our campuses.

What you have just seen is but a segment of the body of a speech. A fully developed outline is divided into three main sections: an *Introduction,* which stimulates audience interest, paves the way for good relationships between the speaker and his audience, and discloses the speaker's subject and possibly his particular line of attack; the *Body* or *Discussion,* which is the major part of the outline, unfolds the steps in the development of the speaker's theme; and the *Conclusion,* the capstone to the entire talk.

REHEARSING THE SPEECH

Students often ask, "Should I practice extemporaneous speeches before delivering them to an audience?" The answer is "Yes!" This is the time to spot and iron out problems that become evident only after you try to articulate your thoughts. Rehearsing helps you to test your ideas, fix the outline in mind, and develop an ear for the sound and swing of your talk. But keep thinking out your speech as you talk it out. Should you hit upon especially felicitous words and phrases along the way, make a mental note of them, but don't come to depend upon them. The good ones will probably stick with you and turn up when you speak to an audience. There are exceptions to this rule, of course. For example, it is usually wise to think up a few good sentences as insurance against a fumbling start and an inconclusive conclusion.

Practice beforehand, but avoid turning these private sessions into sterile, mechanized exercises. Begin early and space your practicing. Make each session a means to personal development and an opportunity to enrich your talk.

"May I use notes?" you ask. Use them by all means to report complicated information or extended quotations. Notes insure accuracy and remove the strain of memorizing. Usually there is no reason why you should not use prompting notes, such as a skeleton outline, if your speech is technical or long and if you use them sparingly and unobtrusively. Use practice sessions to acquire skill in handling notes effectively. You will have some assignments, however, in which notes are unnecessary and inadvisable. In any event, your instructor will let you know whether notes are an aid or a hindrance to your progress. When you need notes, these suggestions may help:

1. Make your notes simple.
2. Put them in proper sequence before you speak.
3. Write your notes legibly. (It is best to type them out in doublespaced lines.)
4. Place your notes on the desk or speaker's stand where you can consult them easily.
5. Resist the impulse to retreat into your notes. Use them only to jog your memory and keep you on track.
6. If you read quotations or other material, hold up your card, sheet, or book for easy reading. Look up and out at your audience from time to time.

DELIVERING YOUR SPEECH

All of your preparation is brought to bear either directly or indirectly in the delivery of speech—in your voice, words, and bodily action. Your goal in private practice, in the classroom, and in public is to talk *with* people, not *at* people.

THE CONVERSATIONAL NORM

Make a point of analyzing some invigorating conversation you over-hear, and you will quickly perceive that *interaction* among participants is its most vivid characteristic. Listeners respond to the speaker through the alert posture of their bodies, changing facial expressions, bursts of laughter, sounds of protest or agreement, and still other overt signs of involvement. Speakers, through their words and comments, their voices and manner, respond to the developing reactions of the listeners. An analysis of this interaction suggests two key concepts that underlie it, basic components of all good speaking: *empathy* and *rapport.*

Empathy is a process by which you involve yourself imaginatively and sympathetically with the thoughts and feelings of another person. You adopt his interests, try to see things as he sees them, to feel as he feels, even though you may not subscribe to his views. Empathy is the opposite of self-preoccupation and egocentric behavior. When both the speaker and listener project themselves into the mind and emotion of the other, the interaction that follows is known as *rapport,* the hallmark of good speaker-audience relationship. Without rapport, the communicative act is always incomplete and therefore imperfect; sometimes it is completely blocked.

Since lively conversations exemplify the attributes of communicative delivery, the conversational norm furnishes the best guide to the delivery of all speech. Qualities of voice and action that characterize lively conversation—directness, animation, variety, and spontaneity—are appropriate to all speech, formal as well as informal. Many people suffer from a mistaken notion that public speech calls for an oratorical manner that is mysteriously different from the natural mode of their more private speech. The truth is that if you can talk easily, directly, and responsively in conversation, happily, you may proceed with assurance in adopting the conversational norm of informal speech for your public speeches—with only two precautions.

Remember, not all conversation qualifies as good conversation. We are seriously misguided if we accept as our models the mumblers and bumblers we hear on all sides. To take our standards for public speaking from the dull, rambling, inept conversations we all overhear (or engage in) every day of our lives is to heap undeserved torture on listeners. Remember, too, that public speech differs from conversation in several obvious ways. The speaker does all or most of the talking; audience response is largely covert rather than overt; more people are present; and the speaker usually stands in front of an audience, often on a platform. Accordingly, the public speaker must alter his delivery through heightened output to accommodate himself to these special conditions. Even so, he can and he should retain the *sense of communication* that is rooted in elements characteristic of good conversational speech.

How to Talk with People

Here are several suggestions that will help strengthen your delivery in both conversation and public speech.

Idea consciousness should supplant self-consciousness. The first requisite of good delivery is an evident interest in what you are saying and in the people with whom you are talking. Given this interest in your subject and your listeners, many of the most common problems in delivery will vanish. Even a highly polished delivery will seem false and empty unless you are motivated by a desire to share your ideas and feelings with your listeners. As soon as you make delivery an end in itself, your speech becomes an artificial, devitalized act.

Think of what you are saying while you are saying it. Mental and emotional drifting can be spotted in a second, for the speaker's manner and voice will give him away. You have listened to people talk from memory or from a manuscript who obviously did not have their minds on what they were saying—and no one else did, either.

An extemporaneous speaker, of course, has no choice but to keep his wits about him. He must think as he talks and talk as he thinks. We expect talk to go forward with fluency, but not at the expense of the speaker's thoughtful reactions to his own remarks. Do not be distressed if you have to pause now and then to pick out the right word. Listeners regard occasional hesitations, on-the-spot revisions, or short digressions as signs of an active mind at work. Rattling glibness betrays a rattling mind. No speaker is really communicating unless he is in touch with what he is saying as he says it.

Respond to your audience. Think about what you are saying while you are saying it, but *think about it in relation to your audience.* Every audience sends out signals. Tune in on them to see if they carry messages of understanding, puzzlement, interest, boredom, weariness, or disapproval. Ask yourself: "Am I making myself heard? Would another example help? Am I spinning this out unnecessarily? Did this sound too flippant?"

Most audiences will go more than halfway in giving you a fair hearing. But if you see that the audience is backing off or slipping away, take positive steps then and there to reestablish contact. Perhaps you need to change pace, or increase or decrease the force of your delivery. Don't hesitate to break in and underscore items with remarks like these: "The point I'm trying to make is this. . . ." "I want this to be perfectly clear. . . ." Throw out some questions: "Have you ever had this experience?" "Have you ever thought of it in this light?" Pointed remarks and questions help to retrieve wandering attention.

A good audience is a stimulus; a difficult audience is a challenge. But speech without any audience at all is a fiasco. Hold on to your listeners by talking things over *with* them instead of just talking *at* them.

Use your voice to carry meaning and feeling. The greatest value of the conversational norm is that it guides you in the use of your voice. Listen to the ordinary conversations around you. You will hear pleasant and unpleasant voices, clear and slovenly enunciation, good and poor diction —dialectal differences, mispronunciations, and grammatical errors. But through it all will come remarkable purposefulness and vitality. There will be exceptions, to be sure. But people do have a way of making their voices work for them. A student asks a question, and an instructor replies; a foreman directs the workman on a job; a girl explains to an anxious housemother why she is late; the cast talks over the play after rehearsal. These people are not thinking about their voices, but they have important business on their minds. Accordingly, their voices are remarkably flexible and expressive.

One of the most common problems among beginning speakers is learning to use their voices with this same flexibility when they are speaking to larger groups. Why do sight-seeing guides lapse into singsong speech? Why do radio and TV announcers, extravagantly extolling lawn fertilizers in one breath and skin balm in the next, speak in souped-up tones? Why do oldtime political orators intone? Why do so many beginning public speakers talk in flat, dull monotones? Speech has become routinized for the sight-seeing guide; announcers who cannot speak from the heart must artificially pump up enthusiasm; the political orator has established bad vocal habits that he thinks are good; and the beginning speaker is inhibited and nervous. In all these cases, *the speaker has lost contact with his ideas and feelings.* His voice has been cut off from its supply of vital energy and has been rendered lifeless. This is the principal cause of breakdowns in voice communication.

Speak with physical animation and directness. Speaking is action in which mind and body cooperate. Bodily action supplements and reinforces words; it energizes thought; it reveals you as a person who is self-confident rather than self-conscious. A listless person fails to sustain interest for very long; an anxious, distracted person communicates his distress; an overwrought person wears us out by trying too hard. A nice balance between relaxation and tension contributes to poise and directness.

People like personal attention. When you look your audience straight in the eye, you are taking notice of them. You are saying, "I invite you to share this information or observation." This simple gesture contributes to good human relationships. It also helps you to adapt sensitively to the reactions of others.

If you are talking to a large group, you cannot focus your attention on everyone at once. Simply shift your attention unobtrusively from one segment of the audience to another, so that no one is excluded. You can do this easily and naturally without swinging your head back and forth like a busy airport beacon. Usually there is no need to single out individuals unless you happen to be especially interested in their reactions. Even then, be careful not to fix them with your eye until they squirm in their seats.

Avoid annoying mannerisms. You have seen speakers shift uneasily in their chairs or pace restlessly up and down the platform. You have seen some who rock back and forth on their heels, jingle coins in their pockets, or aimlessly take their glasses off and put them on again. You have been distracted by speakers who induce little artificial coughs, who clear their throats every few seconds, and who clutter their speech with stray sounds such as *ah, uh,* and *er* or *you know.* These mannerisms call attention to themselves and distract listeners from what the speaker is trying to say. If fellow members of your speech class make you aware of such mannerisms, welcome their criticisms and take steps to eliminate the offending habits.

Observe the courtesies of the occasion. When you are introduced to a stranger, you acknowledge the introduction in a warm, courteous manner. Similarly, when you are introduced to an audience, you acknowledge

the chairman's introduction and greet the audience with a friendly saluta-
tion and remarks appropriate to the occasion.

Good rapport with listeners calls for respect for their feelings. If
someone asks a question, don't brush him off or punish him for his
audacity. Assume that he is asking his question in good faith. Pugnacity,
sarcasm, and defensiveness repel listeners, even when they know you are
being goaded by a boor. A friendly, urbane manner helps to win them over.

OTHER METHODS OF PRESENTATION

Some occasions call for special competence in impromptu speaking,
speaking from a manuscript, and speaking from memory.

IMPROMPTU SPEAKING

Much of our conversation is nothing more than a series of short,
impromptu talks—speech that we have had no opportunity to prepare
beforehand. Suppose you are attending a get-together of twenty or thirty
people. You are all set to sit back and listen to someone else. Suddenly, the
chairman turns to you and asks you to say something to the group. As you
get to your feet, you must swiftly decide on the substance, purpose, and
plan of your remarks. In short, you have to compose and deliver your talk
at the same time.

There is no magic formula to help you become a skillful impromptu
speaker. Actually, the best preparation for impromptu speaking, whatever
the circumstances, is preliminary experience in extemporaneous speaking.
The facility you acquire in finding subjects for extemporaneous speech, in
analyzing and organizing materials, and in adapting your language to the
occasion will immeasurably increase your readiness to deal with impromptu speeches.

SPEAKING FROM MANUSCRIPT

With a manuscript clutched firmly in your hands, you are free from
the fear of making slips of the tongue, from relying on catch-as-catch-can
language, from the danger of running overtime or being cut off before you
have finished. Sometimes these advantages are compelling. Yet few people
read a manuscript with enough skill to communicate successfully. They
plant themselves behind a lectern, bury their faces, and then lapse into a
singsong recital of words while their minds wander off into unknown
realms.

If your material or the situation demands that you use a manuscript,
then make a sincere and serious effort to get your ideas across the barriers.

Here are some suggestions that will help you avoid glaring mistakes when speaking from a manuscript.

Write your speech for the ear and not for the eye. Make sure it represents your best oral style. Keep your sentences short and simple. Weed out the long, complex ones. Favor colloquial words. Use the active voice rather than the passive. Write the talk in your most direct, personal, and graphic style, just as if you were talking person-to-person without a manuscript. Try it out on a friend and ask if it sounds like you.

After you have finished writing your speech, don't toss the manuscript aside and forget about it. Return to it from time to time. Review, rethink, and revise your ideas and language. Make your speech a living, growing thing. You will develop a richer feeling for it. This is the best way to keep your writing from turning cold and to keep your delivery from becoming mechanical.

Maintain contact with your audience while speaking. If you prepare well, you will be free to talk directly with your audience. You will find it easy to catch at a glance the sweep of a sentence, even a paragraph, and to concentrate on getting it across. And if you have your speech well in mind, you can work in on-the-spot comments that will keep it geared to the developing reactions of your listeners.

SPEAKING FROM MEMORY

Memorizing a talk frees you from the manuscript and preserves the advantages of a carefully written speech. Special events, such as a formal ceremonial occasion, sometimes call for speeches that exhibit finesse in composition. If reading a manuscript seems out of place, you may decide to commit your speech to memory.

One hazard of a memorized talk is that it often leads to mechanical delivery. Some people become so engrossed in recalling words and in behaving elegantly that they lose touch with the sense and sentiment that prompted the speech in the first place. Listeners quickly detect a "canned" speech and are likely to dismiss it as a schoolboy performance. A second hazard is that you may forget your speech. The fear of forgetting may itself make your mind go blank.

But you can reduce these hazards. You will discover that skill in extemporaneous speaking will help you when you speak from memory. In extemporaneous speech, you acquire the habit of first focusing your mind on a basic outline of points. Extemporaneous speaking also promotes habits of flexibility and directness that will help you to improvise when necessary and to preserve the conversational norm.

If you memorize a speech, avoid memorizing in rote fashion, line by line. Instead, begin by studying the pattern of ideas you worked up in your preliminary outline. Fix in your mind a picture of the talk as a whole, then take up the separate units as part of a logical structure. You will memorize with greatest efficiency if you spread your study sessions over a period of time.

PREPARATION FOR DISCUSSION

Much of what has been said earlier about preparation for extemporaneous public speech applies here. The principal differences are these: (1) discussion is a group project; (2) it is addressed to a question which can profitably be explored for purposes of better understanding and resolution; (3) it proceeds through unrehearsed conversation among the participants; (4) it is usually guided by a leader appointed in advance; and (5) further guidance is provided by discussion outlines developed from investigation, and prepared by each member of the group in advance. More is said about this in chapters 11 and 18.

It should be emphasized that discussion, properly conceived, is a creative process. Thorough preparation is desirable, and the discussion outlines will record this preparation; but the discussion itself coalesces, clarifies, and evaluates the ideas recorded in these outlines as these ideas are contributed. It is hoped that new insights will be sparked by this give and take conversation. Members of the group, including the leader, should encourage these creative impulses and be willing to abandon prepared positions, or at least accommodate them to new ideas that appear to have greater merit.

The discussion outlines and the general pattern of the discussion is that of the usual steps in reflective thinking: (1) identify the problem; (2) analyze the causes; (3) clarify values; (4) suggest solutions; (5) weigh the alternative solutions; (6) test the preferred solution. These steps may be unfamiliar to you at this stage of your study. Again we suggest you consult the chapters noted earlier.

A QUALIFYING CONCLUSION

We have suggested class speeches and group discussion as the best exercises for speech improvement. Many of the exercises provided throughout the book are of this kind. They have general utility, because all of the principles of speech are brought into play. It is sometimes wise, however, to work on specific speech skills. For example, experience in reading good literature aloud has values of its own, and is also one of the best means to cultivate good vocal usage; similarly, pantomime and acting out parts from a script made up as you go along, as in creative drama, are often good exercises in developing the use of the body in communication. Written speech composition will help you attain a good oral style, a style that is likely to have more distinction than one developed exclusively through extemporaneous speech. These and others can be used profitably as your teacher may direct.

QUESTIONS FOR DISCUSSION

1. What are the values and limitations of extemporaneous speaking?

2. What are the best models for practice in speaking? Why these preferences?

3. Discuss the values and limitations of the "idea-oriented" speech class and the use of "common sources."

4. How do you prepare for oral exercises in the speech class?

5. If the comment below is a fair appraisal of our communication skills, what remedies would you suggest?

> Most children soon learn to talk the language of the people around them. Yet few of them continue their verbal maturing throughout life. Few of them, in adulthood, are so able to say what they want to say—with confidence, precision, beauty, and a sensitive awareness of what is fitting in the situation —that the communicative experience holds more of success than of failure. In no area of our maturing, in fact, is arrested development more common than in the area of communication. It is so common that it is not even noticed; it is taken for granted as natural. The person who is mature in his communicative powers is noted as an exception to the rule. The person who is immature—halting, clumsy, obscure, rambling, dull, platitudinous, insensitive—is the rule. (H. A. Overstreet)

EXERCISES

1. A series of open-forum assignments on controversial subjects stimulates good delivery. Each talk should be extemporaneous. Reserve half of the period for questions and answers. Appoint a chairman to preside. In the open-forum period, insist that each person stand when he speaks and that no one speak for more than one minute. Allow time for a critique of all the aspects of delivery in this chapter.

2. Make a short extemporaneous talk. After the other speakers scheduled for the day have spoken, you will be recalled to expand on the points of your talk or to offer additional ones. Invite the rest of the class to comment on your poise and communicativeness in your two appearances. Were there any differences? Analyze the differences.

3. Divide the class into three or four groups and have members of each group investigate independently a topic of general interest to the group. Appoint a leader for each group. On a scheduled day, have the leader open the discussion of the general topic in an easy, informal way. As the discussion proceeds, the leader will invite each member to rise and speak briefly to some point on which he is prepared to speak extemporaneously.

4. Each member of the class contributes two nontechnical subjects that are suitable for short impromptu talks. Then each person draws two subjects other than his own. After thinking them over, he rises and speaks briefly on the one he chooses.

5. Choose a subject, investigate it, and write out your talk; word for word. Test your writing on someone who knows you well, to see if it is in keeping with your best oral style. Be as communicative as you can when you read the speech to the class.

6. Prepare a short talk that will be largely extemporaneous. Write out and memorize only short passages of it. After you have delievered it to the class, find out if your listeners were able to detect the portions you memorized. If they were, try to find out how they managed to spot them.

7. Choose a passage of prose or poetry. Prepare a short introduction and a conclusion that enforce the point of your passage. Read communicatively, as if you were talking with people.

4. Guidelines for Listening and Criticism

In a speech class we listen to speech—conversation, discussion, debate, public speech, reading aloud—for two main purposes. The first is to grasp the speaker's message, to understand it and to appreciate it fully in all of its implications so that we will be in a position to react to the ideas with questions and comments if such an opportunity is provided. The second purpose is to listen and observe so that we will be in a position to offer helpful suggestions for speech improvement. What were the speaker's strengths and weakness? Why and how did he succeed or fail?

In your speech class, as elsewhere, you will respond vigorously to arresting ideas for their own sake, and you will thereby contribute to a lively forum that furnishes the best kind of audience any speaker could want. But in a class where improvement in speaking is a primary objective, or when you are listening to speech for the purpose of improving your own speech, you are cast in the role of a critic. In this role, you will need to be aware of the totality of the speaking process if you are to be helpful to the speaker and make gains for yourself.

LISTENING FOR IDEAS

Chapters 15 and 16 analyze kinds of listening and responsibility for listening, and offer suggestions for good listening. Here we are concerned mainly with listening in the speech class. Your first class responsibility is to make certain that your *own* speech merits careful listening—that it is your fully prepared best effort. Your second responsibility is to give others the attention you expect; both experiences can be rewarding.

If a speaker cannot command your attention, something is wrong with him or you or both. You have no obligation to listen to an unprepared speaker who is conspicuously operating below his level of competence, or to one who is dealing with trivia. But remember that "sauce for the goose is sauce for the gander." The time will come very soon when you will be asking for attention. Uncharitable behavior on your part as a listener, may very well be your unwelcome reward as a speaker.

One of the best tests of listening is the ability to sum up what a speaker has said in ways that will be acceptable to him. If each member of the class submits a short précis of the speech, and the speaker grants these to be fair summaries of his remarks, it is likely that communication has taken place.

Listening to understand what a speaker has said does not necessarily mean you agree with him. You may wish to question his assumptions and argue with his conclusions, but first be reasonably certain that you do understand what he has said. With this assurance, unless proprieties dictate otherwise, real gains can be made by engaging in a discussion of the speaker's ideas. Awareness on the part of the speaker, that his ideas are under scrutiny and that they may be challenged, provides motivation for him; the listener's knowledge that reaction to these ideas is a normal expectation makes listening more worthwhile.

Listening to *understand* a speaker's ideas is not the only potential reward of listening. Good speech, no matter what the primary purpose, can be a rewarding emotional and spiritual experience. It can also be entertaining. Nor do we discount completely the appreciation that comes from listening to speech that is artistically constructed and delivered, even though this should never be done for display.

LISTENING AS A CRITIC

In general, it is expected that favorable evaluation of a speech will correlate with accurate and appreciative reception of the message, but this is not necessarily the case. A speaker may convey his message in spite of such deficiencies as poor use of his voice, fuzzy organization, or objectionable personal behavior. The critic has an obligation to the speaker and to the class to point out strengths and weaknesses. The acuity with which he does this is a good indication of his own mastery of basic principles.

WHAT CRITICISM MEANS

If you recoil from the word *criticism,* it may be that you equate it with fault-finding, as you do when you say, "You're too critical—too negative. Don't stick pins in me." Perhaps you have come to prefer substitute words such as *comments, suggestions,* or *reactions.* The fact is, however, that the word *criticism* has a well-established and scholarly meaning for which there is no adequate substitute. For those who use the word in a professional sense, it does not imply negation; it is associated with *appraisal.* In all branches of the humanities, the word *criticism* is as meaningful and useful as is the word *diagnosis* for the physician.

Criticism may be defined as an intellectual process by which we seek to understand and to assess a work of art by applying to it the principles appropriate to that art form. Until we know what principles distinguish any art form, we are without criteria for judging it. Given these criteria, the critical process involves analyzing speech objectively to pinpoint strengths and weaknesses in the talk you hear—your own and that of others. Looked at in this way, criticism is an essential procedure for improving the quality of discourse.

SPEECH AS THE OBJECT OF CRITICISM

Although our immediate interest is in the criticism of classroom speech, our approach to criticism must take into account all speaking— speech under any circumstances that we can imagine—long talks and conversational tidbits, prearranged talk and speech that accidentally falls on our ears. Merely to note the range and variety of our daily speaking-listening experience justifies the conclusion that of all forms of human expression, speech is undoubtedly the most evanescent. You can return to a painting or statue to check your initial responses. By rereading a novel or poem, or anything that is in written form, you catch meanings that escaped you the first time through. Not so with speech. Usually you listen without benefit of text. You seldom have artifacts to consult after the event. Normally, you take in the wholeness of the speaking event, now or never, with all of your senses acting like antennae picking up signals.

A speech critic performs multiple acts, simultaneously or in rapid succession. He looks, listens, and searches for half-hidden meanings, probes for implications, and tries to analyze all the subtle interactions among speaker, audience, and occasion. He does more than follow the speaker's words. His criticism is complex. He considers voice, gestures, style, subject, or whatever single features we might name, but he judges the value and effectiveness of speech from the *wholeness* of the event.

The complexity and dynamics of speech place a heavy load on the critic's power of attention. He must listen to understand the speech and must continuously isolate, analyze, and evaluate essential elements that affect the value of the enterprise. Some factors may escape his attention because of the strong competitive or compensatory influence of other rhetorical elements. Thus a great voice may create the illusion of great ideas. Conversely, great ideas may escape notice because they move sluggishly on a thin trickle of voice. Sometimes a glamorous personality half-hypnotizes listeners into believing that the speaker is saying something important. Later, the few people who read the text in cold print or listen to a transcription learn to their chagrin that they had mistaken malarky for a message. A speech that sounded fine in class may come close to sounding like gibberish when you hear it on tape. Because of the fleeting nature of speech and its susceptibility to rhetorical distortions, the art of criticism is demanding. It is mastered only by effort, discipline, and considerable experience.

To make close criticism, you will find a text, recording, or—if at all possible—a film with sound track to be invaluable. In live recordings, you can examine in detail various features of speech—ideas, structure, style, and aspects of delivery; but even so, to repeat a fundamental truth, the fullness of a speech exists only at the moment of its delivery in the presence of an audience. When you listen to it live, you are closer to the wholeness of the speaking event than you can ever be again.

Let us turn now to practical suggestions that you can put to use in criticizing classroom speeches.

PARTICIPATING IN CLASSROOM CRITICISM

As you listen to your classmates, you will hear a variety of views on many subjects coming from people of diverse backgrounds and personalities. You may be attracted by some views and personalities, repelled by others. As you listen, you are tempted to extol a speaker whose views support your own, especially if these views are under attack; or to denounce a speech that runs counter to your thinking. We are all prone to biases, but we must control them. A fair-minded critic is on guard lest he vote his private prejudices. He neither endorses a poor case in behalf of a cause of which he approves, nor does he withhold approval of a strong case for a cause he dislikes. One mark of maturity in a critic is his ability to judge speech by its artistic merits rather than his private predilections.

The most helpful criticism is specific and analytical, or diagnostic. As we have said, the principles of good speech discussed in chapter 2 are, presumably, the standards you will apply. But certain of these principles may be the focus of a given assignment. These matter should be given special critical attention in as specific terms as possible. To say merely that "your delivery is poor" or that "your analysis is weak" or that "your outline is fuzzy" or that "your gestures are great" is not very helpful. In what way is the delivery weak? Where does the analysis break down? Pinpoint your criticism.

You can often go one step further. What appears to be the *cause* of the specific weaknesses you point out? Does it appear to be nervousness, poor preparation, class distractions, a poor subject, or a misunderstood assignment? Since all the principles of good speech operate together, failure to handle one may be the cause of problems with others. Such criticism is diagnostic and can be as helpful in analyzing strengths as weaknesses.

The way in which you express your comments makes a world of difference in the way they are received. Rapport between critic and speaker is just as important as it is between speaker and audience. A speech class is doomed if members get in the habit of backslapping each other or if they look for opportunities to trade low blows. Criticism is productive when intelligence, integrity, and good will prevail. When thoughtful observations are accompanied by evidence of respect for a speaker's feeling, they are almost always welcomed. Frankness is essential, but so is tact. A dogmatic, opinionated statement is resented and often provokes reprisals that destroy class morale.

To their credit, students sense these things without exhortation. Intuitively they tend to open their critiques by stressing a speaker's strong points before indicating matters that need to be improved. This is sound procedure. Without putting it into words, most students realize that criticism must be expressed in a stimulating manner and made persuasive to the speaker before he will act on it.

METHODS OF REPORTING CRITICISM

Methods of reporting criticism vary with the assignment. If it is a group discussion, a debate, or several speeches on the same subject, criticism should follow the completion of the project. Similarly, if a single speech provokes discussion of the ideas presented, it is disruptive to intrude critical comments on the speech so long as the discussion is profitable. As we have said before, the comments stirred up by the original remarks may be fully as worthy of criticism in their own right.

With good reason, students will respect the criticism of their teacher more than that of their fellow students. But student criticism of the speech of their peers is an important learning experience for the critics and a test of their speech competence as well. Such criticism can be handled in a variety of ways: oral comment in class after each speech or after an assignment has been completed; or written comment checked by the teacher and selectively referred to the speakers for discussion with them at a later class meeting.

Student criticism, of course, does not preclude criticism by the teacher—presented orally, written on student outlines, or handled privately in the case of sensitive personal problems.

THE SPEECH CLASS: A SUMMARY

We have no wish or right to be narrowly prescriptive in the conduct of the speech course. There are many variables to be considered. Important among these are the special interests of teachers and students, the maturity and "speech competence" of the students, and the time and place allotted to the course. There is a basic purpose, however, that this book is designed to serve: the development of competent, resourceful speakers and listeners who are able to deal with significant ideas responsibly and graciously both in public and in private.

We think this will be accomplished best in classes where provocative questions bearing on the philosophy and principles and methods of speech developed in the text are discussed openly and critically; where the oral exercises deal with substance of sufficient consequence to invite stimulating forums; where speech criticism is conducted as an important learning experience; and where mutuality in purpose contributes to class morale and commitment to high standards of excellence.

Academic rigor for the sake of "blood, sweat, and tears" is an anathema to any worthy student, but a demanding course that makes a significant contribution to his education is respected. This is what we want your speech course to be.

QUESTIONS FOR DISCUSSION

1. What human faculties enter into "listening?" Your ears, of course, but how about your eyes, your mind, your emotions? Compare the meanings of "attention," "perception," and "reaction" to listening.

2. What correlation would you expect between listening for ideas and listening as a speech critic? Is it possible to give a speaker a high grade for his ideas and a low grade for his speech? Or a low grade for his ideas and a high grade for his speech?

3. Is the concentration expected of a speaker any more or less than that reasonably expected of a listener?

4. How would you compare the personal relations between speaker and audience with those between critic and speaker?

EXERCISES

1. Make this an exercise in comparative criticism. Select a major speaking event that you may listen to on television. If possible, make a tape recording. Write your criticism of the speech based on your TV viewing. Now play back the tape recording. What differences did you pick up between the TV version and the taped version of the speech? How significant are these differences in your judgment of the speech? Look for the newspaper accounts of the speech and take note of the criticism you find. What seems to be the basis or criterion of criticism that you found in the press? Final-

ly, what insights into the art of criticism did you acquire from this exercise?

2. Attend a speaking event on campus. Write a précis of the talk to prove to yourself and others that you understood what was said. Then go on to write an appraisal of the talk, using the thirteen principles of good speech as your standards. Have a classroom discussion of the event, using student critiques as the bases for a criticism of criticism.

3. Find the text of a speech that once excited a great deal of attention but one that you have never read. Examples might be Wendell Phillips, "The Murder of Lovejoy" (1837); William Jennings Bryan's convention speech of 1896; Franklin Roosevelt's first inaugural address, 1933. First read the text without benefit of additional material. Then look up newspaper items on the speech and its times, general histories, and biographies of the speaker. With benefit of these materials and the exercise of historical imagination, reconstruct the speaking event by putting it into the context of its times. Comment on the meaning of the speech with and without the historical context.

4. Read two or three essays on the criticism of individual speakers that you find in W. N. Brigance, ed., *A History and Criticism of American Public Address,* 1943. Select one for an oral report. In your speech, make clear how the critic went about his job, what his findings were, and your judgment of his criticism.

5. Verbal Communication: Voice and Diction

We defined speech in chapter 2 as "the communication of ideas and feelings through visible and audible symbols originating in speakers, listeners, and observers, and in the settings in which communication takes place."

The audible symbols of speech are produced principally by voice—sounds, words, phrases, and articulate speech. This verbal communication is discussed here as voice and diction and elsewhere as oral composition and style.

The visible symbols of speech are produced principally by bodily action—posture, movement, and gesture. These and other visible symbols and signs are discussed in the next chapter as nonverbal communication.

Since all speech takes place in settings with different physical and psychological characteristics, it is inevitable that the visible and audible stimuli arising from these sources enter into and affect the interaction among participants.

All of this interaction is a function of *stimuli, perception,* and *reaction* or *response.* As we go along, we shall see that these stimuli are usually sensuous—perceived by the senses, principally sight and hearing; but in a complete analysis touch, smell, and taste would also enter in. It is not difficult to imagine situations in which these other sense perceptions would affect response. It is also true that some stimuli are *supersensory* in character, induced by recall, reflection, and imagination, but evoking response as surely as direct sensory observation.

Perception of the stimuli entering into communication may be *conscious* or *subliminal.* There are degrees of awareness of the sources of our responses to stimulation. Sometimes we know, or at least we think we know, why we are responding as we are; in other situations, we may react intuitively to stimuli below the limen of consciousness without full awareness. These intuitive judgments, hunches, or feelings, rightly or wrongly, can affect response.

The reactions or responses to these stimuli may be *intellectual* or *emotional* in character, and they may be manifested *overtly* or *covertly*. Typically, reactions are mixed with respect to these rather arbitrary distinctions.

WHY YOU SPEAK AS YOU DO

Voice and articulate speech are the principal carriers of the audible symbols of speech. We arrange words into sentences and organize sentences to represent our ideas and feelings, but in verbal communication we employ the nuances of voice and diction to express these ideas and feelings. The way you use your voice and diction is largely determined by organic, environmental, and personality influences; but all are subject to correction, reeducation, and improvement.

ORGANIC FACTORS

If you are healthy and robust, you are more likely to have a strong, vibrant voice than if you are frail and weak. A small larynx with short vocal cords produces a higher-pitched voice than a large larynx with long vocal cords. A cleft palate or poorly aligned teeth may cause a lisp. Chronic hoarseness is frequently caused by malformation of the larynx. Adenoids impair nasal resonance. A hearing deficiency may result in blurred speech or vocal monotony.

If your trouble springs from organic problems, arrange for a medical examination before you undertake voice training.

ENVIRONMENTAL FACTORS

A child's environment furnishes models for his own speech. By trial and error, he perfects the form of speech that meets with surest acceptance. We talk very much like the people with whom we communicated while our speech habits were being formed.

Geographic environment influences the rate of our speech, tonal patterns, our articulation and pronunciation. Even an untrained ear can detect differences between speech that is indigenous to the Deep South and speech that is indigenous to parts of New England. Skilled linguists can detect dialectal differences within relatively small geographical areas.

Home and community environment may affect our speech for good or bad. A child who is reared in a discordant home may speak in a voice that reflects tension. A child surrounded by people who speak English with a foreign accent may learn to speak English with the same accent.

Speech patterns determined by environment are learned and therefore can be unlearned. New and more desirable habits can be substituted through directed exercises.

PERSONALITY FACTORS

Your voice is a mirror of your personality. A person who talks loudly and with exaggerated heartiness or who gushes over trivialities is probably insecure in his relations with others, is overcompensating for his timidity, and is overanxious to please. We recognize a whining, complaining voice as belonging to a person who feels mistreated, abused, and discriminated against. And we can spot the flat, impersonal tone and the monotonous lack of inflection of the inhibited person who tries to shield himself from the intrusion of outsiders.

If you recognize that your voice lacks confidence, warmth, vibrancy, or expressiveness because of poor personal adjustment, you have taken the first step toward improvement. Your speech course offers a favorable environment for reevaluation of yourself and redirection of your vocal habits.

EFFECTIVE USE OF THE VOICE

The source of energy for the voice is the breath stream, which sets into vibration the vocal folds (also called cords or bands) that are housed in the larynx. Since speech occurs as the breath is exhaled, exhalation needs to be controlled, steady, and adequate. Inhalation needs to be silent, quick enough not to interrupt continuity, and accomplished without tension in the neck and throat. The vocal folds, then, are the vibrator. Vibrations are built up or resonated principally by the pharynx, mouth, and nasal cavities—all located above the larynx.

With this equipment we produce sounds of varying degrees of loudness, at different pitches, with distinctive qualities, and of varying durations. Breathing (the source of energy) is particularly important in loudness and duration; phonation (the vibration of the vocal bands) is the most important factor in pitch and a determining factor in vocal quality; and the resonators are of great importance in bringing out qualities of tone.

The human voice, like other sounds, has four physical characteristics —force, pitch, quality, and time. Properly controlled, these four elements contribute to effective use of the voice.

FORCE

Talk loudly enough to be heard easily and quietly enough to be heard without annoyance. With attention and practice you can bring force under

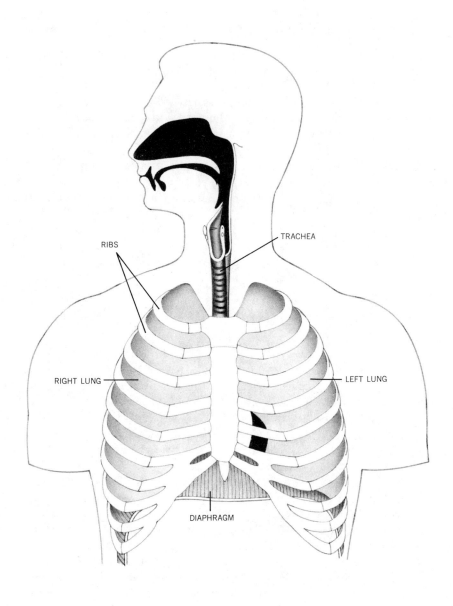

RIBS

TRACHEA

RIGHT LUNG

LEFT LUNG

DIAPHRAGM

Above: The respiratory mechanism. On facing page: (top) Sagittal section of the head and neck. (bottom) Superior view of the vocal folds. (Drawings by Lorelle Raboni)

44

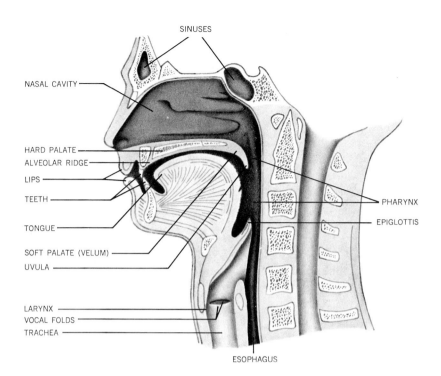

SINUSES

NASAL CAVITY

HARD PALATE
ALVEOLAR RIDGE
LIPS
TEETH
TONGUE
SOFT PALATE (VELUM)
UVULA

LARYNX
VOCAL FOLDS
TRACHEA

PHARYNX
EPIGLOTTIS

ESOPHAGUS

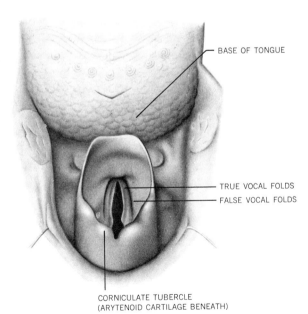

BASE OF TONGUE

TRUE VOCAL FOLDS
FALSE VOCAL FOLDS

CORNICULATE TUBERCLE
(ARYTENOID CARTILAGE BENEATH)

45

control. If people do not hear you, it may be that you need, not just more volume, but finer control.

Varying the force of your voice to convey meaning and feeling is a much more subtle matter. *Stress*—making a word, sentence, or point "stand out"—is an important part of it. Added loudness serves to underline what you say; so does reduced loudness. Any notable departure from your normal level of loudness serves to draw attention. This means that you can use variations in loudness to mark anything that you want to emphasize. Such variations also help to reduce monotony in speaking.

PITCH

Is your habitual pitch level the best pitch level for you? In what ways can you use variations in pitch sensitively and meaningfully?

Each person uses one pitch level more frequently than any other. This is the level on which he most often begins speaking and to which he returns after shifting up or down the scale. It is his *habitual* pitch level.

For each voice there is one pitch level or a small band of pitch levels at which the voice operates most easily and most effectively. This is called the *optimum* pitch level. To achieve best results, try to make your habitual pitch level the same as your optimum pitch level.

Many people begin speech training with a notion that they would like to "lower their voices" because they admire low-pitched voices. Whether this is a realistic purpose depends on the capacity of a particular person's vocal mechanism. If you owned a fine violin, people would think you foolish if you tried to make it sound like a cello. The two instruments operate in the same fashion, just as two voices do. But the cello has larger and longer strings and a larger and differently shaped resonating cavity. The violin's most beautiful tones are considerably higher than the best tones of the cello. A person who attempts to force his pitch down to the level used by a public speaker or actor whom he admires may be sacrificing tonal beauty in the process. Even though his father's voice is a bass-baritone, his may be a tenor. On the other hand, some people continue to talk at a childish or early-adolescent pitch level long after their matured vocal mechanism has become suited to a lower pitch.

Listen to yourself and see if you detect a harsh, gravelly quality, especially when your voice moves down the scale (as at the ends of sentences). If you do, it may mean that you are forcing the pitch of your voice uncomfortably low. On the other hand, do your high pitch levels (as when you accent a word) sound thin, sharp, or strained? If so, your habitual pitch level may be too high.

An expressive voice moves up and down the musical scale continuously in an infinite variety of patterns. This variation in pitch, which we call *melody,* is one of the most important factors in conveying emotions and meanings. Consider this sentence: "You are not going out of the house today." Say it with a continuous downward inflection, and it has the authority and finality of an order. Use a rising inflection, and it becomes a simple question. Leap to a high pitch on the word *not,* and it takes on a threatening tone. Use a gliding inflection upward and then downward on the word *you,* and it becomes contemptuous. For greatest effectiveness, melody should be combined with variations in force and rate, but melody itself permits more subtlety of expression than does either force or rate.

Monotony in melody is of several types. The true *monotone,* who literally does not vary from a single pitch level, is comparatively rare. A more common offender is the speaker who shifts back and forth among three or four notes in a repeated pitch pattern that is quite unrelated to the meaning of what he is saying. Such a pattern seems colorless and dull. The person who ends every sentence on a rising inflection seems indecisive and lacking in self-confidence. A speaker who repeatedly uses heavy downward inflections seems dogmatic and aggressive. True melody demands the use of changes in pitch to supplement and emphasize the intellectual and emotional content of speech.

QUALITY

Vocal quality is the most sensitive indicator of emotion in speaking and it is the least subject to direct control by the speaker. The *quality* of a sound is determined by the relations between the overtones and the fundamental tone (the basic pitch).[1] These relations are determined by the vibrating mechanism and the resonators. The muscles involved in voice production respond to the emotion of the speaker. This response is almost involuntary—it is largely beyond the speaker's control, except as he is able to control his emotions.

It is very hard to disguise or simulate emotion, because vocal quality always gives clues to one's real feelings. A mechanical approach to varying vocal quality produces artificial effects. Sincerity of emotional expression stems from sincere involvement in the emotion itself.

TIME

We have all heard speakers who rattle along at a rate far too fast to be understood, and others who speak so slowly you could almost take a nap between words and phrases. These extremes are both undesirable, and yet there is no one ideal rate of speaking. What is good for one speaker in one environment, in one situation, for one subject, will not necessarily

---

[1]Do not confuse *pitch* and *quality.* Sound the identical pitch on the piano and the violin and note the differences in the sound. These are differences in *quality.*

be good if one of these factors is altered. How, then, can you find a good rate of speaking?

THE SPEAKER'S TEMPERAMENT AND PERSONALITY

The speaking rate of a slow-moving person will naturally vary from that of an excitable, high-strung person. Follow your individual pattern, as long as it does not hamper intelligibility, annoy your listeners, or seem inappropriate to what you are saying.

THE SPEAKER'S ENVIRONMENT

As we have seen, speech habits (including our rate of speaking), are formed on the basis of models provided for us early in life. In some sections of the United States, people speak more rapidly than in other sections. Your speaking rate should be determined largely by what your listeners are used to.

THE SITUATION

Use a slower rate in addressing a large audience than in intimate conversation.

THE CONTENT OF THE SPEECH

Complex ideas, statistics, or problems that the audience has not previously considered take longer to grasp than more simple or more familiar statements. In expressing some emotions, such as joy and excitement, we usually speak more rapidly than when we are expressing grief or reverence.

Duration is the time spent in pronouncing a single word or phrase. *Pause* is the space of silence between words or phrases. The two combine to determine the over-all rate of speech.

Pauses are the punctuation marks in speech. Use them:

1. To separate ideas and to set them apart as units of thought. "He rose awkwardly, / looked about furtively, / cleared his throat, / shifted his weight once or twice, / and finally began to speak."
2. To point up an important idea that you are about to express. "The most dangerous force operating today to undermine our political structure is / apathy of the electorate."
3. To give yourself time to organize your thoughts. But don't use too many pauses for this purpose, or prolong them excessively. Be especially careful to avoid the vocalized pause "er."

Pauses provide a natural opportunity to inhale. If you find yourself interrupting phrases by gasping for breath, practice deeper breathing and give more attention to spacing your inhalations so that they come at logical stopping places. If you talk on and on without pausing for breath, your audience will wonder whether you will make it to the end. Practice phrasing your thoughts to allow for more frequent pauses, and avoid trying to talk on the last molecule of air you can squeeze from your lungs.

ARTICULATION

Articulation means the adjustments and movements of the organs involved in producing speech sounds and in joining these sounds to form words and phrases. As we use it here, the term has about the same meaning as *enunciation.*

The sounds of spoken English include vowels, diphthongs, and consonants. Four actions are essential in producing *vowel sounds:* The vocal folds vibrate, producing voice; the opening into the nasal passage is closed or reduced; the tip of the tongue is held down behind the lower front teeth; and the mouth is opened to permit the sound to come out. How widely you open your mouth varies with different vowels, as do the shape of the lips and the position of the tongue.

A *diphthong* is a continuous blending of two vowel sounds to form one syllable. For example, say these two sounds rapidly, one after the other: the *ah* in *father* and the *oo* in *hoot.* The resulting sound is the diphthong *ow* in *cow.*

Consonant sounds are formed by interrupting or restricting the breath stream. For example, say the word *up.* Notice that you produce the consonant *p* by closing your lips and stopping the breath stream. Then say the word *his.* Here the consonant *is* is produced by forcing air through a narrow aperture formed by tongue and teeth.

ARTICULATING VOWELS AND DIPHTHONGS

Whether your voice is pleasant may be determined by the way you produce vowels and diphthongs. Let your ear be your guide. Try for clear, mellow, resonant intonation. Avoid harsh, guttural, strident tones.

If you are careless about producing vowels and diphthongs, you will also impair intelligibility. Poor production of these sounds will cause listeners to confuse your words and thus mistake your meaning. If you say *tar* when you mean *tower,* you can hardly expect your listeners to know what you are talking about.

ARTICULATING CONSONANTS

The consonants are most important in giving distinctness and clarity to speech. Poor enunciation results largely from a failure to produce consonants with precision. Improvement depends upon finer control over the action of tongue and lips in relation to the gum ridge and teeth. If this contact is not sharply made, the sound produced by releasing the contact is weak. Poor enunciation can usually be improved by more active precise formulation of consonant sounds.

ASSIMILATION OF SOUNDS

We seldom give speech sounds their full value as we talk. This is all right so long as we do not seriously impair our vocal quality and so long as we identify sounds clearly enough for listeners to understand us. Stilted speech that results from loving attention to each individual sound is either an affectation or a bad habit.

Speech sounds are affected by their neighbors. Omissions and glides and carry-overs from one sound to another are inevitable in free-flowing, easy speech. This sort of natural adjustment is called *assimilation.* Say this sentence: "Pat takes science," Notice that one *t* serves for both *Pat* and *takes,* and one *s* for both *takes* and *science.* More assimilation is admissible, of course, in conversation and informal speech than on occasions where considerable volume is required.

PRONUNCIATION

Good pronunciation depends on the speech sounds you choose in saying a word and the syllable or syllables you choose to accent in a word. Suppose you use the same vowel sound in *pour* and *poor,* or in *but* and *full;* or suppose you use the final consonant sound of *rage* in *garage,* or the initial consonant sound of *chill* in *charade,* or say *bus* exactly like *buzz;* or suppose you accent the wrong syllable in *pretense, cigarette, infamous.* These are examples of errors in pronunciation. They are failures to conform to good usage in sound or accent, and they may occur even though your articulation is perfect.

STANDARD PRONUNCIATION

If you have traveled through the United States, you were probably impressed by the variety of pronunciation patterns you heard. Even within a single large city, varying patterns of pronunciation are noticeable. Pronunciations in the various sections of the United States, and at different social levels within any one section, differ in many particulars.

The greatest uniformity in pronunciation occurs among educated speakers. Less uniformity exists at lower cultural levels. When a given pronunciation becomes the predominant usage of educated speakers over a large area, it is accepted as a *standard* pronunciation. A pronunciation that is limited to less-educated speakers or to a very small area is termed *substandard.*

DIALECTS OF THE UNITED STATES

By far the largest number of words in English have one "correct" pronunciation—i.e., one pronunciation that all cultivated speakers of English prefer. There are, however, certain groups of words that are pronounced with a slight difference in various large geographical areas.

A *dialect* is any pattern of pronunciation that is commonly used in one geographical area, but that differs somewhat from the usage of other areas.

A *provincial dialect* is a pattern of pronunciation that is limited to a narrow geographical region and that is not accepted by good speakers over a large area.

A *standard dialect* is a pattern of pronunciation that is used by most good speakers in a large geographical area, but that differs somewhat from the predominant good speech of another large area.

In the United States there are *three standard dialects:* (1) *Standard Eastern,* which is used in eastern New England and in New York City; (2) *Standard Southern,* which is used in the states that roughly made up the Confederacy; and (3) *Standard General American,* which is used in the rest of the United States.

The General American dialect is spreading in usage, because it is the most common form of pronunciation in radio, television, and movies. The Eastern dialect most closely resembles standard British pronunciation, which is the model for stage diction.

Each of the three major dialects has a beauty of its own, and none is superior to another. All are standard and entirely correct. The criterion of good pronunciation is what is preferred by the majority of educated, careful speakers in a large geographical area. The best choice for an individual is the best speech of his own area.

USE OF THE DICTIONARY

You can improve your pronunciation if you get in the habit of using a good dictionary. Referring to a dictionary is futile, though, unless you know how to interpret what you find there.

Many people think that a dictionary's function is to *prescribe* pronunciation. But if you read the preface of several dictionaries, you will discover that the editors have attempted rather to *describe* the pronunciation used by most good speakers.

Other people think that when a dictionary lists more than one pronunciation for a word, the first is the "preferred" pronunciation. Actually, when several pronunciations of a word are used by large numbers of good speakers, the dictionary lists all of them. The order of listing is simply an attempt to indicate their relative popularity. It does not mean that any one pronunciation is superior to the others.

But how can you decide which pronunciation is "preferred"? When you have pronounced the word in each of the ways listed, choose the one that sounds most familiar to you. That pronunciation is likely to be the one most frequently used by good speakers in your dialect area. It is, therefore, the preferred pronunciation for your dialect.

In using a dictionary to improve your pronunciation, be sure you understand the symbols it uses. Mispronunciation of the key words cited by the dictionary to identify sounds will result in mispronunciation of the words you are checking. It will do you no good to know that the *a* in *any* is pronounced like the *e* in *end* if you pronounce *end* as *ind* (a substandard pronunciation common in some areas). Although the key-word system of indicating pronunciation is always open to this misunderstanding, an awareness of the problem and care in identifying the pronunciation of the key words will help you to avoid most mistakes.

SUGGESTIONS FOR SELF-IMPROVEMENT

1. FIND OUT HOW OTHERS REACT TO YOUR SPEECH

Ask for frank opinions. What is good and what is bad? Do you project your voice? Is your vocal quality pleasant, jarring, or distracting? Do you speak distinctly? Is your pronunciation accurate? Sampling the reactions of others enables you to judge how well you communicate.

2. LEARN TO LISTEN OBJECTIVELY TO YOURSELF

This is difficult but essential. Frequent recordings of your voice on a disc, tape, or wire recorder will help. If the result seems unflattering, don't jump to the conclusion that the recording is bad. It is more likely that you are getting the full impact of some defect in your voice for the first time.

3. LISTEN ANALYTICALLY

Casual listening, however objective, won't help you spot problems that need attention. Analytical listening means the ability to isolate your individual characteristics of volume, quality, pitch, and rate, and the elements of your articulation and pronunciation. You will need the ability to detect fine distinctions. This may require ear training.

4. DRAW UPON VISUAL, TACTUAL, AND KINAESTHETIC IMPRESSIONS

Some parts of your vocal mechanism are hidden from view, but you can observe the functioning of others with the aid of a mirror as you perform exercises. The sense of touch will help you identify and reshape your articulatory habits. For example, you can feel the point where your tongue tip touches to form a *t* or where your lower lip comes against your teeth in forming an *f*. Through kinaesthetic impressions you can acquire the *feel* of a relaxed pharynx, the degree of tension in the tongue when a particular vowel sound is formed, or the relaxation of throat muscles not needed in phonation.

5. PRACTICE

A finer control over voice, articulation, and pronunciation is possible through daily work-outs. Start with the exercises at the end of this chapter and collect others to meet your needs. If your problem is relatively minor, it can usually be cleared up quickly. Should your problem be deep-seated, then patience, time, and work will be required to reform your speaking habits.

QUESTIONS FOR DISCUSSION

1. Read the quotation below and comment on the questions that follow:

> . . . Our voice tells a good deal about us. It may reveal something about our physical condition: that we are tired or sleepy, alert and energetic, tense or relaxed; that we have adenoids; that we have been shouting or smoking too much; or that we are sick or well. It may reveal important characteristics of our personalities: that we are aggressive or submissive, introvert or extrovert; that we have or that we lack self-confidence. It may be indicative of our moods, showing when we are happy or sad, excited or depressed. It may indicate quite clearly our attitude toward the situation in which we find ourselves, even though we may desire to conceal that attitude. Our voice may show that we are interested or bored, that we are surprised or disappointed, that we are embarrassed, angry, pleased, hostile, sarcastic, or incredulous.[2]

   a. To what extent are these revelations by voice perceived by listeners? How valuable are they?

   b. As far as voice is concerned, is a speaker at the mercy of his physical condition, his personality, his confidence, his moods, his attitudes, his emotions? What corrective measures, if any, might be available?

[2]James M. O'Neill (ed.), *The Foundations of Speech* (Englewood Cliffs, N.J.: Prentice-Hall, Inc., 1941), p. 200.

2. Voice is the carrier of words in speech. How does voice affect the impact of words in articulate speech? Consider vocal *force, pitch, quality,* and *time.* How much meaning and feeling would you sacrifice if you spoke in a monotone—no variation in force, pitch, quality, or time?

3. Which of the standard dialects of the United States do you speak? Should a person moving to another geographical region attempt to use the dialect of that region? Is he at a disadvantage in communication?

EXERCISES

1. Stand erect before a full-length mirror. Support your weight on both feet, with the center of support toward the front of each foot. Imagine that one string is tied to the top of your head, and that another is tied to your breastbone; imagine that you are being held up by these two strings. Try to "grow upward" in the line of these imaginary strings. Be sure your shoulders and neck are relaxed; your body should be erect but not stiff. Now your lungs are free to fill with air. Remember that slouching crowds the chest cavity and hampers breathing.

2. Place your left hand lightly on your breastbone, and your right hand across your abdomen between the naval and lower ribs. Take a quick, silent breath. Watch your two hands; the left one should remain steady, for the breastbone should not move (nor should the shoulders rise); the right hand should be forced outward, since the abdominal wall is forced against it when the diaphragm pulls downward against the viscera. Watch the lower ribs also. Do you see the lower chest expanding? Now you have inhaled in an easy, natural manner for speech, "packing the breath against your belt."

Remaining erect and keeping the breastbone steady, *gradually* force the breath from your body by pulling inward with the abdominal muscles. Your left hand on the breastbone should remain steady; your right hand should pull inward as the abdominal muscles contract. As you exhale, say the vowel *ah.* Prolong it, keeping the tone smooth and steady.

3. Slowly repeat the question, "Who are you?" five times per breath. The first time, use a small inhalation and control the exhalation so that the words are loud enough to carry to a person five feet away. Next, imagine you are speaking to someone ten feet away; then twenty; then forty. Beware of tightening the throat or raising the pitch level as you increase your strength of tone. Make each successive question louder by taking a slightly deeper inhalation than the time before, and, on exhalation, by pulling inward more firmly with your abdominal muscles.

4. In the following selection, underline the words that need greater force to carry emphasis. Practice reading the poem as you marked it.

Teach me to feel another's woe,
   To hide the fault I see;
That mercy I to others show
   That mercy show to me.
          —Alexander Pope

5. Each of the following sentences has an obvious mood. Read each one aloud, pausing and varying the rate of your speech to convey the particular mood.

Life is a narrow vale between the cold and barren peaks of two eternities.
                                  (*Robert Green Ingersoll*)

I wish I knew what to do about it.
Let me tell you the wonderful news!
Will you tell me how to get to Vine Street?
Why don't you look where you're going?
I'm too tired to go another step.

6. Hold your head erect. Now let the neck muscles relax until your head drops forward on your chest. Be sure you don't pull it forward, but let it drop of its own weight. Rotate your head slowly toward the right shoulder, then to the back, to the left shoulder, and front again, letting it fall of its own weight, relaxed. Keeping your muscles relaxed, read the following sentences. Then read the three lines from Matthew Arnold and listen critically to your tone to detect any return of tension.

Ah, how easy this is!
I will relax and relax and relax.

The sea is calm to-night.
The tide is full, the moon lies fair
Upon the straits—
          —Matthew Arnold

7. Using various melody patterns, discover how many different meanings and emotional shades you can express with each of the following sentences.

I don't know why you want me to go to the movies with you.
How would you like to move to the moon?
I've always been polite to Tom.
I should change my attitude toward mathematics.

8. Read the following sentences. There should be no nasal sounds.

This is the house that Jack built.
She goes to school every day.
Who left a light gray hat by that chair?

Now read these sentences, giving full nasal resonance to the *m, n,* and *ng,* none to the other sounds.

Nobody expects him to come home.
Turn left at the next corner.
His name must be in the telephone book.

9. Practice reading the following selection aloud, paying particular attention to the way you produce the vowels and diphthongs.

If thou must love me, let it be for naught
Except for love's sake only. Do not say,
'I love her for her smile—her look—her way
Of speaking gently,—for a trick of thought
That falls in well with mine, and certes brought
    A sense of pleasant ease on such a day'—
    For these things in themselves, Beloved, may
Be changed, or change for thee—and love, so wrought,
May be unwrought so. Neither love me for
    Thine own dear pity's wiping my cheeks dry:
A creature might forget to weep, who bore
    Thy comfort long, and lose thy love thereby!
But love me for love's sake, that evermore
    Thou mayst love on, through love's eternity.
                                    —Elizabeth Barrett Browning

10. Practice reading the following selection aloud, paying particular attention to the way you articulate the consonants.

Trust thou thy Love: if she be proud, is she not sweet?
Trust thou thy Love: if she be mute, is she not pure?
Lay thou thy soul full in her hands, low at her feet;
Fail, Sun and Breath!—yet, for thy peace, She shall endure.
                                    —John Ruskin

11. During the next five days, listen for the mispronunciations that other people make. List all that you hear.

6. Nonverbal Communication

Spoken language remains the principal mode of communication, but speakers necessarily use nonverbal stimuli and adapt to them in any setting in which the speaker is in sight of or in proximate contact with his audience. These nonverbal factors affecting communication almost defy classification, but they certainly include the bodily action of the speaker—posture, movement, and gesture; personal characteristics and appearance; and the physical and psychological environment in which the communication takes place. All of these carry meaning and feeling in their own right, and can reinforce or weaken the impact of words.

BODILY ACTION: SOME COMMON MISCONCEPTIONS

CONFINING BODILY ACTION TO GROSS MOVEMENT

Some people think that bodily action refers only to big movements of the entire body or sweeping gestures made with arms and hands. They are suspicious of instruction in bodily action, for they have watched persons who behaved like acrobats rather than speakers intent on communicating ideas.

Eloquent gestures need not involve big movements. The body has hundreds of muscles, and all of them contract and relax. These voluntary and involuntary muscle movements *are* bodily action. An expressive face, a thrust of the jaw, a toss of the head, a shrug of the shoulders—these and dozens of other small movements constitute bodily action.

Big movements are not taboo. Far from it! But bodily action includes more than the gross movements of arms, legs, or the whole body.

TREATING BODILY ACTION AS MECHANICAL

Mechanical gestures, like mechanical phrases, say very little to your audience—except that you have spent a lot of time practicing how to turn

57

them out. Old-time elocutionists often charted elaborate classifications of gestures and worked out precise instructions for making each one. The result was a mechanical speaker whose puppet-like movements had little to do with his thought or mood, but who felt he had to make gestures even when there was no good reason for them.

CONFUSING NATURAL WITH HABITUAL MOVEMENT

Sometimes people insist that good bodily action is whatever "comes naturally." They confuse natural behavior with habitual behavior. We often hold nature responsible for what really is the product of habit, and call something natural only because it is familiar.

This confusion gets us into trouble when we excuse bad habits as being natural. People whose unfortunate habits of posture or gesturing interfere with communication need new habits, no matter how natural the old ones seem. Bad habits are changed by objective self-study followed by corrective exercises.

HOW BODILY ACTION WORKS FOR OR AGAINST YOU

ACTION WINS AND HOLD ATTENTION

A listener can rivet his attention to a fixed point for only a few seconds. You must constantly adapt your matter and manner to his shifting energies. You can catch his ear by keeping your ideas and language lively; you can catch his eye by matching your physical movements to your marching ideas.

An animated window display attracts more attention than a stationary one. A physically active speaker excites more interest than a "stationary" one. A vital speaker stimulates listeners to empathize with him. Listeners respond to a lively speaker much as a fan in the bleachers responds to the backfield in action. When you stir your listeners to participate in communication, you win their active interest.

ACTION COMMUNICATES MEANING

Look about you. Out of earshot but within eyesight you see two people lounging on the lawn. One leans forward in a confidential manner. The other throws back his head and slaps his leg. Both seem to laugh uproariously. You see two other people standing on the sidewalk. Their bodies quiver; one gestures menacingly at the other. Without hearing a single word, you reach conclusions about each conversation, the moods of the participants, and their attitudes toward each other. Action is loaded with meaning.

Physical behavior is an index to personality

Our impressions of a speaker come from his total behavior, from many cooperating cues so faint and fleeting that we can seldom isolate them. For instance, our initial confidence—or lack of it—in a speaker's ability depends upon "something" we sense in his general manner. Not that we actually sit back and muse. "Here's a fellow who walks energetically, has a bright eye, has an easy, comfortable manner, and for these and other reasons warrants my confidence." Still we see these things without realizing it, and we respond favorably to him. In the same way, we respond unfavorably to a speaker whose facial muscles are taut, who shuffles about, and who darts furtive glances here and there as if seeking to escape. His anxiety transfers itself to his audience.

Certain patterns of physical behavior lead us to make snap judgments. Mincing movements suggest a prissy person. A scowling face and a jutting jaw send us off to a neutral corner for safety. The man who descends upon us, gives us a bone-crushing handshake, and flashes smiles on and off like a neon sign puts us on guard and stimulates our sales resistance. Whenever you speak, your listener responds to your mannerisms as well as to your words. He is sizing you up. We may deplore snap judgments, but people go right on making them. The man who totters onto the platform like Casper Milquetoast may have nerves of steel and the courage of a lion, but unless his listeners have a chance to test these qualities on the spot, many of them will never revise their first impressions of him.

Gestures aid in description, narration, and exposition

Gestures supplement words and fill in gaps. A traveler excitedly describes the volcanic eruption of Mt. Parícutin, in Mexico. His arms and hands begin to speak, suggesting clouds of billowing smoke and a flood of white-hot lava. His actions help you to create the scene in your own imagination. Or you are lost and ask a farmer for directions. As the farmer talks, he points north and west to help you get your bearings; his arms cross to suggest an intersection; he moves hand and arm in a sweeping curve to indicate a bend in the road. Indeed, it is difficult to instruct—either formally or informally—without gestures that indicate location, space, size, speed, force, and procedure.

Gestures express conviction and feeling

We speak forcefully with our entire body when we are under the influence of strong convictions and feelings. Even someone who is usually shy and reserved becomes a person transformed. His face becomes mobile; there is a new set to his shoulders; and his arms and hands suddenly go to work without any conscious effort on his part. Unless a person's emotions get out of control, he is at his best when he speaks for a cause that means a great deal to him. His mind and body cooperate in an accent and rhythm of expression that the audience quickly detects and respects. Any one of his gestures—a shrug of the shoulders, a clenched fist, an expression of scorn—may be ambiguous in itself; but in the full context of his unmistakable attitudes and feelings, it will move the audience to give undivided attention and to react correspondingly, with laughter, vexation, or indignation.

ACTION RELIEVES TENSION

Some tension, though we may scarcely be aware of it, is normal even in our day-to-day speaking. Heightened tension is inevitable when you are on the spot—whether you are participating in a conference or giving a public reading or speech. From autobiographies and biographies of great speakers, we learn that before each speech they too built up tensions bordering on stage fright, even after years and years of experience. Norman Thomas, himself a brilliant and seasoned speaker, describes this universal reaction:

> Some degree of nervous tension one must expect before an important speech. At least before certain speeches, especially in a debate or symposium, one shivers on the brink of speech as before diving into cold water. But once in, the speech, like the water, is bracing.[1]

As tensions mount, some speakers freeze in their shoes, unable to think clearly and to find the right words. If this happens to you, take deliberate steps to break the cycle of tension. Change your position. Move about. Make some gestures. Clearly these are only temporary expedients to use in emergency situations. But it is important to shake off your immobility and to loosen up. Physical activity is your best way to gain freedom and relaxation, no matter how awkward it makes you feel at first.

If you don't find some way to relieve dammed-up tensions, they may spill over into random, nervous movements. In effect, these are the body's involuntary and uncontrolled attempts to relieve itself of strain. You have seen a speaker move about the platform in a distracted manner, shifting his weight from one foot to the other, clenching and unclenching his hands, forcing a ring up and down a finger, stretching his neck to relieve the pressue of his collar. Actually this distraught behavior doesn't really relieve the tension; and once the speaker becomes aware of it, he responds to it as a further distraction. And so does his audience.

The way to break up random behavior is to focus sharply on what

[1] *Mr. Chairman, Ladies and Gentlemen . . .* (New York: Hermitage House, 1955), pp. 80–81.

you are saying, then *induce* some purposeful activity that will enforce your statements. The gestures you make may not be the best, but they will help to redirect your energies. With increased poise and self-control, your body will begin to speak purposefully without conscious direction.

CHARACTERISTICS OF GOOD BODILY ACTION

1. VITALITY

Energized speech keeps the listener listening. A person who is alive from head to foot relays his vitality. A droopy, lethargic speaker suggests, in effect, "I'm sorry to take your time. I'll be through soon." A vital speaker mobilizes his audience.

2. VARIETY

Physical flexibility is the key to variety. Unrelieved action wearies an audience. Overworked gestures, no matter how well they are executed, are monotonous. Still worse are unvaried and meaningless gestures, such as the perpetual motion of a bobbing head or chopping the air with an arm and hand. Tension or poor habits usually account for this monotony. Variety is achieved through self-appraisal, a keener appreciation of purposeful movement, and exercises that induce flexibility.

3. COORDINATION

Though varied, gestures may be awkward and disjointed. Any single gesture should mesh smoothly with all parts of a totally responding body. A speaker who bobs his head around but holds his shoulders stiff reminds his viewers of a poorly manipulated puppet. And if he thrusts out his arm and hand mechanically, he calls to mind a badly adjusted mechanism of wheels and springs. When all movements are well coordinated, no single gesture is conspicuous as a detached action.

4. INTEGRATION

Effective action springs from the meanings a speaker is trying to convey. He shrugs, smiles, scowls, points, draws himself up because he is responding to an inner impulse to do so. Action is integrated when it is keyed to a speaker's mind and emotions.

5. TIMING

A good gesture is timed to fit the word or phrase it is intended to enforce. An arm or hand gesture is ludicrous when it precedes the essential word or phrase it is supposed to emphasize, or when it comes as an afterbeat. Poor timing is the result of uncoordinated activity, weak integration between action and meaning, or "canned" gestures.

6. RESERVE

Expend energy freely in speaking, but don't squander it all at once. If you unwind with a terrific burst of gestures, you will soon dissipate your initial impact. Give your listeners the feeling they have when they are driving a high-powered automobile—that there is plenty of power left if it's needed. Listeners grow uneasy when a speaker strains or wilts. End your speech as you begin it, with energy to spare.

7. APPROPRIATENESS

Adapt your action to both the audience and the occasion. A pep rally calls for abundant action from a cheer leader. But exaggerated gestures at a dinner party or in a small group suggest that the speaker is either an exhibitionist or that he suffers from an overheated mind.

HOW TO IMPROVE YOUR BODILY ACTION

1. STUDY OTHER PEOPLE'S PHYSICAL BEHAVIOR

Observe the part bodily action plays in the speech that goes on around you—in lectures, movies, TV programs, and your classmates' talks. Sensitize yourself to the role of bodily action in communication. Note how bodily action works for or against the people you observe. How would you advise those with poor bodily action to improve?

2. GET AN IMAGE OF YOUR OWN CHARACTERISTIC PHYSICAL BEHAVIOR IN SPEECH

This may not be easy. You can get some visual glimpses from candid camera shots, or, better yet, from home movies. But the image also includes a feeling for what you're doing when you're doing it.

Welcome your classmates' descriptions of your physical behavior. Try to see yourself objectively through their eyes. Then check their descriptions by talking before a full-length mirror. If you see an unrelieved deadpan expression or an unbroken frown, remember that is what your audience has to look at each time you speak.

3. FORM A CLEAR IDEA OF HOW TO CORRECT YOUR PROBLEMS

Once you have pinpointed your problems, let your instructor and classmates help you find procedures for correcting them. Short work-out programs in class are particularly helpful. Experiment on the spot with the suggestions that are made and get your classmates' reactions to the results. If you don't understand a suggestion, ask someone else to demonstrate it for you.

4. Devise a specific plan and practice privately

Follow through on helpful suggestions made in class. A posture problem has to be worked at every day, not just when you speak before a group. Devise special exercises for work-outs at home to deal with persistent problems. If your bodily action is inhibited, stiff, and awkward, use pantomime exercises in which you imagine yourself as a tennis player on the courts or a swimmer in a pool. Or read aloud excerpts from dramatic literature that stir up muscular responses in you. Now and then, practice these exercises before a full-length mirror to check the results. After a time, you will acquire the new sense of physical freedom that you need in reading and speaking.

5. Choose subjects for your class speeches that call for physical action

Demonstration talks in which you show how to build a piece of furniture, assemble an apparatus, or execute a dance step—are especially helpful. Or recall some exciting event you have witnessed; then re-create the event with actions as well as words. Speeches on subjects about which you have especially strong convictions induce action.

SOME SPECIAL PROBLEMS THAT PLAGUE PUBLIC SPEAKERS

How should I walk to and from the platform?

The important thing is to make the trip without calling unfavorable attention to yourself. A hesitant manner suggests timidity, and a hurried, nervous walk marks you as overanxious. Shuffling feet suggest indifference. A stilted, strutting, or lilting entry leads to speculation about your personality and makes listeners more interested in proving their hunches than in listening to what you have to say.

Simply walk to your place in a firm, easy manner that tells your audience you have business with them. Once you have finished speaking, make your exit in the same easy, unhurried manner.

Where and how should I stand?

Stand where it will be easiest for you to establish the best contact with all your listeners. Normally, this is at the front and toward the center of the group. Stand as close to your audience as you can without seeming to press in on them or crowd them. Avoid turning your back on any of them. If your listeners are scattered, ask them to move together. This will reduce the strain on you and will give you better contact with them.

Good posture improves appearance and contributes to bodily action. Stand upright but not stiffly. Avoid both the slouch of a bum and the strut of a drill sergeant. And don't drape yourself over the lectern, lean carelessly against the wall, or dangle one leg in midair. The Napoleonic stance, with legs spread far apart, or the oratorical pose, with feet planted at studied angles, is conspicuous and contrived. Make good posture habitual, and you will be free to direct your attention to more important matters.

SHOULD I MOVE AROUND WHILE SPEAKING?

By all means, if you have some place to go. Moving around may help maintain contact with all your listeners. A few steps break the monotony of one position, indicate a transition in thought, and also relieve tension. Roaming restlessly like a caged tiger distracts the audience.

WHAT SHOULD I DO WITH MY HANDS?

When you make your first few speeches, you may discover that your hands have suddenly become as large as violin cases hanging at your side. This is just one sign of exaggerated self-consciousness.

Beginning speakers are often told to drop their hands to their sides when they are not gesturing. But this may look artificial and may make them seem more conspicuous. There's nothing wrong with thrusting a hand into your pocket—but don't forget where you left it. If you are standing near a lectern, feel free to rest your hands on it naturally, without clutching it like a shipwrecked passenger clinging to a floating log. After you get into your speech, your hands will stop being a problem and you will find good use for them.

HOW SHOULD I USE THE SPEAKER'S STAND?

During the first few minutes of a talk, it's comforting and reassuring to have a good, solid speaker's stand as a base of operations. It can, however, become an obstacle instead of an aid. Speakers who grimly attach themselves to the lectern, hide behind it, or drape themselves over it are a familiar and dismal sight. Make a point of moving to one side or out in front from time to time. You will find that your audience is much more interested in you once you come out of hiding.

Sometimes, of course, you have to stay close to the speaker's stand, as when you read from a manuscript. And when you are talking into a microphone fixed to the stand, you must remain relatively stationary. But it is still possible to gesture without pounding the lectern or rattling the mechanism.

APPEARANCE

In the next chapter we discuss "personal relations in speech"—how to make a good personal adjustment in speech, and how to establish good personal relations with your listeners. Your personal appearance is, of course, a factor in these relations; but it is hoped that for many for us, it need not be critical. In judging horses and dogs and beauty contests we understand that conformation and grooming are important considerations. This doubtless is as it should be, but any fair-minded person will surely recoil from the idea of judging speakers by these standards. Before we dismiss this whole matter as frivolous, however, consider these observations.

Before the popularity of long hair for men and boys, we can document cases in which boys were dismissed from school and men denied jobs because they wore their hair too long; pantsuits and miniskirts have been factors in the employment of women; and television ads dress hucksters up like doctors to sell their nostrums. Many professions and trades have their stereotypes marked by dress and even personal characteristics. Clergyman, policemen, military personnel, professors, and nurses are examples.

To press the matter of appearance in speakers is to yield to prejudices and perhaps even to bigotry. Certainly this is the case in any factors beyond the control of the speaker; and while conventionality in matters of dress and grooming is probably the safest guide, not all speakers are conventionally oriented. Some have even capitalized on their eccentricities with telling effect.

SETTING

Speech always takes place in a setting with physical and psychological characteristics. These characteristics include the place and time, and other relevant circumstances such as temperature, noise level, and detracting or facilitating factors. Such settings may be accidental or planned. In any case, they affect communication—sometimes peripherally and sometimes with great impact.

Examples include conference rooms carefully designed for face-to-face discussion; great cathedrals, churches, and synagogues as places of worship; and classrooms and auditoriums in amphitheater style with tiers of seats around a central area. Often acoustical treatment and temperature controls are provided.

Other more informal settings include the family living room, the athletic field, quiet retreats that invite picnics and bonfires, the social rooms of dormitories, and even parked automobiles.

The setting for speech can infuse emotions and attitudes that reinforce the words and actions of speakers and listeners. Or, if the setting is not fitting to the occasion, it may be a significant barrier to communication. The skill of the speaker is unquestionably a factor in establishing an environment favorable to the reception of his message. Evocative speaking, discussed in chapter 21, provides some of the most suitable methods. But our special interest here is in the atmosphere created by the setting itself.

This factor in communication may be called *mood*. In terms of *reaction*, it is a cluster of emotions, attitudes, and feelings that affect response. So defined, you can speak of the mood of the speaker or the mood of the audience. In terms of *stimulus*, it derives from the time, place, and circumstances of the setting, with or without the efforts of the speaker. So defined, we may refer to the mood of the occasion or the setting. Rapport is established when the mood of the participants is in optimum accord or agreement with the mood of the setting.

Skillful speakers usually know when the mood is right to press their case. Even the inexperienced soon learn that time, place, and circumstance can often make or break their best rhetorical efforts. Fortunately, speakers and listeners are not completely at the mercy of inhospitable settings. If they cannot choose a setting to their liking, there are many resources discussed throughout this book that can be used to create facilitating moods. These same resources can be used to take full advantage of the most favorable settings.

As a footnote, we might observe that the classrooms in which speech classes meet may leave a great deal to be desired. Gains can sometimes be made by staging certain assignments in different surroundings. But the problems imposed by barren, unprepossessing settings are not confined to classrooms, and speakers have to learn to surmount these barriers.

SUMMARY

Of all nonverbal signs or symbols entering into speech, the *bodily action* of the speaker is most directly perceived and most completely within the control of the speaker. For these reasons we have treated it prescriptively in some detail. Although the influence of *appearance* and *setting* is more circumstantial, and thus less amenable to prescriptive treatment, all speakers and listeners will profit by an awareness of these factors.

QUESTIONS FOR DISCUSSION

1. Read the quotation below and comment on the questions that follow.

> How truly language must be regarded as a hindrance to thought, though the necessary instrument of it, we shall clearly perceive on remembering the comparative force with which simple ideas are communicated by signs. To say, "Leave the room" is less expressive than to point to the door. Placing a finger on the lips is more forcible than whispering, "Do not speak." A beck of the hand is better than, "Come here." No phrase can convey the idea of surprise so vividly as opening the eyes and raising the eyebrows. A shrug of the shoulders would lose much by translation into words. (Herbert Spencer)

    a. To what extent can bodily action be reduced to conventional signs such as those cited by Spencer? Make a list of such signs.

    b. Would you expect these signs to differ from one culture to another, and from one language to another? Do they have more or less universality than spoken symbols?

2. How would you expect changes in setting and mood to affect speaking and listening? Does your speech class provide opportunities to accommodate to such changes? How might this be accomplished?

3. The silent movies had to get along without sound, and radio had to get along without sight. Are these significant limitations? How are compensations made?

EXERCISES

1. Select two sites, one a building on campus, the other a building in your home or city. Devise a one- or two-minute report to instruct a stranger on how to get from one building to the other. Use bodily action and blackboard sketches to supplement verbal description.

2. Prepare a how-to-do-it talk on directing an orchestra, interpreting the gestures of football officials, or administering aid at the scene of an accident. Use bodily action as an aid to communication.

3. Prepare a report on a process, an operation, or an institution. Tell how stage sets are built; explain the structure of the United Nations organization; describe the layout of your college library; report on prospecting for oil. Use visual aids, but also use gestures to suggest height, width, distance, direction, movement, relationships.

4. Recall an exciting event you witnessed firsthand—the finals of a tennis match, a rescue, a parachute jump, fighting a fire or a swollen river, climbing

a mountain, a mock political convention. Try to recover the excitement you felt at the time. Make use of bodily action to depict the event and to communicate your excitement.

5. Pick a short story with lots of action in it. Read part of it to the class. Make it come alive.

6. Choose a subject about which you have strong feelings. Make up your mind that the time has come to speak out. Deliver your talk with force and energy that do justice to your convictions.

7. Listen to comments about other people. Do any of them express stereotyped judgments based on appearance and physical behavior? Write up the results of your observations and present them to the class.

8. If circumstances permit, hold your speech class in different settings for certain assignments (in a large auditorium, in a conference room, out-doors).

7. Personal Relations in Speech

Speech takes place in a variety of settings, for different purposes, with different participants. The ways people adjust and perceive each other are inevitably factors in all communication, and, in some cases, these adjustments and perceptions are critical in determining response. There are two closely related problems involved: how to make a good personal adjustment in speech, and how to establish good personal relations with your listeners. These are really two sides of the same coin.

THE PERSONAL FACTORS INVOLVED

The ways in which people relate to one another are important factors in all human endeavor, be it within the family, the school, the church, business and industrial organizations, labor unions, political parties, or social clubs. It is difficult to think of many institutions or shared enterprises in which this is not the case. Many organizations have paid personnel whose job it is to maintain good public and internal relations. In large operations, the lines of communication between individuals and offices are studied carefully to insure smooth working relations. The final answer, however, will be found in the people who do the communicating, their capacity to get along with their associates, and to relate to one another in ways that will get the job done with a minimum of friction and misunderstanding; or to put it positively, with sensitive accommodation to other people involved. People have been hired and fired because of this ability or the lack of it.

It is very difficult to pinpoint the personal factors that count in communication. Aristotle, whose work on speech is comprehensive and useful to this day, puts it this way:

As for the speakers themselves, the sources of our trust in them are three, for apart from the arguments (in a speech) there are three things that gain our belief, namely, intelligence, character, and good will. Speakers are untrustworthy in what they say or advise from one or more of the following causes. Either through want of intelligence they form wrong opinions; or, while they form correct opinions, their rascality leads them to say what they do not think; or, while intelligent and honest enough, they are not well-disposed (toward the hearer, audience), and so perchance will fail to advise the best course, though they see it. That is a complete list of the possibilities. It necessarily follows that the speaker who is thought to have all these qualities (intelligence, character, and good will) has the confidence of his hearers.[1]

This counsel is analytical rather than prescriptive and leaves us with several questions. What do *intelligence, character,* and *good will* mean in behavioral terms? How can these sterling attributes be translated into conduct in speaking that will serve the speaker and his listeners? How can we proceed to mend our own limitations, if any, to achieve the good speaking relations promised by these attributes?

PERSONAL ACCOMMODATIONS IN SPEECH

Ask yourself this question: What personal behavior do you usually associate with intelligence, character and good will? We suspect that most people take *confidence,* tempered by some modesty, as a sign of competence and intelligence; *sincerity* as a sign of integrity and character; and *friendliness* as a sign of good will. This simple answer hardly does justice to the complexities involved, nor does it specify conduct. But it does suggest behavior within the reach of any person. It is possible, with some guidance, for any speaker to present himself confidently, be sincere in what he advances, and be friendly and well disposed toward his listeners.

Suggestions are given throughout the book that will guide your personal behavior in speaking. First of all, however, it is comforting to know that conduct which helps you do your best will be well received by your listeners. Such conduct, including posture, movement, gesture, and sensitive vocal inflections should be comfortable, in good taste, and motivated by what you are saying. Confidence in your message, an evident desire to get your message across, and cordial attitudes toward your listeners provide a sound basis for self-assurance and self-possession, earnestness and genuineness, and sympathetic mutuality between yourself and your audience.

These suggestions may still be less specific than you might wish them to be. Our counsel here is intentionally couched in broad categories and

[1]The Rhetoric of Aristotle, II. 1. Translation by Lane Cooper.

general terms. We have learned through long experience that narrowly prescriptive advice on such behavioral matters fails to recognize individual differences, and often leads to mechanical applications that are less effective than no advice at all.

LISTENER REACTION TO THE SPEAKER AS A PERSON

If the speaker can control his confidence, sincerity, and friendliness, he will be able to speak with greater assurance. We need to ask next: how do listeners react to these accomodations?

Ask yourself another question: How do I react to a speaker who appears to be confident in his views and presentation, sincere in his recommendations, and friendly toward me? Again reactions may vary, but we suggest that most people will respond to confidence with *respect*, to sincerity with *trust*, and to friendliness with reciprocal *cordiality*.

If you are uncertain in your answer, try another question: How do you react to speakers who are timid and uncertain, or conceited and overbearing; who are apathetic or guileful; who are hostile or wary, condescending, and overly solicitous? We hope and believe we know the answer!

Now you may have a question for us: Why should I care about the personal qualities of the speaker? I can listen to what he has to say if I choose to, go along with him, or forget it, and forget him too. These are brave words. The choice *is* yours to exercise, but you exercise it at your own peril! If you can assess the speaker's message without regard to his personal credentials, so much better. You can let his case stand or fall on its own merits. But if you lack the capacity or the opportunity confidently to evaluate the speaker's message, you will be well advised to check his credibility. The means at your disposal often are no more or less than your on-the-spot impressions of the speaker—his confidence, his sincerity, and his attitude toward you. Improvisational as this may be, it certainly is prudent to guide your assessment by the most reliable signs available.

Depending on how personally involved you are and how important the matter is to you, you will be concerned about the personal qualifications of the speaker. Moreover, you will be most concerned about the qualities that most directly affect the outcome in which you are interested. You obviously would be more interested in the personal qualifications of a speaker recommending how you invest your life savings than of a speaker telling a funny story at a dinner party. We have all been entertained by speakers whose personal qualifications, except as entertainers, leave something to be desired. As much as we might prefer personal credentials more to our liking, the matter is certainly more critical when these qualities make a real difference.

HOW TO IMPROVE YOUR PERSONAL ADJUSTMENT IN SPEECH

Now that we have identified some of the desirable personal behaviors in speech, we will suggest ways and means of strengthening yourself in these qualities. It is lame to start with an apology, but we have no magic for you here. We can say, however, that we have seen many students improve their speech substantially by acquiring a better understanding of their personal resources and by learning to use them with greater sensitivity. The suggestions which follow have been found helpful.

1. SELF-APPRAISAL

This is the first step. What kind of a person are you? What are your personal assets and liabilities? What are your intellectual, emotional, moral, and social qualifications? Be as objective as you can about yourself. Self-depreciation and overcompensation are typical responses to real or imagined weaknesses, and they often are our undoing. In either case, we exaggerate the problem in our own minds, and then respond in ways which hurt us with others out of all proportion to the original provocation.

Adopt positive attitudes. Be realistic in self-appraisal, but always work with a positive image of yourself at your best.

2. COMPARE YOURSELF WITH OTHERS

Observe the personal behavior of others when they speak. Why do you respond favorably to one speaker and not to another? What are the special strengths and weaknesses of these speakers in personal adjustment and human relations? How do these strengths and weaknesses compare with your own? Which of the speakers you have heard show the personal qualities you would most like to possess?

Cicero, in his *De Oratore,* tells the story of a young Roman, Sulpicius, who made great strides as a speaker by deliberately modeling himself after Crassus, one of the distinguished orators of his time. Cicero cautions the student to select the best model and "to strive with all possible care to achieve the most excellent qualities of the model he has approved," without imitating mannerisms in "pose or gait" or other eccentric habits.[2]

You can often pick up valuable pointers by studying the personal qualities and adjustments of other speakers. No one wants you to make yourself a carbon copy of another speaker, however successful he may be. But to emulate the best qualities of good speakers is a way of profiting by their experience.

[2]Cicero's *De Oratore,* II. XXII.

3. Plan a role for yourself

In preparing for a speech or conference, planning the disposition of your personal resources may be as important as planning your case. Ask yourself these questions: What will be in good taste? What conduct will be appropriate? What approach will do justice to my cause? What behavior and what attitudes will help convey my ideas?

If you make firm decisions on these matters beforehand, you will avoid mental and emotional drifting when you begin to speak. But what is more important, you will narrow the areas in which tensions are most likely to develop.

4. Master your fears

A realistic appraisal of personal relations in speech should convince anyone that there is very little to be afraid of. But in spite of this rather obvious fact, few of us are immune to fears and apprehensions, even in situations where very little is at stake. Why is this? How does it affect the personal impression we make on our listeners? What can be done about it?

The analysis of the basic causes of fear need not detain us here. Such analyses have occupied psychologists, psychiatrists, psychoanalysts, and even philosophers, for many centuries. At the risk of oversimplification, we suggest that stage-fright stems primarily from *self-consciousness* and *self-interest:* We don't want to make a fool out of ourselves, and we don't want to fail our cause.

Both of these fears are perfectly normal and healthy if kept under control. Those rare individuals who don't care what other people think of them, and who are indifferent to failure, are not likely to make effective speakers. The primary need is adequate self-possession in situations where self-consciousness and self-interest are likely to panic us. Although it is true that few speakers do themselves justice when fear takes over, it is comforting to know that audiences are less allergic to a few symptoms of nervousness than they are to overweening ingratiation or pompous conceit.

We have no patented formula for overcoming stage-fright, but suggestions given elsewhere in this book will be helpful here: Prepare thoroughly so you know you have your subject in hand; converse with your audience rather than orate at them; deliberately assume a confident manner and confident physical posture even though you don't feel confident; move around a bit to loosen up and let off steam; don't try to speak from memory; use notes and a speaker's stand for first practice if they make you feel easier. And if you are speaking in class, remember that one of the primary purposes of the class is to give you opportunities to speak in situations where you can develop skills which will give you good reason for greater confidence.

5. PROFIT BY EXPERIENCE

In spite of your best efforts, you may sometimes come away from a conversation, conference, or speech with the sick feeling that you have handled yourself very poorly indeed. The best therapy for this feeling is to make an objective analysis of what went wrong, devise a plan for improvement, and resolve to do better next time.

Every speech you give really consists of three speeches—the one you give in anticipation, the one you give to your audience, and the one you give to yourself on the way home. This third one is often the best of the lot, for then the pressure is off and you can profit by your mistakes while they are fresh in your mind. If you make these "third speeches" standard practice, you are likely to do better with the one that counts.

HOW TO IMPROVE PERSONAL RELATIONS WITH YOUR AUDIENCE

We have suggested that confidence, sincerity, and friendliness are personal qualities to which listeners respond favorably. Objective analysis of yourself, observation and study of other speakers, commitment to a personal role, mastery of your fears, and critical appraisal of your own speaking will help you achieve these qualities. But you must earn the right to the assurance that these qualities imply. You don't turn these qualities on and off like a water faucet, and no amount of adjuration from us, your teacher, or anyone else will substitute for self-discipline.

The question before us now is *how* your personal behavior as a speaker is perceived by your listeners—*how* it wins respect, trust, and cordial relations. In other words, *how* can you capitalize on your personal qualifications to gain personal acceptance. We have five suggestions. The first two are basic; the others are special applications for many situations.

1. REVEAL YOUR BEST SELF

Every time you speak, you make certain choices in *what* you say and *how* you say it. Your personal impact as a speaker is determined primarily by these choices and the reaction of your listeners to these choices. Most of the audible and visible symbols you use to convey your ideas and feelings—words, syntax, context, construction, intonation and inflection, posture, movement, gesture—are within your power to control. You make these choices, and every choice you make says something about you. Here is the way one writer describes it:

When an individual makes a voluntary selection of words to use in any human situation, he describes himself. To be sure, a person may recite, "Two plus two equal four" without giving himself away. But if he talks of anything more intimate than that—anything about which he has a free choice of what to say and how to say it—we do not have to listen long before we can guess what we can reasonably expect of him as a human personality.

That words reveal personalities is not accidental. Language serves the purpose of giving public form to otherwise private thoughts. Words, in short, get people out into the open. They may think they are talking about something quite other than themselves—about a stranger who cuts across their lawn; or about an editorial in the morning paper; or about an educational experiment, a minister's sermon, a housing project, a strike, a radio program. But it is *they* who are doing the talking, who choose the words and the tone of voice, and who, with those words and that tone of voice, recite their own philosophy, their own attitude toward human beings and human arrangements.[3]

The list of controllable factors is endless. We have mentioned some. Others include the subjects you choose to discuss, the emotions you display, the interpretations you make, the stories you tell, the evidence you present, your attitudes toward yourself and others, and so on. Out of the welter of clues, the listener traces out his opinion of you as a person.

You will soon discover, if you have not already, that most people are pretty shrewd in their judgment of speakers. A clever actor may be able to simulate qualities he does not possess, but he usually gives himself away in the hearing of critical listeners. Confidence, sincerity, and friendliness will usually be taken as signs of competence, integrity, and good will, but these qualities are hard to fake. It is a sad fact that many able men fail to win respect, trust, and cordial relations with their listeners because they are poor speakers. The capacity to conduct yourself in ways that reveal your best self is an important part of the art of good speech.

2. ADAPT TO YOUR AUDIENCE AND TO THE OCCASION

An understanding of your listeners and sensitive awareness of the circumstances under which your speech is being received will often dictate the choices you should make in developing your subject and presenting your speech. Adaptations can always be made within the limits of accuracy, honesty, and good taste.

Your answer to the following questions may indicate how you can modify and adapt your speech: What interest is the audience likely to have in my subject? How well informed is the audience on my subject? What attitudes do my listeners have toward my purpose and my stand on the subject. How do my listeners regard me as a person? What opportunities

[3]Bonaro W. Overstreet, *Freedom's People* (New York: Harper & Row, Publishers, 1945), pp. 60–61.

will my listeners have for participation? How do my listeners feel toward one another? What physical distance exists between me and my audience? Does the physical situation aid or impede speaking? What is the mood of the occasion? What, if any, are the time limitations?

It is true that you cannot always know the answers to these questions, but it is equally true that many speakers have alienated their listeners by misjudgments and improprieties.

3. ADAPT TO YOUR REPUTATION

People have a tendency to form an opinion of a speaker before they ever hear him. They draw on press reports, public relations releases, personal associations, conversations with people who know him, introductory remarks by the chairman, and many other clues. This initial impression may work for, or against, you as a speaker.

For example, the subject of James Brown's speech is "Let the People's Voice Prevail." His argument is a solid one, yet his listeners greet it with raucous laughter. Such is the price of Brown's reputation as the Machiavelli of Siwash. But reputations work the other way too. Helen Green is known as a thoroughly democratic person. So when she defends the right of a social organization to be as exclusive as it pleases, she receives a fair hearing, even though most of her listeners disagree with her position. John Jones has flown fifty missions in a Sabre-Jet and has been decorated for bravery. Even though he has a quaver in his voice, none of his listeners will question his courage.

You may discover that your reputation has followed you into your speech class. You will either have to live up to it or else live it down.

4. MAKE A GOOD FIRST IMPRESSION

First impressions have a way of growing into lasting impressions. You meet a person for the first time and you make a quick appraisal of him. Once this judgment is made, you are likely to stick with it unless later evidence forces you to revise it. A speaker who makes a poor opening has to work hard to overcome this disadvantage. And one who makes a strong impression at the start can draw on this strength throughout the conference or speech.

5. GIVE INFORMATION ABOUT YOURSELF

A speaker usually provides a certain amount of information about himself during his speech—either inadvertently or for a specific purpose. That specific purpose is often to establish himself as someone who knows what he is talking about: "I have always been a friend of the farmers; I should like to take this opportunity to make my voting record on farm aid a matter of public record. . . . I have three sons in service and I know how vital this matter is to you. . . . I spent two years of my professional life in the Orient and I have seen these things for myself. . . . I wrote the labor platform and I have kept my promises to the working men and women of America. . . . You can't tell me anything about dormitory food; I've been eating it for four years."

We all issue such guarantees—both in conversation and in public speech. The very fact that we do is proof of how important this matter of personal status is both to speakers and listeners. We know that in one way or another we must establish ourselves as worthy of our listeners' attention if we hope to get a fair hearing. But remember that careful listeners will check your credentials, and a false guarantee is sure to be detected.

SUMMARY

In this chapter, we have tried to deal with a matter of great importance in all communication—the personal relations among participants. Any analysis, ours included, immediately encounters the enormous variability in human personalities and the resulting individual differences in interaction. We have drawn on our own experience and the available studies to generalize certain relations: confidence as a sign of competence; sincerity as a sign of integrity; friendliness as a sign of good will; and the reactions to these signs—respect, trust, and cordiality. We have also given suggestions for improving personal adjustment and personal relations with listeners. Most of these adjustments and reactions to them operate in all social contexts, even when speech is only minimally involved. When communication is the primary purpose, they may be critically important.

QUESTIONS FOR DISCUSSION

1. Read the following excerpt and discuss the questions in the last few sentences:

> Among the virtues cherished by good Americans, "sincerity" looms large. To say of a man (oddly, not of a woman) that he is "sincere" is a seal of approval stamped with satellite words like clean-cut, upright, God-fearing, neat, hard-working, polite, respectful and regular. Sincere Americans might well be toilet-trained at the age of three months.
> They always, moreover, look you straight in the eye. No shiftiness. "You can count on this man, Bob—he's *sincere.*"
> Now, there's nothing inherently wrong in these attributes, but there may be in the fact that so many Americans not only confuse "sincere" with "honest," but accept the *appearance* of sincerity as the ultimate proof—in public or private figures—of sincerity itself. Classic examples of the sincere gaze and the sincere statement abound in the very recent past.

The English don't buy this sort of thing. Neither, conspicuously, do the French. Both peoples may respect the serious man and the pure conscience, but their private translation of sincerity is usually tedium. Who has not been numbed by the uninflected drone of the sincere speaker? Conversely, can a speaker possessing imagination, wit, fantasy or humor be—since he is clearly not serious—truly sincere?[4]

2. How do these habits and manners contribute to good personal relations in speech? What would you add?

The person fit to be a maker of a free society shows his fitness:

By habits of verbal accuracy. He speaks with conviction only when he is sure of his facts and reasons, and is careful to qualify as opinion that which is merely opinion. In this respect he contrasts sharply with the person whose positiveness of tone is an ingredient added to an opinion to make it sound like a fact.

By habits of verbal generosity. He does not find it necessary, through sarcastic jibes or cruel innuendoes or verbal browbeatings, to add to the world's burden of sorrow.

By a manner that encourages give and take. He is capable of enjoying the drama of mutuality in speech—not merely of monologue. He can sound convinced and modest at the same time, for he has both character enough to hold a conviction and knowledge enough of human fallibility to realize that he is capable of error. He does not find it humiliating to acknowledge ignorance. Nor does he retail, to the gratification of his own ego, conversations in which he has outshone someone else—and which any shrewd listener suspects of having been improved by repetition and after-the-fact polishing.[5]

3. Analyze and discuss the personal qualities recommended in this chapter and the relations among them. Is *confidence* a sign of competence? Is *sincerity* a sign of honesty? Is *friendliness* a sign of good will? How reliable are these signs? If you disagree, what personal qualities would you recommend?

4. Do listeners respond to confidence with *respect;* to sincerity with *trust;* to friendliness with *cordiality?* If you don't accept these correlations, propose others.

EXERCISES

1. Write an analysis and appraisal of your own personal qualifications in making a satisfactory adjustment in speech. What are your strengths and weaknesses? What special problems do you face? What steps can you take to meet these problems?

[4]Marya Mannes, "The Sincerity Trap," *Newsweek,* September 10, 1973, p. 14.
[5]Overstreet, *Freedom's People,* pp. 64–65.

2. Write an analysis and appraisal of some speaker you admire—a speaker whose personal qualifications enable him to make effective adjustments in speech. Make a list of his special strengths—the personal qualities you admire and the ways he manages his personal resources. Conclude your paper with a list of specific suggestions for your own speaking.

3. Use the analysis in Exercise 2 as the basis for a class speech. Characterize the speaker you are discussing and explain what you believe to be the personal resources that contribute to his strength. Be specific. Give examples drawn from the speech or speeches you have heard him deliver.

4. Bring to class a published speech that exemplifies the methods a speaker uses to establish his competence on his chosen subject. You may have to read the speech more than once to discover all the methods he uses. Read the speech to the class; then tell what methods you think the speaker has used to establish his competence.

5. Prepare a short talk in which your primary aim is to establish your competence to speak on a particular subject. Try to win your listeners' confidence without parading your qualifications. If you are describing an event, and if you were present when it occurred, say so. If you are talking about another person, tell your audience how well you know him. The important thing is to establish your right to talk about your subject, but to do so unobtrusively.

8. Speaking with a Purpose

All significant speaking is addressed to a purpose. The talk that goes on around us may be idle chatter serving no purpose other than breaking silence. But when purpose asserts itself, overtly or covertly, both speaking and listening are directed and energized.

PRIMARY PURPOSES

The universal purpose of all speech is to get a *response.* When we communicate with others, we translate ideas and feelings of our own into symbols that others can see and hear, in the hope that they will react to them in meaningful ways. In short, we seek a response of some kind from someone.

At first sight, the conceivable purposes of speech seem too numerous to classify. After all, anybody can talk about anything for any reason under the sun. But if we look more closely, we find that there are four primary purposes that encompass all the important objectives of speech. These basic purposes will guide you in identifying and accomplishing your specific purpose.

INQUIRY

Much of our speaking is a search for information or insights. We may simply ask someone a question in the hope that they can give us a helpful answer. Or we may try out our ideas on another person to see what he thinks of them. Or we may join with a group of people to discuss a common problem, in the hope that we can solve it or at least understand it better.

The common denominator in all speech of this sort is *inquiry*—or call it exploration, problem solving, investigation, or discovery. The occasion may be private conversation or public deliberation, but the purpose is always this searching for knowledge and understanding. In a sense, when we speak to inquire, we are doing what the scientist does in his search for facts and hypotheses. The laboratory and the conference table may have little else in common, but both can yield new insights of great social significance.

REPORTING

Most of you will be called on to make reports—in class, to business associates, to your clubs, and innumerable informal reports to friends and other people whom you meet in your daily activities. Here you are presenting information to your listeners. In your capacity as a reporter, you are not searching for information—you already have it. Your purpose now is to inform or to instruct others who hope to learn from your report. What they do with this report may be of real concern to you, but your job as a reporter is well done if you have conveyed your information clearly, accurately, and in ways that sustain the interest and attention of your audience.

Reporting, like inquiry, is one of the four primary purposes of human discourse. It complements both inquiry and advocacy in the deliberative processes, but it is a distinguishable purpose in its own right.

ADVOCACY

The speaker who seeks to convince or persuade is an advocate. The advocate is not content just to provide his audience with information. He wants his listeners to adopt a specific attitude toward a proposition or to take action on it. He marshals arguments and appeals in support of a predetermined position—a position to which he is committed because he believes in it or simply because he has chosen to support it.

Advocacy is the third important purpose of speech. We practice it every day in selling, advertising, promoting, campaigning—in representing and defending causes that are important to us. Much of the practical decision making in our society is accomplished by advocates who defend competing ideas and yield to majority votes.

EVOCATION

The fourth primary purpose of speech is to inspire or to entertain. Here the speaker's intent is to evoke an emotional response, to intensify or allay feelings. You inspire people to greater efforts, comfort a friend in distress, tell a story to get a laugh, call for faith, reminisce, give encouragement, share your fears, stir up anger and resentment, express affection.

Such emotional experiences may be deeply moving, exciting, and exhilarating to the listener. Or they may be quieting and consoling. They may be pleasurable and entertaining, or stern and demanding.

All good speaking involves human emotions, of course, but in evocation the speaker's *central* purpose is to engage these emotions in a special way. Evocation is an end in itself, to be enjoyed or valued in any way the speaker and his listeners see fit.

SECONDARY PURPOSE

Although a speech should be dominated by one of the above primary purposes, the methods of other primary purposes may play secondary, supporting roles. For example, a speaker whose primary purpose is inquiry will almost always do some reporting, and may occasionally slip into the role of advocate. Advocates often use the reporter's approach in developing their case, and they have been known to use the techniques of inquiry for persuasive purposes. Similarly, entertaining and inspirational speaking may be employed in such secondary roles.

A speech is organized in relation to the four primary purposes. (The organization of a speech will be discussed in chapter 11.) Each has its own basic structure dictated by the logical responsibilities imposed by the purpose; in speaking, these structures are adapted to the audience and occasion. Such accommodations often include methods and materials normally associated with one of the other primary purposes. In this secondary role, they may serve logically necessary functions, or they may introduce diversions that have their own rewards. In any case, they must be kept subordinate to the primary objective. If a speaker's primary purpose is inquiry and he succeeds only in advocating his own point of view, his inquiry has failed; if his primary purpose is reporting and he succeeds only in entertaining he has failed as a reporter.

THE SPECIFIC PURPOSE

Your specific purpose is your immediate goal in speaking to a particular audience. You should be able to state your specific purpose in a way that will point to your central idea and make clear precisely what you hope to accomplish. This statement should also indicate your primary objective. If inquiry is your primary purpose, you might put your statement of specific purpose this way: "How may we establish more efficient study habits?" or "We intend to investigate capital punishment as a deterrent to crime." If reporting is your primary purpose, your statement of specific purpose might be: "My object is to recount the highlights of the national Delta Sigma Rho Congress," or "I wish to explain the essential differences between boogie and cool jazz." If advocacy is your primary purpose, you might express your specific purpose this way: "My purpose is to urge the abolition of spring football practice," or "We must organize to oppose universal military conscription." If evocation is your primary objective, your specific goal might be expressed this way: "I wish to entertain my audience with an account of the rise and fall of Jenkins' Corners," or "I wish to stimulate appreciation for the poetic qualities in the sermons of John Donne."

Always phrase your specific purpose beforehand for your own guidance. If you are to investigate a subject efficiently and organize a speech effectively, you need a clear and concise statement of purpose.

When, where, and under what circumstances you should disclose your specific purpose to your audience is quite another matter. Most often, perhaps, it is wise to state your purpose at the outset, so that your listeners will know precisely what you are trying to do from the very beginning. Sometimes, however, it may be wise to withhold your purpose until later. And there are times when you may decide never to state it at all. If your objective is controversial and likely to arouse a hostile reaction, pave the way for your proposition before submitting it directly. If you are after an emotional response of any kind, it would probably be naïve to spell out your purpose for your audience. Your purpose and your development of it can be implicit rather than explicit in any speech.

STATING YOUR SPECIFIC PURPOSE

Your statement of specific purpose should be:

1. A COMPLETE SENTENCE

Usually, a question is the most satisfactory form for speeches of inquiry. A declarative sentence is suitable for reporting, advocacy, and evocative speaking.

Inquiry: "Are telephone operators becoming obsolete?"
Reporting: "There are four basic procedures to be mastered to qualify for a position as telephone operator."
Advocacy: "Telephone operators should receive a ten-cent-an-hour pay hike."
Evocation: "Your telephone operator may be your life line."

2. ONE CENTRAL IDEA

Your statement must present one idea, and only one. Many speakers find it difficult to compress their purpose into a unified sentence. They confuse supporting arguments or other lines of development with their specific purpose. Notice the confusion in this statement: "I want to acquaint my audience with Franklin D. Roosevelt's message to Congress in 1941 asking for a declaration of war against the Japanese Empire, because the step he was proposing was an important one in modern history, and it literally affected the entire world." Only the first part of this statement, ending with the word *Empire,* expresses intention or purpose. The rest of the sentence is a justification for talking about Roosevelt's message. These reasons should appear later, in the speaker's development of his talk.

3. CLEAR AND PRECISE

Be as terse and explicit as you can. Avoid ambiguity and vagueness. The statement "The best way to check inflation is to increase income taxes" is far more precise than "Something ought to be done about high prices."

ULTERIOR PURPOSES

A speaker may have a purpose in the back of his mind that he never reveals to his audience. This *ulterior* purpose is some indirect end toward which the speaker is moving, but which is unrelated to the form and substance of his talk. A candidate for a job might present a report on novel methods in advertising, but with the ulterior purpose of impressing his prospective employers. Speaking contests are good examples. Each speaker hopes to win the contest—that is his ulterior purpose. But each speaker tries to achieve this success by speaking to some specific purpose that is completely unrelated to winning or losing. Similarly, in your speech class, your ulterior purpose may be to win a good grade. But your speeches will be planned to inquire, report, advocate, and evoke in order to secure a specific response that is unrelated to the grade you get.

MIXED PURPOSES

The four primary purposes may be represented as a continuum of purpose: You talk to discover; you report what you have discovered; you advocate what has been reported; and you entertain and inspire in the light of ground achieved. In communication where one speaker plays the dominant role, his purpose is dictated by his own interests and those of his listeners. But in situations where speakers and listeners exchange roles, it is not unusual for people to find themselves at different points on this continuum with respect to the matter under consideration. Thus in conversation or unstructured discussion, these people can be expected to participate at *their own level of interest and comprehension.* You ask a question (inquiry); I answer (reporting); the next speaker agrees or disagrees and argues his position (advocacy); and all of this may prompt someone else to tell a story that lightens the conversation or inspires to greater effort (evocation).

If these individualistic responses prove to be unrewarding, the situation may be rescued by competent leadership and more structured procedure. These matters are discussed in chapters 18, 19, 20, and 21 where special methods serving each of the primary purposes are set out in some detail.

QUESTIONS FOR DISCUSSION

1. Do the four primary purposes of speech encompass *all* the important objectives of speech? What are the values and limitations of this classification as you see it?

2. It has been suggested that speech serves a fifth primary purpose as *therapy* in counseling, sensitivity training, "talking out your problems," and other techniques for tension reduction and personal adjustment. Do such therapeutic objectives constitute a primary purpose with methods unique to this purpose?

3. Discuss the ways in which primary and secondary purposes are related.

4. What ethical and moral questions are involved in the purposes of speech? What determines the worthiness of purpose? Does a worthy purpose justify the means of securing it?

EXERCISES

1. Prepare a short talk based on (a) one of the four primary purposes set forth in this chapter and (b) a full and precise statement of your specific purpose. Speak to these purposes, but withhold any statement of them when you deliver your talk. After your speech, have your listeners write statements of what they understood to be your primary purpose and specific purpose.

Are your listeners in agreement? Now read to them the statements of your intentions. Did any of the listeners fail to recognize your intentions? What reasons do they offer for possible failure to understand your primary and specific purposes? How do you explain the discrepancies, if any? What conclusions may you draw from this experience?

2. Assume that you are to prepare a five-minute talk on each of the following statements of purpose. Is each an acceptable statement? If not, revise it to make it an acceptable statement of specific purpose. Then identify each specific purpose with some primary purpose that it might serve.

   a. The best way to keep down weight is to push yourself away from the table.
   b. College students are taller today than they were a generation ago.
   c. The owners of a big business are the American public.
   d. Something needs to be done about high prices and extravagance and lack of self-discipline.
   e. Radio and television have made "whistle-stop" presidential campaigns an anachronism.
   f. How should we study for the final examination in this course?
   g. Making assets out of our liabilities.
   h. Evansdale needs a public library and a swimming pool.
   i. The British Monarchy.
   j. There are many satisfactions in owning your own home, and you can finance it as cheaply as you can rent a house.
   k. Our vanishing forests and Indians.

3. Pick out a big, inclusive subject such as theater, fashion, door-to-door selling, Texas, trains, chemistry, automobiles. Divide this large subject into four subtopics, each suitable for a short class talk. Formulate a primary purpose and a specific purpose for each. Now prepare a speech on one of the topics. Have the class evaluate your talk in light of your avowed purposes.

4. Analyze the printed text of a speech that you find in a newspaper, in *Vital Speeches of the Day,* or in an anthology. Prepare and present a report that answers these questions:

> Who gave the speech? When? Under what circumstances?
> What is the speaker's primary purpose?
> What is the speaker's specific purpose? If it is not stated explicitly, what do you believe it to be?
> Is there any evidence that the speaker had an ulterior purpose? If so, do you regard it as commendable or justifiable?

5. Have four members of the class choose a single topic that is of interest to all of them. One will use this topic as the basis for a speech of inquiry. A second will use this topic for a report; a third for a speech of advocacy; and a fourth for an evocative speech.

9. Speaking About Worthy Subjects

All of the basic principles of speech are wrapped up in what you choose to talk about. A speaker's potential may never be realized if he repeatedly talks about trifling and inconsequential matters. We have emphasized that the most significant speech addresses personal and social problems in the spirit and method of serious deliberation. We have suggested that aptitudes and skills mastered in this kind of setting will serve you well on other occasions. We have also recommended idea-oriented speech classes where speakers and listeners are held accountable for *what* they say as well as *how* they say it.

This emphasis on deliberative speech and the idea-oriented speech class does not mean that your selection of subjects is limited to world-shaking matter of policy. Nor does it mean that what we regard as the best model for practice is the only good model for practice. Later chapters give careful attention to many types of speeches that you will enjoy experiencing and can profit by. In this chapter we suggest speech subjects that lend themselves to the methods serving each of the main purposes of speech.

Personal factors are deeply involved in what you choose to talk about and the purposes to which you direct your remarks. We respect these individual differences; they can make a speech class more interesting. But always remember that when you take the time of the class, you have a responsibility to make this a rewarding experience for your listeners.

The spirit of our recommendations will be met if you talk about matters, big or little, close to home or far away, past, present, or future that have contemporary relevance beyond your personal orbit, and provide exciting springboards for class discussion. If your speech gets no comment or fails to set off reactions, you may have selected the wrong subject.

Under many circumstances, you do not *choose* a subject. It chooses you. You are confronted with it as when someone asks you for directions, or when the agendum for a meeting is presented to you, or when topics emerge in a discussion. But in a speech class, unless the teacher assigns topics, you usually make the choice yourself.

FINDING SUBJECTS: A PERSPECTIVE

The key factor in your search for subjects is *reaction.* A worthy subject for speech is not simply an event you have read or heard about. Neither is it a book, a memory, an acquaintance, or a concept. The subject lies (1) in your reaction to the book, event, person, or idea; and (2) in the possibilities it opens for inviting the reactions of other people. Finding subjects is not like picking up rocks or seashells. It is a creative process in which reflection, imagination, and experience set your mind in motion.

REACTING TO THE WORLD AROUND US

Ours is an age of revolution—revolution in transportation, in human relations, in communications, in education, in weaponry. Man is in revolt against repressive political systems, the inhumanity of machines, art forms, deprivation, disease. Religious and ethical systems are being reexamined, questioned, and sometimes repudiated. All of us have some part in the pageantry of our times. We exist, we act, and we talk in the context of a restless environment. This is our world, to be fashioned meaningfully through the power of human discourse.

But not all worthy subjects are world-shaking. Good subjects often reside in commonplace and even prosaic topics. The word *transportation* may suggest space flights to the moon, or it may suggest the hazard of scooters on a throughway, parking problems, or the incidence of bicycle thefts on campus. Ordinary conversational tidbits about haircuts, hairdos, and hair dyes become arresting when you catch their psychological and cultural implications. Spending a few minutes of reflective observation in a supermarket can send your mind in many directions—the effect of motivational research on packaging, the value of artistic displays, soft music and selling, our dependence on truckers, petty thefts, and courtesy in the check-out lines.

Often we are blind to good subjects right before our eyes—the effect of pesticides on food, the condition of our hospitals and schools, the roads we travel, and the billboards that block our view. A commuting student once complained he had nothing to talk about because he missed out on all of the campus activities. Encouraged to inspect his immediate environment more closely, he asked himself, "What do I look at each day without really seeing?" Among the things he listed were three used-car lots, each covering a city block. He took new interest in these car lots, asking questions such as these: Why do people dispose of cars that still have years of service left in them? Who buys these cars? What special sales pitch is used to sell them? Is there any other country in the world where you would find acres of used cars in a large city? What does the used-car business say about our economy? Does it mean that we are an enterprising or an extravagant people? Out of these questions grew the subject for an extremely interesting class talk: cars as a status symbol in our society.

REACTING TO THE IDEAS OF OTHERS

Be alert to possible subjects for speech as you scan the newspapers, listen to lectures, dinner conversations, or talks in your speech class. Jot down the ideas that turn up. A conversation on hypocrisy in religion may suggest a talk on hypocrisy in education, the law, or the home. A student who explained the theory of majority rule prompted a classmate to explain the doctrine of consensus practiced by the Society of Friends. A critic of the social ethics of advertisers aroused a member of the class to champion the advertising industry as essential to a free economy. A creative listener uses what he hears as a springboard to related topics.

PROBING PERSONAL EXPERIENCES AND EXPECTATIONS

Nothing you say has meaning for others until it first has meaning for you. What is it like to travel the Trail Ridge Road in the Colorado Rockies at an elevation of over twelve thousand feet? Better ask the person who has made the trip. Does Boris Pasternak's *Doctor Zhivago* have the stature of a Tolstoy novel? Who can attempt to answer the question unless he has read both Pasternak and Tolstoy? How effective is the Woman's Judiciary Board in handling disciplinary problems on campus? A member of the board can offer facts that outweigh the opinions of the casual observer.

Oddly, students with special abilities and enthusiasms often dismiss rewarding subjects because of a mistaken notion that only fellow-specialists are interested in them. Here is a ski enthusiast, a collector of antiques, a cartoonist, an accomplished gardener. Here is someone wrapped up in thermodynamics, automation, puppetry, theater-in-the-round. Often your best subjects are your special interests. These are the things you can speak about with authority and enthusiasm. Through them you open a world only dimly known to others.

Examine your life as an unfolding process. Each of you has gone through infancy, childhood, adolescence, and into adulthood. Looking back over the years provides new insights, and looking ahead thrusts forward new questions and goals. A retrospective view of high school may reveal the way to revise study habits. A forward look into a law career may lead one to attend police court, an experience that may be stimulating or dismaying. Both experiences contain the raw materials for speech. Stretching out before you are a career, travel, marriage, parenthood, and active citizenship. Clustered around these experiences are scores of questions that open subjects for talk.

USING THE FOUR PRIMARY PURPOSES OF SPEECH AS GUIDES TO SUBJECTS

INQUIRY

All of us carry in our heads unresolved questions that may perplex others too. When there is so much pressure to get into college, why do some students cut classes once they are admitted? Why does mononucleosis seem endemic to college students? You go with some friends to see a play. Some find it obscene, others do not. You decide to make a speech of inquiry on the question, "How does one judge whether or not a dramatic work is obscene?" You attend an evening lecture and discover that the audience is largely made up of townspeople and faculty. Why do so few students turn out for these lectures? You ask, "Should the university calendar be cleared of all extracurrricular activities one night each week, to be known as Cultural Activities Night?" You cringe when you read the morning's headline: "Convicted Murderer to be Executed Tonight." You are aroused to revive the long-standing question, "Should capital punishment be abolished?"

It is good practice to consult daily newspapers, news magazines, and current journals of opinion. They are filled with ideas and subjects suitable for discussion.

REPORTING

Here are just a few subjects that students have used successfully in making reports.

Reactions to crisis: bailing out of an airplane
The proposed honor system
My life on a dude ranch
Uses of classical mythology in our modern world
Frontrunners in the presidential sweepstakes
How the Secret Service protects the president
The life history of a bank check
Susie: a case study of a cerebral palsy victim
A new development in automation
The physiology of nutrition
Basic principles underlying cone reentry
How a television show is put together
The process by which a new nation gains membership in the United Nations
The function of a computer's memory core

Make a list of things you have done, have seen, heard, or read that might be worked up into informative speeches that you would enjoy making.

ADVOCACY

We engage in advocacy whenever we seek to influence the belief or action of others. We engage in it daily. "Next time, take the train. . . . The Greeks get all the breaks on this campus. . . . If you don't start smoking, you won't have the problem of stopping. . . . You can lose weight on a high protein diet."

Cause-minded people never run out of subjects for speeches of advocacy. They are quick to encourage, defend, or denounce political, social, economic, educational, literary, or religious change. Here is a random list of propositions that students have used.

> There is too much pressure to go to college.
> A student judiciary should replace the faculty-student committee on discipline.
> We need uniform traffic signs and signals throughout the Western world.
> Everyone should take a vocational aptitude test at the end of his sophomore year.
> Daylight saving time is a hoax.
> The library stacks ought to be opened to undergraduates.
> Pesticides are homicide.
> Fashions make fools of us.
> One foreign language should be required for graduation.
> A computer is a creature without compassion.

We have not included the many public policy questions that are current in your town or city, your state, or the nation. Make such a list for your own use.

EVOCATION

Your class offers opportunities for entertaining speech and for inspiration. We advance the civilizing process by illuminating accounts of men and women whose lives have enriched our own. Our love of the beautiful, our devotion to country, and our religious and humanitarian impulses impel us to share our feelings. These have been the titles of moving speeches:

> Albert Schweitzer's reverence for life
> Jane Addams changed Chicago
> St. Francis of Assisi
> A Scoutmaster saved my life
> My favorite parable

The versatility of Robert Frost
John Glenn is more than an astronaut
The tragedy of John F. Kennedy

Classes have been entertained by light-touch speeches with titles such as these:

The secret language of women
My dog thinks he's people
Dollar signs without sense
What is "funny"?
How I tell my friends from apes

Basically, subjects for evocative speeches arise from your personal sense of values and find expression in either the inspirational or the light-touch speech.

FINDING SUBJECTS: SOME COMMON MISEVALUATIONS

All this advice on how to find subjects will be wasted on a person who habitually misevaluates himself and his responsibilities in speaking. What are some of these misevaluations?

"I'M NOT AN AUTHORITY ON ANYTHING."

Being an authority is a relative matter. It depends on the situation and the problem at hand. If you have had first-aid training, you may take charge at the scene of an accident, but you will give way when the doctor arrives. Similarly, without being a psychologist, your job as a camp counselor may have qualified you to report on how unruly children were changed into socially cooperative youngsters.

Know what you are talking about. The more you know, the better; but it is wise to indicate the limits of your knowledge on a topic. Authoritativeness is never absolute. We might as well sew up our mouths if we have to know everything there is to know before we speak.

"NOTHING I CAN SAY WILL INTEREST MY AUDIENCE."

This lament arises from the false assumption that good subjects spring only from unusual experiences. Students complain: "She was in summer stock; all I did was go to summer school. . . . Lots of people in my class have been everywhere; I've never been outside the state. . . . He worked in Glacier Park; I worked in a service station."

Anyone who has ever listened to a boring travelogue knows that it is not the exotic experience *per se* that insures interesting talk. This point was brought home to one student who habitually drew unfortunate comparisons between his opportunities and those of others in the class. Having helped his father keep alive a family grocery store, he was encouraged to draw upon his personal experiences. He spoke with unmistakable authority on the threat of big business to small enterprise. The favorable reactions to his speech convinced him that audiences respect ideas and attitudes gained from firsthand experience, even if the experience is not glamorous. He saw, too, that he had needlessly belittled himself.

"I HAVEN'T ANY BURNING ENTHUSIASMS."

The subject you choose doesn't have to make the blood pound at your temples. You are not expected to set off a crusade or campaign in a five-minute talk. True, some people have more excitement in them than others. But all of us have interests that lead to worthwhile topics for class talks. Furthermore, as free men and women, we are under some obligation to strengthen our involvement in social and political affairs, and to think and talk about these matters.

"NOBODY HAS SUGGESTED ANYTHING THAT APPEALS TO ME."

This clinging-vine attitude is rooted in the false notion that our own education is always somebody else's responsibility. You may pick up some good leads from something somebody else said or wrote. But in the final analysis, your own mind needs to reach out, take hold, and make the selection. You will never be able to speak convincingly until you can claim the subject as your own.

"I HAVE PLENTY OF TIME TO THINK UP A SUBJECT;
I DON'T SPEAK FOR A WEEK."

You may have met this grab-bag specialist. The night before he is scheduled to talk, he scans a newspaper for the first time in days, gives an ear to a radio commentator, glances at some predigested magazine articles, or prowls through the dormitory badgering anyone available with a "Hey, I've got to make a speech tomorrow. Know any good topics?"

A last-minute speech is a talk of desperation—a batch of jumbled, pointless remarks on a topic chosen at random. There are no short-cuts to good speech. You have to live with an idea long enough to get acquainted with it. Select your subject early, so that you will be on familiar terms with it before you introduce it to others.

TESTING YOUR SUBJECTS

IS MY SUBJECT LIKELY TO YIELD SOLID VALUES FOR ME AND MY AUDIENCE?

Some occasions call for small talk, but people who talk about only trivial things betray trivial minds. They cheat themselves and others. Discriminating listeners judge us by our interests. What you choose to talk about reveals how well you live up to your social responsibilities.

AM I ABLE TO DEAL WITH THIS SUBJECT COMPETENTLY?

Ask yourself, "Do I already know enough about this topic to discuss it responsibly?" If not, "Do I know how and where I can find the information I need?" If so, "Do I have the background to understand and interpret the material?"

DOES MY SUBJECT FIT THE INTERESTS AND BACKGROUND OF MY AUDIENCE?

An archaeologist returning from excavations in Egypt may hold fellow archaeologists spellbound with an account of complicated techniques for excavating and preserving remains. The same subject would probably fall flat in a speech to an interior decorating class. Here the archaeologist might be well advised to talk about tastes in home furnishings during various periods of Egyptian history.

IS MY SUBJECT APPROPRIATE TO THE OCCASION?

A church group in a college town wanted to promote understanding and good interfaith relationships among students of different religions. Invited to a dinner meeting were Mohammedans, Hindus, Buddhists, Christians, and Jews. The main course of the Friday dinner was ham, the only prayer was to the Christian God, the only song was a Christian hymn, and the speaker topped it all off by extolling the Christian missionary spirit. So many blunders may seem incredible, but any blunder that offends the sensibilities of individuals and groups—their rituals, conventions, taboos—cuts off lines of communication.

IS MY SUBJECT MANAGEABLE?

Beginning speakers often make the mistake of choosing subjects of almost unlimited scope for a five-minute talk. They try to take a cross-continental trip instead of a short excursion. Instead of talking on "advertising" in all its phases, confine yourself to one specific aspect of the subject, such as ethics in advertising, artistic television commercials, scenery and signboards, hidden persuaders in our supermarkets.

QUESTIONS FOR DISCUSSION

1. Radio and television programs are frequently criticized for their intellectual and artistic vacuity. The producers of these programs reply that they are giving the people what they want. Should speakers—you, for example—operate on this same principle? To what extent are the subjects of your speech limited to the capacities and interests of your listeners?

2. Much of what is said in this chapter is oriented to speaking in public. Discuss the applications to conversation and discussion. To what extent are subjects suitable for public discourse acceptable for social conversation?

3. Do you ever feel at a disadvantage in social conversation because you think you have nothing to talk about while the chatter goes on all around you? This is an important question for many people and it is relevant to our study. Is the problem a result of your own limitations, or the general tone and level of much of our social conversation?

EXERCISES

1. Start now to build a classified list of potential subjects for speeches. Be alert to possibilities in the classroom, while reading a newspaper or magazine, while watching TV, in conversations, while studying, and while listening to your classmates speak.

2. Think of three people you know well, and think of one subject you would like to hear each one talk about. Now apply the same test to yourself. Of all your experiences and interests, what might the class most enjoy hearing you talk about? If you still have doubts, ask your friends for their opinions. Prepare a short extemporaneous talk on the subject you choose.

3. Prepare a short talk on an occupation. Your speech should answer questions such as these: What is the nature of the work? What qualifications are required? How useful is it? What future is there in it? How interesting is it likely to be? What are some of its disadvantages? Here are some suggestions:

Playwright	Teacher	Radio and TV
Landscape gardener	Farmer	commentator
Personnel director	Clergyman	Professional football
Electrical engineer	Salesman	player
Commercial artist	Psychiatrist	Space pilot
Novelist	Fashion model	Nurse
		Architect

4. The lives of famous or infamous men and women—their ideas, pursuits, and deeds—serve as good subjects for speech. Choose someone who interests you greatly, then phrase a question or two you would like to ask him or her. From the writings by or about the person, figure out the answers he or she might give to your questions. Prepare a talk based on your questions and answers. Here are some examples of questions.

Albert Einstein: "Does a scientist have a social responsibility with respect to his specific research?"

Albert Schweitzer: "Why did you choose to pursue your philosophic, medical, and musical talents in an African jungle?"

Here are the names of other people to whom you may wish to put a question.

Frank Lloyd Wright	Greta Garbo	Norman Thomas
Ralph Waldo Emerson	John Glenn	Martin Luther King
Winston Churchill	Franklin D. Roosevelt	Arthur Conan Doyle
Dwight D. Eisenhower	Adolf Hitler	Mark Twain
Charles Darwin	Van Cliburn	Emily Dickinson
Eleanor Roosevelt	Babe Ruth	Charles Lindbergh
Leonard Bernstein	Ernest Hemingway	Robert Frost
Lee Harvey Oswald	Lyndon B. Johnson	Adlai Stevenson
Sam Irwin	Walter Cronkite	Richard M. Nixon

10. Exploring Subjects

There are two kinds of preparation for speech: *direct* and *indirect.* The distinction is that all your experiences—including reading, travel, work, play, family background, religious commitments, and formal education—*are* preparation for speech. They are *indirect,* in the sense that these engagements are *not* undertaken as a preparation for speech, but are, nonetheless, sources upon which you will necessarily draw in all of your speaking. As you mature, we hope that these life experiences will be extended, deepened in ways that will contribute to your effectiveness as a speaker.

A brief review of the basic principles of speech and the assumptions upon which they are based will show you that *direct preparation* for speech, beyond your indirect experiential background, is usually essential for best results. Certainly this applies to any speech of special significance, and it almost always applies to exercises in self-improvement in speech.

The regimen proposed here for exploring your subject *is* direct preparation. And it is demanding. You may not need to go through all the steps proposed, and you may already be familiar with some of the resources discussed.

PRELIMINARY SURVEY AND ANALYSIS

MAKE A PRELIMINARY INVENTORY

First, take stock of what you know or think you know about your subject before you scout out the "authorities." This kind of concentrated brain-cudgeling will jog your memory and stir up some original thinking. Talk that draws slavishly on the ideas and material of others sounds bookish and smells of somebody else's ink.

Make a list of your discoveries—key factual items, ideas, hunches, and questions that you can use as they stand or investigate further. What you turn up will probably look like a grocery list. If you were to turn this list over to someone else, it probably would not mean much to him. No matter, this is a sensible way to begin. It is a strictly personal record of self-investigation that may both please and dismay you. Some of your insights may excite you as genuine discoveries, but you will probably find some gaping holes that need to be filled in your background of information.

ANALYZE YOUR AUDIENCE IN ITS SETTING

When you work up a speech, visualize the audience as they will be when you meet them. For example, if you are getting ready for a ticklish conference, think of the people who will be there. Consider the range of their information, interests, and prejudices. Which points are urgent? Which points need to be mentioned without laboring them? Which points have to be introduced gingerly, or dropped altogether? Keep the time limits in mind.

Here is an actual case in which a little preliminary analysis of the audience and the occasion would have saved the day. A local civic group invited a public official, who was an expert on conservation, to explain proposals for reducing pollution and for checking the alarming depletion of local water resources. The speaker unwound with a detailed history of the government agency he represented, and then he sketched its nation-wide organization. A half-hour of this, and the audience was summoning up courage for a sprint to the nearest exit. Public meetings are plagued by speakers who drag in material extraneous to the business at hand. Get into the habit of thinking about your audience's expectations as you explore your subject. Guard against allowing your private interests or even the seemingly logical dictates of your material to dominate your approach.

INTEGRATE YOUR INITIAL SURVEYS

You are now ready to make some tentative decisions. Go over your preliminary inventory again, this time with your audience in mind. Select the points that look most promising as big headings for your speech. Under each, list the observations and notations that are directly related to it. You may not be able to include all the items from your preliminary inventory, but you may come back to some of them later on. Your new list is an organized guide to further exploration of your subject. Let us look at a specific example of how you can put your preliminary survey and analysis to work.

THE THREE STEPS ILLUSTRATED

The experience of a student—we'll call him Arthur Lewis—provides us with an instructive example. You won't duplicate his procedure in every detail when you work up your own preliminary survey and analysis, of course, but you will have a clearer idea of how to go about it.

Lewis took this subject for a class speech: "The values of mastering a foreign language." A number of things had led him to his choice—his own progress in mastering French, his pleasure in overcoming an early phobia toward foreign languages, his trip abroad, and a story in *The New York Times* that reported an appalling deficiency in foreign languages among college students. As he proceeded, Lewis kept this purpose in the back of his mind: "I want to convince members of my speech class that they owe it to themselves to master at least one foreign language before they graduate."

STEP ONE: LEWIS' PRELIMINARY INVENTORY

Lewis pondered his subject, analyzed it in various ways, and came up with this list of leads.

My summer abroad.

The study of foreign languages as an aid to English (debatable).

Being able to speak a foreign language helps to confer culture (belongs to the genteel tradition; probably not very convincing today).

With isolationism breaking down, the ability to read and write in a foreign tongue helps us to relate ourselves to our new world.

Today there are student exchange programs that enable us to live and study abroad.

Leadership in your chosen vocation makes language facility of practical value.

Business is becoming increasingly international. Many large department stores hold night classes in French, German, Italian, etc., for buyers and sales personnel.

Knowing a foreign language will help you professionally by giving you access to professional literature from abroad. Many professional meetings are held in foreign countries.

Government service is badly in need of specialists in almost all lines of work who can speak the language of the country.

You may want to enter graduate school someday, and you may have to show ability in one or more foreign languages.

Your pleasure in traveling abroad on vacations will be doubled if you can speak a language besides your own.

Opportunities for language study at our college.

Language phobia? How I overcame mine.

New techniques and aids in learning a foreign language.
Which language or languages should you study? Some of the variables that will affect your decision.
Government subsidies to colleges and students who undertake a concentrated program of language study.

STEP TWO: LEWIS' ANALYSIS OF HIS AUDIENCE IN ITS SETTING

Through earlier speeches and class discussion, Lewis had already sized up the other eighteen members of his class. They were preponderantly freshmen and sophomores, people who still had plenty of time to make course decisions. About a third of the class were women, and he noted that their speeches ran to "cultural" subjects; most of the men seemed to favor more "practical" topics. He had a hunch that a few of his classmates would fall right in with his purpose; that some had already had a skirmish with a foreign-language course that left them reluctant to tackle another; that about half the class had thought little about the matter.

Not satisfied with guesses, Lewis put together a little questionnaire and asked each member to fill it out. The answers sharpened his analysis. He learned that (1) only three people talked or read a foreign language with any fluency, (2) a scattering of the class members had taken a high-school or college language course but had no strong desire to go on, (3) most of the class had no plans to elect a foreign-language course, and (4) several insisted that they lacked aptitude.

STEP THREE: INTEGRATING HIS AUDIENCE ANALYSIS WITH HIS
PRELIMINARY INVENTORY

Now that he had worked up an audience profile, Lewis was ready to make some tentative decisions on which items in his preliminary inventory would best serve his purpose. Now he had to pick and choose. He decided to concentrate on (1) the lifelong personal satisfactions that knowing a foreign language would bring, (2) the practical benefits, and (3) some novel and interesting ways to learn a new language.

Looking over his inventory, Lewis crossed out some of the items (though he decided that he might be able to mention a few of them in passing), and rephrased others. He settled on three big headings, under which he grouped other items from his inventory.

Fluency in a foreign language is a passport to travel and living abroad.
Two personal experiences from my summer abroad.
Interview some students who have lived abroad.
Consult brochures on student exchange programs re language requirements and suggestions.
In today's world, your business and professional future may hinge on your ability to write and speak another tongue.
New job opportunities are opening as business becomes increasingly international.

> Your chances for government service are greatly increased if you can speak the language of another country.
>
> New devices and techniques make learning a language pleasant and speedy. How Professor Andrews teaches his language courses in French. (Check with him on the results of his three-year experiment.)
> The language "lab."
> Records and tapes that have helped me.
> My experience in learning French at the "language table" in McCullen Hall.
> Opportunities for language study at our college.

Lewis now felt satisfied that his preliminary explorations had opened the way to directed inquiry. He had no intention of freezing his analysis or settling for the information that he had on hand. He needed to know more, and he was quite willing to scrap or revise his analysis if further probing turned up something better.

EXTENDING THE INVESTIGATION

Your own preliminary analysis will put you on a trail that you can follow as far as you need to go. Along the way, you will encounter new ideas, points of view, facts, examples, illustrations, and all the other things that will enrich your perceptions, thinking, and speaking. You will not use everything, but in subtle ways "everything" will show through as you talk. Here, then, are some suggestions for pushing deeper into your subject.

INTERROGATION AND OBSERVATION

TALK OVER YOUR IDEAS WITH SOMEONE WHOM YOU CAN COUNT ON TO LISTEN AND GIVE THOUGHTFUL REACTIONS

As writer Robert Penn Warren aptly remarks, "Very often it is in conversation during the germinal stage of a project that I stumble on my meanings, or they stumble on me. . . ." If possible, arrange interviews with people who have special knowledge of your subject.

USE PAPER-AND-PENCIL DEVICES FOR COLLECTING INFORMATION

When you want to survey specific attitudes and practices, try your hand at working out simple questionnaires and opinion polls. Since most of us lack the time and the special knowledge needed to prepare and use these devices scientifically, be realistic about the results. Be aware of their limitations and make those limitations clear to your listeners.

TAKE A FIELD TRIP TO SEE FOR YOURSELF

This may mean that all you have to do is inspect a project so that you can talk about it with more familiarity; or it may mean some sleuthing. Agnes Watson kept hearing the charge that college students who drove cars were a menace to the citizens of Moresfield. She decided to investigate the charge. She went directly to the proper municipal offices and checked over the records of accidents during the past academic year. She interviewed a judge in traffic court. She talked to several traffic patrolmen. Her report was acclaimed as a masterful example of careful and productive field work. And incidentally, she learned that it was better to base her beliefs on research and critical thinking than on loose talk.

PUBLISHED SOURCES

For many subjects, the only place you can find the information you need is in the library. Logically, then, you will need a working knowledge of the basic tools and resources that you will find there.

REFERENCE BOOKS

Learn to use *Guide to Reference Books* by Constance M. Winchell. Although this guide is primarily for librarians, you will find it invaluable and easy to use. We can list here only a few of the types of standard reference work listed in the Winchell *Guide.*

Encyclopedias are surveys of knowledge organized on a topical basis. Outstanding are the *Encyclopaedia Britannica, The Encyclopedia Americana,* the *New International Encyclopaedia,* and their supplements. You will also find encyclopedias that cover special fields, such as the *Encyclopaedia of the Social Sciences.*

Then you will find many collections of short biographies of prominent people based on time periods, geographical areas, and occupations. Outstanding collections of national and international figures are the *Dictionary of American Biography,* the *Dictionary of National Biography* (English), *Who's Who in America, World Biography,* and *Current Biography* (international). *Biography Index* is a guide to current biographical materials.

When you want factual data about the contemporary world, look in the Winchell *Guide* for the yearbook that is most likely to contain them. You will find that *The World Almanac* is a compendium of facts for each year. *The American Yearbook* is an annual record of events in politics, economics, business, social conditions, science, and humanities. *The Statesman's Yearbook* supplies information on governments of the world, on population, religion, education, crime, finance, industry, and so forth. The *Statistical Abstract of the United States* is a source book of facts covering social, political, industrial, and economic subjects. *Facts on File* is a weekly world-news digest. And there are many others.

Two well-known dictionaries are Webster's *New International Dictionary of the English Language* and *Funk & Wagnall's New Standard Dictionary.* The *Oxford English Dictionary* and *A Dictionary of American English* are invaluable for information on the history and usage of words.

BIBLIOGRAPHIES

A bibliography is a list of works on a particular subject. By looking in the *Bibliographic Index* you can locate lists of works on a great variety of subjects. *The Reference Shelf* series supplies bibliographies on timely, controversial questions that have been debated in schools and colleges.

BOOKS

The card catalog is an alphabetically arranged index to all the resources of your library, primarily to books. The cards are usually filed in three ways—according to author, title of book, and subject of book. The speediest way to find an item is to look for it under the author's name or the title. But subject headings, in addition to supplying a third place to look for a particular item, often provide a list of additional works on your subject. If you cannot find your book in the card catalog, and if it was published in English during the twentieth century, look for information about it in *The United States Catalog* or its supplement, *Cumulative Book Index*. Look in the *Book Review Digest* to locate reviews of a book and to find short summaries of these reviews.

PERIODICALS

The Reader's Guide to Periodical Literature is indispensable in exploring subjects for speeches. It will pay you to study carefully its system of abbreviated entries. Use *Poole's Index to Periodical Literature* for articles published in the nineteenth century. Scholarly articles in the humanities and sciences are listed in *The International Index to Periodicals.*

INDEXES TO SPECIAL FIELDS

These indexes list all types of publications in a special field—books, articles, pamphlets, bulletins, and so forth. Examples are *Educational Index, Industrial Arts Index,* and *Public Affairs Information Service.* Look in Winchell for a guide to the special field you have in mind.

UNITED STATES PUBLIC DOCUMENTS

The *Monthly Catalog* is a current bibliography of government publications and tells you how to order them. *The Congressional Record* contains congressional debates, speeches, extended remarks of congressmen, and Presidents' messages.

NEWSPAPERS

The New York Times Index, published since 1913, is a chronological and alphabetical index to that paper's news items and other features. Actually, this index serves as a master key to current affairs reported in other newspapers as well.

RECORDING YOUR MATERIAL

Human memory is fickle. A good set of notes will save you from little and big errors, and will spare you a return trip to the library to recover information that you have looked up before. Writing a thing down carefully and thoughtfully increases accuracy. A good investigator checks on himself as well as on his sources of information.

There are four kinds of notes that you will want to make. Put a symbol on each card or slip of paper to show what type of note it is.

1. *Verbatim notes* contain somebody else's words and data exactly as he expressed them.
2. *Paraphrased notes* embody somebody else's ideas and data in your own words.
3. *Summary notes* are digests of a book, article, speech, interview, or conversation.
4. *Personal "idea" notes* are a record of your original thoughts and observations on a particular subject.

Each card or slip, in addition to the note itself, should carry a subject heading, designation of the type of note it is, the writer's name, a full and accurate statement of the source from which it is taken, and the page number. Sometimes information such as the library call number, the writer's identity and special qualifications, and any appraisal you care to make of the work proves valuable too. At the top of the next page is a sample note card containing the minimum essential information.

Here are some useful rules for note taking.

1. Put notes for only one subject on each card, slip, or sheet.
2. Check and double-check your note against the original source. *Get it right* before you go on.
3. Never distort by lifting material out of context. Be faithful to the writer's or speaker's intended meaning.
4. Write legibly and follow a consistent style.
5. Before you file a note, be sure that you have indicated what type of note it is and have included all other necessary information about it and your source.

QUESTIONS FOR DISCUSSION

1. When you are speaking, when and how should you document the source of facts, opinions of others, and other supporting materials?

2. Consider the usefulness of discussion and conference as preliminary exploration of a subject *before* reporting or advocating.

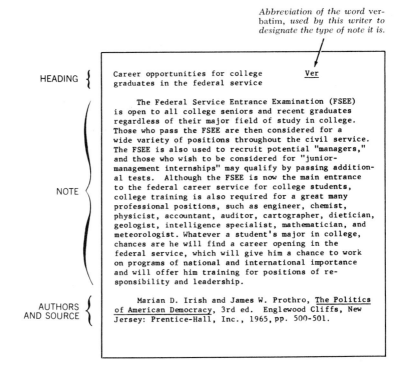

Abbreviation of the word ver-batim, used by this writer to designate the type of note it is.

HEADING { Career opportunities for college   Ver
           graduates in the federal service

NOTE {
The Federal Service Entrance Examination (FSEE)
is open to all college seniors and recent graduates
regardless of their major field of study in college.
Those who pass the FSEE are then considered for a
wide variety of positions throughout the civil service.
The FSEE is also used to recruit potential "managers,"
and those who wish to be considered for "junior-
management internships" may qualify by passing additional tests. Although the FSEE is now the main entrance
to the federal career service for college students,
college training is also required for a great many
professional positions, such as engineer, chemist,
physicist, accountant, auditor, cartographer, dietician,
geologist, intelligence specialist, mathematician, and
meteorologist. Whatever a student's major in college,
chances are he will find a career opening in the
federal service, which will give him a chance to work
on programs of national and international importance
and will offer him training for positions of responsibility and leadership.

AUTHORS
AND SOURCE {
Marian D. Irish and James W. Prothro, The Politics
of American Democracy, 3rd ed. Englewood Cliffs, New
Jersey: Prentice-Hall, Inc., 1965, pp. 500-501.

3. In what ways, if any, would you expect the exploration of a subject for an evocative speech to differ from the preparation of other types of speeches?

4. What kind of a reading and listening program might best improve your indirect preparation for speech?

5. What college or university courses are likely to provide the best preparation for speech?

EXERCISES

1. Prepare an extemporaneous talk. Turn in to your instructor the following items:

a. Worksheets containing your preliminary survey of the subject.

b. A list of all your sources of information.

c. A few sample note cards.

2. Schedule a series of reports on specific reference material in your library. Have one speaker report on *The United States Catalog*, a second on the *Oxford English Dictionary*, a third on the *Encyclopaedia of Social Sciences*, and so on. Report on the purpose of the reference item, its history, its scope and limits, its location in the library. Explain how to use if efficiently.

3. Organize the class into teams of two or three investigators. Have each team interview a librarian who is in charge of one department of your school's library—the circulation department, the reference room, the reserve room, the documents department, the archives, the order department, the periodical department. Each team should seek information that is pertinent to an understanding of the materials and functions of the one department, and then hold a short discussion on its findings before the rest of the class.

4. Choose a topic on which you can make a firsthand investigation. Survey campus opinion, arrange interviews, make a personal check on conditions for yourself. Check and double-check your methods, data, and results. Make a report on your investigations.

5. Inform yourself on a speaker's habits and methods of preparation. Interview an outstanding clergyman, businessman, public official, or instructor. Or you may wish to read up on a speaker's work habits in biographies or in special studies such as those contained in *A History and Criticism of American Public Address*, edited by W. N. Brigance and Marie Hochmuth.

11. The Organization of Speech

All speech profits by organization unless it be exclamations, laconic remarks, or frivolous conversation. In this respect, speech is like most significant human activities—purposes are set, plans are made, and action proceeds on the basis of these plans. One of the most demanding requirements of leadership in any undertaking is the capacity to analyze a situation, see the critical issues, and then devise and guide a plan of action in cooperation with others. Both analytical and creative skills are required. Speakers, no matter what their purpose, assume leadership roles when they command the attention of others. If they are well organized—know what they are going to say, and have a tightly conceived plan of saying it—their chances of capitalizing on this leadership opportunity are greatly enhanced. You will soon discover that the organizational skills essential to effective speech will help qualify you for leadership roles in many human endeavors. This is a bonus worth your best effort.

THE ROLE OF ANALYSIS IN ORGANIZATION

The speech outline is the plan of the speech. This plan develops, first, from analysis of your subject in relation to your purpose, and second, from an analysis of your audience and your setting. Subject and purpose are analyzed to reveal critical questions, salient points, and vital issues necessary to your purpose. The analysis of audience and occasion reveals how best to deal with these matters to achieve your purpose without compromising your logical responsibilities. The best speech outlines, then, organize the essential considerations in ways that invite attention and interest, and provide a sound basis for the response sought.

THE LOGICAL STRUCTURE OF SPEECH OUTLINES

Logical analysis is related to purpose. We discuss below the logical patterns best suited to the several purposes of speech.

THE LOGICAL STRUCTURE OF INQUIRY

The American philosopher, logician, and educator, John Dewey, sets out the nature and logical conditions of both social and scientific inquiry in his book, *Logic: The Theory of Inquiry.*[1] This work refines an earlier analysis presented in a little book, *How We Think.* We quote:

> Upon examination, each instance [of inquiry] reveals more or less clearly, five logically distinct steps: (1) a felt difficulty; (2) its location and definition; (3) suggestion of possible solution; (4) development by reasoning of the bearings of the suggestion (5) further observation and experiment leading to its acceptance or rejection; that is, the conclusion of belief or disbelief.[2]

In our chapter 18, dealing with the nature and methods of inquiry, we recommend a variation of these five steps as a logical framework for organizing speech that conducts or invites inquiry. Typically, such speech proceeds through group discussion although a single speaker can address an audience in the spirit and method of inquiry.

In preparing an outline to aid you in inquiry, the following questions will serve as major headings: (1) What *is* the problem? (2) What are the *causes* of this problem? (3) What *values* should be served by a solution to this problem? (4) What are the possible *solutions?* (5) What are the *relative merits* of these solutions? (6) How can the best solution be *tested?* The outline is completed by listing the critical questions in each of these six areas. Presumably, the exploration of these questions will yield answers that identify the problem, determine causation, establish criteria for evaluating solutions, suggest possible solutions, assess the pros and cons of these proposals, and so far as possible, test the solution that appears to provide the best answer to the problem.

THE LOGICAL STRUCTURE OF REPORTING

Typical forms of discourse in reporting are exposition, description, and narration. One or all may enter into a single report, but usually one is dominant. The speech outline that organizes such a report is topical; each of the main topics is developed through subtopics, and these secondary topics are developed through topics subordinate to them. The degree of refinement, of course, varies with the need for clarification.

In a topical outline, the subject being reported may be regarded as a "whole," and the main points as "parts" of that whole. Similarly, the main points may then be taken as "wholes" with their subordinate points taken

---

[1](New York: Henry Holt and Company, 1938.) See especially chapter 6, "The Pattern of Inquiry," pp. 102–20.
[2]John Dewey, *How We Think* (Boston: D. C. Heath and Company, 1910), p. 72.

as "parts." Rigor and tightness are achieved if the "wholes" are divided on the basis of a common variable, and if the "parts" are all-inclusive and mutually exclusive.

THE LOGICAL STRUCTURE OF ADVOCACY

The structural outline for advocatory speech begins with a proposition and supporting statements. The proposition is the claim the speaker is making, his proposal, or his recommendation; the supporting reasons are the arguments he offers in its behalf. The advocate analyzes his proposition to discover the issues, and these issues are phrased as the main supporting reasons. The primary reasons are then supported by secondary reasons and these, if necessary, by tertiary reasons. This process is refined until premises are reached that are self-evident or amenable to evidential support.

The nature of issues and kinds of reasons are discussed in later chapters. Suffice it to say here that the outline achieves logical rigor if the supporting reasons establish the validity of the proposition or the premises to which they are immediately subordinate.

The basic difference between the advocate's and the reporter's outline is that the reporter seeks understanding and clarification through exposition, description, and narration, while the advocate seeks conviction and action through reasoning and argument.

THE STRUCTURE OF EVOCATION

The outlines of speech to inspire or entertain are usually a relaxed form of the topical outline. Here the reaction sought is an emotional response. Under these circumstances, the speaker's concern with logical structure is quite properly minimal. This is not to say, however, that a speech outline is unnecessary. Quite the contrary is true.

ADAPTING LOGICAL STRUCTURE TO AUDIENCE AND OCCASION

There are cases in which a straight-forward logical presentation will serve your purpose: for example, you may be more interested in demonstration than persuasion (and in some circumstances such a presentation is the best kind of persuasion). In most cases, however, it pays to accommodate these structural patterns to the interests and needs of your listeners and to the occasion. Fortunately, this can be done without compromising your own integrity or that of your subject. Here are some ways to make your speech outlines work for you *and* your listeners.

1. Limit your purpose

Time and the patience of your listeners impose practical limits on the scope of your speech. If you propose too much, you will either oversupply your listeners with information or have to settle for a shallow treatment of your subject. By narrowing your objective, you can keep the demands of your speech within manageable limits.

2. Omit logically necessary points already accepted by your listeners

Nothing is gained by laboring the obvious. Narrow your speech outline down to the critical points affecting understanding and acceptance. Focus on the matters that count.

3. Accommodate your outline to secondary purposes

Although your speech will have a primary purpose—to inquire, to report, to advocate, or to evoke—any one or more of these purposes may enter in as a secondary purpose. Your speech outline should be sufficiently flexible to admit organizational patterns suitable to these secondary purposes. Such intrusions will result in mixed structures, but flexibility is preferred to rigidity.

4. Phrase the points in your outline in clear, stimulating language

The typical barrenness of a tight structural outline can profitably yield to more vivid language without loss of logical impact. Since the phraseology of the outline is likely to emerge in the speech, it pays to phrase the questions, points, or premises in your outline as you wish them to appear in your speech.

5. Vary the sequence of points

Arrange your outline to take your listeners from where they are to where you want them to go. Let your listeners' needs and interests determine the order of development. You may wish to start with matters most likely to engage interest, hold controversial points until later, or build to a climax. Sequence can be determined psychologically without impairing logical structure.

6. Include examples and other illustrative materials that have motivational values

Amplification beyond the logical requirements of your thesis will often pay dividends in closer attention and stronger appeal. Specificity and concreteness have both logical and psychological values. Such amplification usually appears as support for the subordinate points in the outline.

7. DESIGN YOUR OUTLINE STRATEGICALLY

Strategic planning to achieve your purpose need not compromise logical responsibilities. Since your purpose is achieved in the response of your listeners, maneuvers and tactics that help you get your message across are invaluable aids to persuasion. You can be inventive and ingenious in deploying your resources without being tricky or dishonest.

8. PATTERN YOUR OUTLINE ARTISTICALLY

All speech profits by effective oral style. The arrangement of ideas and the relations among them shown in the outline contribute to clarity, vividness, and energy in style. Stylistic distinction of any kind suffers if the outline is ragged and disjointed. Moreover, a good outline paves the way for a smooth development of the subject with easy transitions and flowing continuity. Keep working it over until this is achieved.

9. PROVIDE AN INTRODUCTION AND CONCLUSION

Most speech outlines should provide opening and closing remarks that lead listeners into and out of your speech graciously and arrestingly. The section that follows discusses the divisions of the outline, including introductions and conclusions.

DIVISIONS OF THE OUTLINE

Organized speech has a beginning, a body, and an ending. You can spot these divisions most clearly in public speech, but you will find them in informal talk, too. Don't think of them as formal and rigid. Rather, think of them as functions that the speaker must somehow perform. These divisions are closely knit, and their boundaries are sometimes indistinguishable. In outlines for public speech, these parts are usually labeled *introduction, body,* and *conclusion.*

THE INTRODUCTION

The introduction to your speech is an invitation to listening. It should create good relations between you and your audience and pave the way for your subject. The length, ingenuity, and degree of formality of these opening remarks will vary with circumstances. These circumstances include the attitudes of your listeners toward you and your subject, the degree to which this audience is informed in the area you plan to cover, and their personal involvement (if any) in these matters. They may also include your personal interest in the subject, your competence with respect to it, and your reasons for discussing this subject with these people.

It is hardly possible and certainly unwise to try to prescribe formulas for introductory remarks that will be fitting in the great variety of situations you will meet as a speaker. Suffice it to say, it is wise for you to plan a beginning with considerable care, keep it as brief as possible, relevant to the circumstances at hand, and appropriate in style and mood to the occasion.

The outline of your speech should include provisions for the introduction and it should be treated as a separate section of the outline (as indicated in the sample outlines presented later). The introductory outline may consist of little more than a sentence or two, or a paragraph, or a short outline of your opening remarks. The important thing is that it provide adequate cues in legible form to guide your opening remarks.

BODY

This division of your outline is the main part of your speech. It contains all the main points and subpoints by which you explain or support your topic or thesis.

1. How many main points and subpoints do I need?

This is a little like asking, "How many legs does a table need?" It depends on the size and shape of the table, how strong the legs are, and where they are placed. Some tables stand well on one leg, some on two, and some need four or more.

In a short talk, it usually is wise to limit yourself to between one and five main points. One thing is certain: If you try to cover nineteen main points in a five-minute talk, you will be in a hopeless position. Either limit your purpose and therefore the number of your main points, or reexamine your analysis of the subject and combine some of your main points into a few bigger points.

The same answer holds for the subpoints. Do not spin them out beyond your own needs or those of your audience. If your outline goes beyond two or three degrees of subordination, try recasting it into a simpler form.

2. In what order should I arrange my main points and their subpoints?

The answer to this question lies in your subject or in the special needs of the audience and occasion.

The points in a topical outline may be arranged in one of several different ways. If you discuss labor organizations in the order of their appearance on the American scene, you would be following a *time sequence*. If you compare the mountain ranges of the United States, region by region from east to west, you would be using a *space sequence*. A speech explaining the physical needs of a school district might take up these needs in an *order of priority*—classrooms, laboratories, a lunchroom, and a gymnasium. Points in a speech analyzing the composition of the *New York Times'* Sunday edition might be arranged according to the *interests of the audience.* Speeches of instruction often move from the *familiar to the unfamiliar* or from the *simple to the complex.*

Customarily, logical outlines open with arguments that establish a *need for change* or a *cause for action.* There are times, however, when it is wise to depart from this formula in order to accommodate your speech to the psychology of your audience. If you know that your audience has a keen interest in one of your arguments, capitalize on that interest. Open with that argument. Then again, if you feel that all your arguments will sustain interest but that one is especially strong, you probably would use it as a clincher or climax. Should your audience be divided on a controversial issue, open with the point that is likely to win agreement, in the hope that your other points will be given a more favorable hearing.

3. SHOULD I WRITE TRANSITIONS INTO MY OUTLINE?

Transitional sentences link together points in your speech, offering a terse concluding reference to or summary of one point while foreshadowing the next. For example:

> Having defined automation, let us consider its benefits to our economy.

> We have declared that our first human "good" is survival, but that alone is not good enough. What other distinctly human values justify the human experience?

A speech may be overloaded with forced transitions, but the omission of these bridges is a more frequent fault. If your outline is tightly woven and if you have worked on transitions in your rehearsals, chances are that you will move easily and naturally from point to point without laboriously writing transitional sentences into your outline.

4. SHOULD I USE COMPLETE SENTENCES OR KEY PHRASES?

It is usually better to use complete sentences for main points and major subpoints, particularly in the body. Complete sentences force one to think through all the points clearly and to express them with precision. If you want to refer to an outline while you are speaking, then reduce your formal outline from complete sentences to key phrases.

THE CONCLUSION

A good conclusion ends smartly and strongly. Use the conclusion as a capstone for your speech, not as a dumping ground for leftover items. Think out your conclusion beforehand and make it part of your outline.

As in the case of the introduction, it should be a separate part of the outline labeled "conclusion."

The conclusion can present a brief summary of the main points of your speech, emphasize what you regard as most important, or make a plea for acceptance of your thesis or the course of action you have recommended. Sometimes, one or more of these objectives can be accomplished by a story, an illustration, or an example that conveys the central idea of your speech in capsule form.

Planned conclusions are important for two reasons: They provide terminal facilities for speakers who find it difficult to bring their remarks to an orderly ending; and they give any speaker an opportunity, which he presumably has earned, to come to terms with his listeners in ways that will win the response he seeks.

HOW TO USE OUTLINES IN SPEAKING

As we have seen, the outline is the map or blueprint of your speech. It is a final record of your preparation and the selections you have made to present to your listeners—the ideas, the lines of thought, and the supporting materials. If you are to speak extemporaneously, you will compose the language best designed to develop the outline as you speak, but whatever method of presentation you choose, the outline is the guide to the composition of the speech.

For first practice you may be more comfortable if you have the outline before you as you speak. The dangers here are obvious: You are tempted to use the outline as a crutch, hide yourself in your notes, and lose contact with your audience. If you feel the need of notes, your outline can be condensed to a few key sentences or phrases that will give you the guide lines you need. Be certain that these notes are legible, in convenient form, and that you are thoroughly familiar with them. Then refer to them only as necessary.

The alternative to notes is to keep this condensed version of your outline in your head. In this case you speak extemporaneously from a memorized outline. As you gain experience in speaking, you will find this approach considerably less demanding than you might expect it to be.

In a discussion group, it is hoped that each participant is equipped to raise and explore the relevant questions. The discussion outlines are resources for such questions. In this case, the discussion may not follow your outline because others share in the speaking and new ideas may emerge in the discussion.

Good speakers have, or develop, *analytical skills*—the capacity to bring issues out of a welter of irrelevancies and deal with them cogently and persuasively. Good speakers also have *creative skills*—the perception, imagination, and courage to come up with new ideas or new interpretations of old ideas that serve to integrate conflicting views. The situations in which you have a chance to speak abound with opportunities to exercise these analytical and creative skills, often without benefit of an outline prepared in advance. *But the need for disciplined organization is no less!* Here is where the experience in organizing your efforts provided by written outlines in your speech class will give you the assured resourcefulness needed.

SAMPLE OUTLINES

The sample outlines that follow illustrate organizations suitable to the four primary purposes of speech. They also illustrate the basic principles of all outlining—coordination, subordination, and appropriate symbolization.

SAMPLE DISCUSSION OUTLINE

The discussion for which this outline was prepared followed a class speech of more than ordinary vehemence in which it was proposed that the physical education courses required of all students in the university be abolished.

Should the University Abolish Required Courses in Physical Education?

I. What is the problem?
   A. What are the present requirements?
   B. Does the alleged dissatisfaction with these requirements constitute a serious problem?
      1. Attitudes of students?
      2. Faculty attitudes?
      3. The positions of the department of physical education? The health service?
II. What are the causes of the problem?
   (If opposition does exist, what are the causes of these complaints?)
   A. How adequate is the present program?
      1. The courses?
      2. The teachers?
      3. The facilities?
   B. Are there any measurable results of the present program?
   C. How does the program affect other academic requirements?
   D. Are students simply trying to escape a requirement?

     E. Are the costs of the program relevant?

III. What should be the objectives in this area of student health?

     A. What are the responsibilities of the university for student health and exercise?

     B. Is freedom of choice for the students a worthy objective?

IV. What solutions to this problem should be considered?

     A. Complete abolition of the program?

     B. Reduction of the requirement? How?

     C. Make the program optional?

     D. Strengthen the intramural program?

     E. Broaden the base for excusing students from the requirement?

     F. Keep the requirement, but revise and strengthen the program? How?

     G. Keep the requirement as it now is?

V. What are the advantages and disadvantages of these proposals? What should our recommendation be?

     A. Is an optional program most satisfactory?

        1. Might it not encourage a strengthening of the present program to make it more attractive?

        2. Might it not lead to a better intramural sports program?

        3. Would it remove student objections and meet university responsibilities?

        4. Would students avail themselves of the opportunities of such a program without being required to do so.

     B. How does such an optional program compare with other possible solutions?

VI. What is the best way to test such a program?

     A. What has been the experience of other colleges and universities with optional programs?

     B. Could we adopt it for a year or two on a trial basis?

SAMPLE OUTLINE FOR A REPORT

The Anonymous Doctor

INTRODUCTION

I. The pathologist is a doctor's doctor.

     A. He works directly with internists and surgeons.

        1. His job is to analyze and interpret disease tissue.

        2. Every accredited American hospital has at least one pathologist.

     B. Since he does not treat patients, his work is little known by the public at large.

II. You owe it to yourself to learn more about his role.
   A. When you are a patient, this knowledge will add to your confidence in hospital procedures.
   B. Knowing about his work may suggest professional opportunities to you—a career as a doctor, technician, nurse, or hospital administrator.

BODY

I. The pathologist is an indispensable partner to other doctors.
   A. His diagnostic reports may save both the patient and the surgeon.
      1. He warns the surgeon against operations that analysis shows to be unnecessary.
      2. Or he calls attention to an urgent need for an operation.
   B. Often the surgeon calls upon the pathologist to look over his shoulder while he operates.
      1. As a tissue specialist, he may make on-the-spot interpretations of unexpected discoveries.
      2. The surgeon may suspend an operation in progress while the pathologist makes a quick microscopic analysis of tissue.
   C. The pathologist prescribes for preoperative and postoperative care of the patient.
II. The pathologist presides over hospital laboratory work.
   A. Each day brings its routine of laboratory analysis.
      1. Every organ removed in the operating room must be inspected.
      2. Every sample of blood extracted must go under the microscope.
   B. Much of the lab work is done by technicians, but the pathologist has final responsibility.
III. The pathologist is a standard-maker.
   A. As a research man, he contributes to medical knowledge.
   B. He is a watchdog for the profession.
      1. He reports to the "tissue committee" all healthy tissue removed in an operation.
      2. He also serves as a member of the "tissue committee."
         a. This committee reviews and adjudicates doubtful procedures.
         b. It may call on a surgeon to explain his reasons for the procedure in question.

CONCLUSION

I. The pathologist is the patient's anonymous doctor.
II. He serves both you and the medical profession.

SAMPLE OUTLINE FOR SPEECH OF ADVOCACY

Clear the Aisles

INTRODUCTION

I.   A mock political convention simulates a national political convention.
   A. It follows procedures common to the political conventions of the major parties.
   B. It drafts and enacts a political platform.
   C. It brings to campus prominent political speakers from both major parties.
   D. It nominates candidates for the office of president and vice-president of the United States.
II.   Since this proposal involves the whole school, the Student Governing Board is the logical group to get the ball rolling.

BODY

I.   This project would add to our political education, because
   A. It would supplement our academic studies, for
      1. It would strengthen our interest in the history of political campaigns and conventions.
      2. We would apply information about political procedure that we learn in political science.
   B. It would stimulate interest in contemporary political issues, because
      1. We would have to read widely in current sources of information.
      2. It would encourage informal discussion among students.
      3. We would have a chance to hear and meet prominent political figures in person.
II.   A mock political convention would contribute to the personal development of students, because
   A. Many students would have opportunities for leadership in areas of their special interests, for
      1. Money has to be raised and budgeted by students.
      2. There would be publicity and public relations assignments for many people.
      3. Technical arrangements would require students who have knowledge of electronics and lighting.
      4. Staging the convention would bring students of theater and music into the act.

5. All who have political ambitions would gain experience in the art of politics.

B. Students generally would learn a great deal about group behavior, for

1. They would learn what it means to work together in order to get things done.

2. They would gain experience in cooperative decision making on controversial issues among partisans.

III. The convention would instill meaningful school spirit, because

A. Students would get to know each other better, for

1. Each house and dormitory would be organized to act as a state or territorial delegation.

2. Campaign activities are great mixers.

B. It would promote good student–faculty–administration relationships, for

1. Faculty members would be called in as advisers.

2. Students and administrative officers would need to work closely on arrangements.

IV. A mock political convention is a feasible project, because

A. Other colleges and universities have been successful at it.

B. We have adequate building facilities.

C. We can handle the financial side of it, for

1. There is an accumulated surplus of $1,000 in our student activities budget.

2. We can sell advertising space in convention programs.

3. We can charge a door admission for all outsiders.

CONCLUSION

I. We should and can stage a mock political convention, because

A. It confers valuable educational benefits.

B. It will contribute to campus unity.

C. It is a feasible project.

II. I ask that the Student Governing Board endorse this proposal and forward it to the administrative officers for their consideration.

SAMPLE OUTLINE FOR A SPEECH TO ENTERTAIN

The Saga of the Rocking Chair

INTRODUCTION

I. I am going to talk to you about the vicissitudes of an institution of considerable potential in American life—the lowly rocking chair—a questionable objet d'art, but a boon to the leisure time addict.

II. My dictionary defines the "rocking chair," or if you prefer "the rocker" (either is acceptable), as a "chair mounted on rockers or springs so as to permit a person to rock back and forth while sitting." I object to this definition on three counts:
   A. In the first place, it is a tautology: it simply says that a rocker rocks on rockers.
   B. In the second place, it limits the occupant to "sitting." This is not an essential characteristic: you can stand in a rocker (although I do not recommend it) and in the venerable platform rocker you can lie prone if you choose (again, seldom recommended).
   C. In the third place, this definition is much too short and prosaic. Try this one on for size: "The rocking chair is a contraption mounted on a moveable platform, or curved half-hoops, with a seat to accommodate the human anatomy in various postures, that goes back and forth, sometimes with the aid of springs, propelled by the occupant or by some well wisher standing beside, traditionally located to provide a view through the front window, or more recently, to aid in viewing the tube, and in all cases to provide rest for the weary."
III. The saga of the rocking chair is in three parts: First, its unknown origin; second, its untimely demise; and third, its return to a bright future.

BODY

I. My research has failed to reveal the beginnings of the rocking chair, but I do know:
   A. My grandmother's great grandmother had a rocker (I have a picture to prove it).
   B. Whistler painted his mother in a rocking chair, sometime in the last century.
II. But whenever it first appeared, it was destined to die before this century reached the half-way mark.
   A. A victim of the small apartment.
   B. A victim of cartage problems imposed by a mobile population.
   C. A victim of hard-working, restless Americans with no time to rock.
III. Its triumphant return was signaled by:
   A. President Jack Kennedy's affection for the rocking chair.
   B. Certain basic social and economic forces.
      1. Automation gave us more leisure.
      2. The shortened workday and workweek and longer, more frequent vacations.
      3. The longevity of our senior citizens, especially women.

CONCLUSION

I. If the chairs you now sit in were as comfortable as the good old rocking chair, I would prolong this discourse.

II. On second thought, any speaker would have serious trouble competing with this sleep-inducing comfort.

QUESTIONS FOR DISCUSSION

1. Plato, in his *Phaedrus,* has Socrates offer the following suggestions for planning speech. Read this and then discuss the questions below.

> SOCRATES. In advance, a man must know the truth about each particular of which he speaks or writes. He must be able to define each one of them in itself. When he has defined them, he must, in turn, know how to subdivide them severally according to their species, to the point where a division cannot be carried further. By the same method of analysis he must investigate the nature of the soul, and must discover what kind of argument is adapted to each nature. This done, he must settle and order his discourse accordingly, addressing to the many-sided soul a varied speech that touches every chord, a simple one to the simple. Not till then can discourses be artistic as far as it lies in the nature of their genus to be made so, to be controlled by art for the purpose of instruction or persuasion. That is what the whole preceding argument has revealed to us.[3]

a. Compare the advice given here with that set forth in this chapter.

b. How do the logical structures serving the several purposes of speech differ in formal structure?

c. Discuss the ways in which logical structure can be adapted to develop outlines for speech?

2. It is common practice in speech courses to require carefully prepared written outlines to be handed in to the instructor. Discuss the pros and cons of this practice. Will this practice in preparing written outlines help develop organizational skills useful in situations where there is no opportunity to prepare a written outline?

3. To what extent should a speaker be bound by an outline he has prepared in advance? What circumstances might justify impromptu adaptation of the outline while he is speaking?

EXERCISES

1. Each student writes the outline for a speech on the blackboard. Or better still, each outline is typed on a stencil, duplicated, and distributed

[3]Lane Cooper (tr.), *Plato* (New York: Oxford University Press, 1938), p. 68.

to the class. Spend a class period or two analyzing one another's outlines and making suggestions for improvement.

2. Deliver a talk based on a carefully developed outline. Ask the class to jot down your main points and subpoints as they come through while you are speaking. If your prepared outline fails to agree with your listeners' records, either you need to improve your organization or to make it come through better *when you talk.*

3. Focus on introductions and conclusions. Plan and deliver an interesting introduction to a ten- or fifteen-minute speech; you need not go beyond the introduction. Revise and strengthen the conclusion of some speech you have already given. Refresh your listeners' memory on the whole speech, then deliver your revised conclusion.

4. Analyze and outline a short, printed speech. Many speeches have ill-designed and rickety structures. But make an honest and diligent effort to find the main points, to see if they follow in sensible order, and to determine whether the whole outline holds up. Make a thoroughgoing critique of the organization.

5. Divide the class into groups of five or six. Each student prepares a discussion outline on a question agreed upon by his group. Work independently. Then compare outlines in class. Note differences and similarities in each step in the outline. Finally, as a group, agree on a single outline that represents the best efforts of all members of the group.

6. Perform the same exercise (5 above) for speech outlines suitable for reporting and advocacy.

12. The Content of Speech

The content of speech varies with the purpose of speech. *Facts, opinions,* and their *interpretation* are the basic content, and they enter into all speech in different contexts and with different emphases. They are the means of inquiry; they are the substance of reports; the advocate employs them for persuasive purposes; and the evocator uses them whimsically to entertain, or selectively to inspire.

Facts, opinions, and interpretations of these data may be drawn from ordinary human experience, from any specialized field (the basic and applied sciences, the behavioral sciences, and the humanities), or from any area of human knowledge (including philosophy, history, and religion). Information from highly technical and esoteric fields may require translation for the majority of the population. But given a mastery of both the content and the appropriate means of communication, the effective speaker will be able to make both commonplace and erudite matters serve his purposes and those of his listeners.

All these matters are more immediately relevant to the substance of speech and to substantive criticism than any other considerations in this book. Were we to pursue these in greater depth, we would be led into the many areas of knowledge from which they are derived. Such a treatment is beyond our scope, but it should be clear that breadth of experience and education will serve *all* speakers and listeners.

FACTS

Facts are distinct items that we can verify. Facts are objective (they are based on reality), and, like sound money, they are negotiable. Facts are not created. They simply exist. They may be discovered by anyone who cares to look for them and who knows how and where to look. Facts are impersonal. We cannot talk them into or out of existence. Facts are not determined by majority agreement. Whole families have been wiped out because they mistook toadstools for mushrooms.

Most of us like to think we "face the facts." We hear people exclaim with a ring of pride, "I have the facts" or "Let's look at the record!" Since most of us want to talk facts, it is fair to ask: How do we decide what are the facts and what are not? How do we know who has the facts? Here are some ways of evaluating alleged facts.

IS THE ALLEGED FACT CONSISTENT WITH HUMAN NATURE AND EXPERIENCE?

It is hard to believe that a small child fatally injured a grown man by striking him with his fist or that a drug addict was completely cured by a five-day jail sentence. Whenever you offer a factual claim that seems to defy human nature or normal experience, be sure to double-check it before you use it; and if you do use it, be prepared to give an explanation that will make your claim believable. Remember, though, that what strikes us at first as being inconsistent with human nature and experience may only reflect the limitations of our own experience.

IS THE ALLEGED FACT CONSISTENT WITH ESTABLISHED FACTS?

This is a good test for checking up on speakers who tend to make loose or exaggerated claims. If the listeners are in possession of certain established facts, they will reject alleged facts that seem to be inconsistent with what they know to be true. If statistics published in local newspapers indicate a steady over-all rise in crime rate, the incumbent mayor's claim that he has greatly reduced local crime simply cannot be sustained. The mayor may mean that he has waged a vigorous battle against crime or that he has succeeded in reducing the incidence of particular misdemeanors or felonies—but the facts show that he cannot have reduced the crime rate. When such inconsistencies are pointed out, a speaker must qualify his claim, admit his mistake, or explain away the seeming inconsistency. Otherwise he will lose the respect of his listeners.

ARE ALL THE SPEAKER'S FACTS CONSISTENT?

Never be guilty of inconsistencies within your own remarks. A real estate promoter is trying to induce people who live in a crowded city to buy building lots in suburbia. In one breath he claims that suburbia possesses all the advantages of "spacious country living;" in the next breath he boasts that suburbia is so attractive that its population has jumped from three thousand to ten thousand in three years. The wary listener, knowing the town limits of suburbia, concludes that spacious country living and a skyrocketing population are incompatible. If inconsistencies turn up in your remarks, your listeners have the right to conclude that you may be right on one claim and wrong on the other or that you may be wrong on both; but you cannot be right on both.

IS THE PERSON WHO IS REPORTING THE ALLEGED FACT MENTALLY AND MORALLY QUALIFIED?

Without being wantonly suspicious or cynical, be attentive for prejudice, exaggeration, rumor, inaccuracy, poor memory, and downright falsification that impede communication of facts. Guard against people who are given to loose talk or who have a motive for distorting facts. A common human failing is the tendency to report only those facts that support one's vital interests or that prove to be the least damaging to those interests.

CAN THE ALLEGED FACT BE VERIFIED?

Whether you are a listener or a speaker, verify any alleged fact that seems questionable before you adopt it. One way is to make direct observations and inquiries. Do people in your locality believe that the voting age should be lowered to eighteen? Poll representative segments of the community to find out. Has there been a trend in the last five years toward increased juvenile delinquency? Check the records maintained by local law enforcement agencies and news media. Did the death of Ann Rutledge drive Abraham Lincoln to the verge of suicide? Consult the authorities. (Scholars such as J. G. Randall have concluded that the legendary impact of Ann's death upon Lincoln has been greatly exaggerated, if not fabricated.)

There are three ways, then, to verify an alleged fact: make direct observations, check records, and consult authorities.

OPINIONS

An opinion is a person's judgment of a matter that we are asked to accept because he is represented to us as an authority. If an opinion contains factual claims or an interpretation based on facts, we must test it just as we test facts and interpretations themselves. But here we shall talk only about strictly personal judgments that are offered without factual support or interpretation—opinions that we are asked to accept solely because the person who makes them is presumed to be an authority.

Here are some tests that you may apply to personal opinions.

IS THE OPINION OFFERED BY AN EXPERT?

Obviously, we have more confidence in an expert's opinion than in a layman's. But remember that an expert in one field may know little or nothing about some other field and that a layman in one subject may be an expert in another. We may accept a layman's testimony on *matters of fact,* if it stands up to the tests of facts, but we must treat his *opinions* with extreme caution in fields where expertness is required.

For example, the opinion of a distinguished atomic physicist on the amount of energy likely to be released by an atomic explosion carries great weight. But his opinion on our moral right to bomb a city might be less useful than a clergyman's or philosopher's, or your own.

HOW DOES YOUR AUDIENCE FEEL ABOUT THE EXPERT YOU ARE CITING?

If you offer the opinion of an expert in support of a point, your listeners must agree that he is really an expert. If he is unknown to them or if his qualifications are doubtful, be prepared to establish his competence. Show that his training, position, and experience qualify him to speak with authority.

IS THE OPINION BEING OFFERED AS A SUBSTITUTE FOR FACTS?

Most people prefer facts to opinions—when they are available and if they are comprehensible. Sometimes, however, the facts are complicated or technical enough to be effectively beyond the grasp of many people. A homeowner who must decide what type and quantity of wall insulation to install will very likely seek the recommendation of a trained engineer, rather than try to evaluate technical reports that have been published about the relative merits of rock wool, aluminum foil, and other insulators.

Always get the facts and interpret them for yourself whenever you can. But whenever it is difficult to get the facts or to understand them, make use of expert opinion. This is what you do when you accept a physician's diagnosis.

IS THE OPINION BEING USED TO CONFIRM FACTUAL EVIDENCE?

For instance, you might state the facts on athletic facilities for women at your college, draw a conclusion about the need for additional space and equipment, then cite the opinions of members of the athletic staff and administrative officers to confirm your conclusions. Or you might begin with an expert's opinion, and then explain the factual basis for it. Either way, you strengthen your own conclusion by citing expert opinion, and your listeners have a chance to inspect the factual basis of the opinion.

DO THE EXPERTS AGREE?

Expert opinions are stronger and more reliable if you can show that the experts agree. If they do not agree on the important points, your listeners are likely to reserve their own opinions.

INTERPRETATIONS OF FACT AND OPINION

Interpretations are the meanings we give to facts and opinions and the conclusion we draw from them. We make use of interpretations every day. We decide to take the dog for a walk and discover he has disappeared. When and where was he last seen? He was around an hour or so ago. Maybe another member of the family has taken him out. His leash is gone. That must be the answer. We pick up the evening paper and read about a threatened steel strike. An editorial suggests that the government is prepared to take over the plants. Is this a wise move? Can you blame the workers for asking for a wage increase with prices the way they are? On the other hand, can you expect management to absorb the wage increases without raising steel prices? You recall an article in a journal you glanced at a few days ago and pick it up to see what it has to say on inflation.

And so it goes. All these interpretations are based on inferences. We think or reason our way to conclusions from facts—or what we take to be facts—and opinions. Failure to interpret fact and opinion reasonably can be due to a variety of causes. We may wish for certain outcomes and simply rationalize our desires; we may be blinded by prejudice; we may be led astray by exceptional cases and coincidences; we may willfully distort under pressure; or we may lack the comprehension and perception that enables us to discriminate between straight and crooked thinking. In any case, speaker and listeners alike will benefit by an understanding of the several types of inference and by the ability to test their validity.

GENERALIZATION

A generalization is a conclusion that we reach on something common to a whole group of things after we have examined a good sample of the group. Speech abounds with generalizations. In fact, our daily life would be completely disorganized unless we generalized from our experiences and then acted according to our generalizations. When you eat in a restaurant, you act on dozens of tacit generalizations—that public buildings are safe, that restaurants do not put poison in their food, that public eating places are reasonably sanitary, and so forth. Here are just a few generalizations that were made in a single conversation: Country living is more healthful and wholesome than city living; the University Theater produces the best plays in this area; football players are subsidized; labor leaders lack a social conscience; the food in England is terrible.

These examples show how often we use generalizations, and they suggest the danger of making hasty ones. Some of the examples appear to be false, and all of them are open to exceptions. How can you draw generalizations that are safe and useful? Here are some tests.

HAVE YOU EXAMINED ENOUGH SAMPLES?

Our confidence is quickly undermined when we hear a speaker draw sweeping, general conclusions from few or no facts. You are sitting in on a bull session with four or five other students. Each remarks that he is taller than his parents. So you all agree that the present generation of college students is taller than the last. Obviously, this generalization is not based on enough samples. All sound generalizations depend on an adequate survey of the field.

ARE THE SAMPLES EXAMINED TYPICAL OF THE WHOLE GROUP?

Often we have to generalize without having time or opportunity to examine very many samples. So we must be careful to base our conclusions for the whole group on typical cases. Avoid basing generalizations on exceptional or bizarre examples. Suppose you declare that foreign motion pictures are superior to American ones. This conclusion is unwarranted and unfair if you see foreign films that have been carefully selected for export to the United States, but only go to Hollywood's B movies.

HAVE YOU ACCOUNTED FOR THE EXCEPTIONS?

In our enthusiasm or in our desire to make a point, we sometimes overlook the exceptions to a generalization. Suppose we assert that summer vacations are now a standard practice among all Americans. No doubt you can think of many exceptions, and you would be quite right to insist that the generalization be scaled down to fit the facts. We might say that summer vacations are a standard practice among Americans *except for* farmers and other groups who have to work through the summer; or we might say that *many* or *most* Americans enjoy a summer vacation. Better still, if the statistics were available, we might supply the *exact percentage* of Americans who take summer vacations. Almost every generalization needs to be qualified in terms of quantity, time, place, or special circumstances.

ANALOGY

An analogy is an inference based on a comparison of two items. If you can show that the two items resemble each other in all significant respects, you may infer that they resemble each other in an attribute known to belong to one but not known to belong to the other. In contemporary international politics, the controversial opinion that new nations should form democratic governments is based on a tacit analogy between America and any other country that comes into existence by revolutionary means and seeks "freedom."

Apply the following tests to analogies before you accept them as valid.

ARE THE CASES ALIKE IN ALL ESSENTIAL RESPECTS?

This is the key test. The success of a democracy in the newly independent United States in 1776 is no guarantee that it will succeed in any other country if it is smaller, has different traditions and standards of living, and is emerging as a nation two centuries later.

HAVE SIGNIFICANT DIFFERENCES IN THE CASES BEEN ACCOUNTED FOR?

If you discover such differences, you must either show that they do not affect your conclusion, or else qualify your conclusion. Suppose that a colony existed today in which many of the so-called American values and attitudes, learned through textbooks and periodicals, were popular, and the people of that country rebelled against their colonial government for independence. However, the economy of the colony has been entirely agrarian and oriented toward domestic consumption. If you believe that this new country should become a democracy, you will have to show that the difference does not impair your conclusion.

CAUSAL RELATIONS

In establishing a causal relationship, we try to show the probable cause for some known event or condition, or we try to predict the effect of some event, condition, or proposal. We speak of the first of these two methods of interpretation as reasoning from a *known* effect to an *alleged cause*. The following questions will help you test *effect-to-cause reasoning*.

DID THE ALLEGED CAUSE ACTUALLY CONTRIBUTE TO THE KNOWN EFFECT?

This is the first and most elementary test. Often the actual cause is obscure and lies below the surface. Did the men really strike because of poor working conditions? They knew that improvements had been made and that others had already been contracted for. Avoid hasty conclusions. Analyze the problem and scrutinize all possible causes, rejecting those that do not seem to have made significant contribution to the effect. One can be sure that this test is being applied—perhaps unconsciously—when one hears comments such as these: "No, it can't be the fan belt; I just had a new one put on." "Surely it's not a lack of water; why, I watered the plant every day."

IS THE ALLEGED CAUSE THE WHOLE CAUSE OF THE KNOWN EFFECT?

Don't try to explain an effect by a cause that is only *partially* responsible for it. A man's poverty may be charged to his laziness when, in fact, poor health and lack of opportunity may have contributed to it. Whenever a known effect seems "too big" to be explained by the "little" cause assigned to it, treat the explanation with caution.

Is the alleged cause too general and vague to explain the
known effect?

If the known effect is too "little" for the "big "cause assigned to it,
look for a more specific cause. To say that Frankie's misbehavior at school
is caused by a wave of juvenile delinquency sweeping the nation fails to
tell us much about Frankie's problems. This alleged cause, even if it is
remotely true, is too big and too far removed from Frankie's immediate
difficulties to help us straighten him out.

Now let's reverse the process. We have a *known cause* and we want
to predict its effect. This is what we usually do whenever we explain,
defend, or attack a proposed course of action (offered as a known cause).
For example, perhaps someone urged you to attend college because a
college education would broaden your outlook, enable you to meet interesting people, or increase your earning power (alleged effects). A plea to
lower our tariff schedules might be urged in the interest of "trade not aid,"
world economic stability, and world peace (alleged effects); the same plea
might be challenged on the grounds that it would lower wage rates for
American laborers, dislocate industry, and lead to inferior products.

The following questions will help you test *cause-to-effect reasoning.*

Is the known cause sufficient to produce the alleged effect?

Will insulating my house reduce my heating costs by two hundred
dollars a year? Will eating Wheaties make me a champion? This is a good
test to apply to many of the claims of enthusiastic promoters and salesmen.
Never mistake a half-truth for a whole truth.

Will the known cause produce effects other than those
alleged?

Even if insulating my house will save me money in the long run, its
immediate effect may be to throw me into bankruptcy. Certain proposals
for federal aid to education may mean better educational facilities as
claimed, but they may also mean increased federal control of education.
Try to discover *all* possible effects, good or bad, before you commit yourself.

Are the alleged effects too vague to be convincing?

"Turn the rascals out and return to good times" is a familiar political
theme. Because the times are always a little upset in our imperfect world,
this slogan appeals to disgruntled and undiscriminating voters. But before
you accept as probable outcomes the general claims that are made for or
against a proposition, reduce them to specific items. In politics, this would
mean reviewing a candidate's position on definite issues.

CORRELATIVE RELATIONS

Correlative relations are simply implied relations between two or more items. You take the presence or absence of one as an *indication* of the presence or absence of the other. You take the familiar red-and-white barber pole as a sign of a barber shop. You interpret dark clouds to mean wind or rain. An open front door is taken to mean that someone is home. Rainy weather on election day is sometimes taken as a sign that the rural vote will be light.

As with other methods of interpretation, we must test the reliability of the correlative relations that we hear and use.

IS THE KNOWN ITEM A CERTAIN SIGN OF THE ALLEGED ITEM?

How close, how sure, how constant is the relationship attributed to the two items? We can answer these questions only after making close and repeated observations. If we're looking for a barber shop, we may head for the red-and-white pole with confidence. Less convincing are these inferences: "If he's so smart, why isn't he rich?" "The food must be good here; the prices are high enough." Unless you have made enough observations to support a firm correlative relationship, qualify your conclusions, present them tentatively, and act on them with caution.

IS THE RELATIONSHIP BETWEEN THE TWO ITEMS REAL OR ACCIDENTAL?

Many superstitions and old wives' tales collapse under this test. Try it on these: Misfortune will stalk you if a black cat crosses your path. Potatoes should be planted when the moon is full. A horseshoe nailed above the door brings good luck.

Racial bigotry and prejudice thrive on accidental relationships. No race or creed is exempt from undesirable members, and thoughtful people are not easily duped by accidental associations. Yet it is tragically true that many people who are usually cautious seize upon the frailest kind of relationship for support when their prejudices are threatened.

HAVE SPECIAL FACTORS ENTERED IN TO ALTER NORMAL RELATIONS?

Black clouds probably mean rain *if* the wind is in the northeast. The party would have been well attended *if* the invitations had gone out on time. The deal was practically in the bag *until* his wife stepped in. Unforeseen conditions often upset what we would normally expect. An important part of the maturation process is the realization that few signs are absolutely reliable. We should try to anticipate as best we can the factors that might upset relationships between signs and that might destroy the conclusions we are tempted to draw or to accept uncritically.

QUESTIONS FOR DISCUSSION

1. Do people really want the facts? Most *profess* to want the facts, but do they really? Do they want the facts in certain areas of their lives and not in others? What happens to facts when they run counter to desires?

2. Discuss this statement: "To disrespect facts, to overlook facts, to becloud facts, to withhold facts—these are the illiberal modes of the propogandist, the shyster, and the dictator."[1]

3. Compare the ways in which facts, expert opinions, generalizations, analogies, causal relations, and correlative relations are properly used in inquiry, reporting, advocacy, and evocative speaking.

4. How are the above "contents" of speech expressed or shown in speech outlines?

5. Read this quotation and discuss the questions that follow.

> ... he [the speaker] must have a thorough and detailed knowledge of the special sciences which mainly concern the art of Rhetoric—that is, ethics and politics, above all, since they have to do with the conduct of men as individuals, and with men in groups. Of course he must have an adequate knowledge of other special sciences, too; no knowledge comes amiss to the speaker.[2]

    a. What knowledge encompassed by *ethics* and *politics* is of special importance to the speaker? What fields of study in a modern college curriculum would be included?

    b. Is "an adequate knowledge of other special sciences" dictated by the speaker's subject or his need for a general education, or both?

EXERCISES

1. Prepare a short talk alleging at least three facts and specifying their sources. Convince the audience of the reliability of the sources and allow them to question you about the sources. This exercise encourages critical thinking by both speaker and listeners.

2. Maintain a list of statements alleging facts that raise some doubt in your mind. Conversations, public speeches, and printed material are good sources for such statements. The resultant list will be heterogeneous and may include statements by friends and other students. Apply the five tests for facts offered in this chapter. Present some of your analyses to your class

[1]Hoyt H. Hudson, *Educating Liberally* (Stanford, Calif.: Stanford University Press, 1945), p. 20.

[2]Lane Cooper (tr.), *Aristotle's Rhetoric* (New York: D. Appleton and Company, 1932), p. 155.

and allow others to evaluate your reasoning. Confine the discussion to the factual acceptability of the statements.

3. Find a news story, editorial, magazine article, or advertisement to which you take exception because of (a) the alleged facts or omission of facts, (b) the opinions offered in behalf of the contention, or (c) the interpretations made of the alleged facts and opinions. Discuss the claim or contention, the support offered in its behalf, and your objections on the grounds suggested in this chapter.

4. Choose as your subject for a talk some problem about which you have limited knowledge and no settled opinion. It may be a problem in politics, medicine, architecture, literature, agriculture—any field. Locate some articles and speeches by people who seem to write and speak as authorities on the matter. Then find out all you can about the qualifications of these people. What tentative conclusions may you draw about the subject based on the several opinions and their sources? Discuss your findings and conclusions.

5. Prepare and present a talk in which you develop your subject *primarily* by means of *one* of the four methods of interpretation: generalization, analogy, causal relations, or correlative relations. Most of us use all these methods in our daily speech, but this time you are to concentrate on one method. Make your inferences as tight and invulnerable as you can. After you have spoken, ask the class (a) to identify the method of interpretation you employed, and (b) to apply the appropriate tests of inference listed in this chapter.

6. Analyze the printed text of a recent speech. Identify statements of alleged fact, opinion, and interpretation of fact and opinion. Which predominate? After testing these statements, are you prepared to accept or reject the speaker's conclusions? Did you detect any significant fallacies? Present a written or oral report of your findings.

7. For this exercise, select the printed text of a speech by which the speaker won your confidence because of his respect for facts, his discriminating use of opinions, and his sound interpretations of facts and opinions. Offer it to the class as a model of straight thinking. Briefly review the speech as a whole for the class, point out its merits, and read portions of the speech to illustrate and enforce your conclusions about it.

13. Developing Ideas

Although facts, expert opinions, and logical arguments may speak for themselves, they frequently need to be energized before they become meaningful to an audience. It is a *fact* that thousands of families "on the wrong side of the tracks" live in crowded, ill-ventilated, rat-infested housing, but this fact will have greater impact if you can tell a vivid, firsthand story of the plight of one of these families.

This chapter presents tested methods for amplifying and dramatizing your ideas. These methods are *not* substitutes for facts, expert opinions, or the reasoning process. Rather, they are supporting devices that help you to project your material with impact. Skillfully used, these methods will endow your speech with clarity, warmth, color, human interest, and emotional appeal.

METHODS OF AMPLIFICATION

DEVELOPMENT BY DEFINITION

Define important terms that may be unfamiliar to your listeners or that may be misunderstood. No one should take liberties with well-established meanings, but when a term has several possible meanings, make clear the one you are using.

A definition establishes boundary lines. It places a term in a general class or category and then shows how the term differs from other members of the class. If you can offer an example that further pinpoints your meaning, so much the better.

Suppose you wanted to define the word *manslaughter*. You might say, "Manslaughter means killing another human being without malice. If someone kills a person in self-defense or through reckless driving, he may be charged with manslaughter but not murder." Here you place manslaughter within a category of actions called killing. Immediately you draw distinctions, pointing out that manslaughter is limited to the killing of human beings, not other forms of life. And you add that it must be done without malice, which distinguishes it from murder. Finally, you offer two examples of killing under circumstances that warrant the charge of manslaughter.

Often we need to define our terms with great precision. Other times we wish only to highlight an already familiar term by throwing out a few points of reference that will help our listeners catch the special sense and importance we attach to it. Notice the somewhat satirical vein in which Robert M. Hutchins, former president of the University of Chicago, sets forth his conception of a university. Notice too how he first classifies his term, then separates it from other "communities."

> A University is a community of scholars. It is not a kindergarten; it is not a club; it is not a reform school; it is not a political party; it is not an agency of propaganda. A University is a community of scholars.[1]

DEVELOPMENT BY EXAMPLE

An example is a *specific case in point* that supports or explains a general statement. Listeners appreciate examples that are relevant and that facilitate understanding of a point. There are *real* examples and *hypothetical* examples. A *real* example is an actual case that can be documented. A *hypothetical* example is one that you create for the occasion. The following excerpt from a statement by Adlai E. Stevenson to the United States Senate Subcommittee on Foreign Relations in 1963 is replete with real examples that support his general point:

> I said a moment ago that the agenda of the Seventeenth General Assembly was a virtual compendium of the ongoing problems of the modern world. Listen to this list of trouble spots and sore spots: the Congo . . . the Gaza strip . . . Southern Rhodesia . . . South West Africa . . . Yemen . . . West New Guinea . . . and the Arab refugee camps.
>
> Mark this string of contentious issues: Chinese representation . . . North Korea . . . Hungary . . . colonialism . . . Troika . . . and sovereignty over natural resources.
>
> Consider, if you will, this list of universal concerns: disarmament . . . nuclear testing . . . outer space . . . world food . . . world trade . . . world science . . . and the training of manpower for economic and social development.[2]

In this instance, the listeners were familiar with the examples, and the speaker had only to name them to make his point.

[1] *Vital Speeches of the Day,* May 20, 1935, p. 547.
[2] Adlai E. Stevenson, *Looking Outward,* ed. Robert L. Schiffer and Selma Schiffer (New York: Harper & Row, Publishers, 1963), p. 122.

Some examples, however, need to be developed in detail before they they become convincing. Observe how Frederick Mayer uses a single example to give impact to his point.

> I can think of one of my students as a freshman. She was a replica of Middle-Town, a product of what Sinclair Lewis described in *Babbitt*. She called Plato–Pluto. Her spelling was atrocious. Her first test was chaos roughly organized. Her taste in music was influenced by Elvis Presley. Three years later she is reading Kafka, Thomas Mann, and Gide. She has just written a superb essay on Albert Camus. . . . She is a different person today —alive, vibrant, idealistic. This shows what education can do.[3]

Sometimes an entire speech is developed through a single master-example. One student, arguing that it is possible for a small town to have a lively cultural life, based her entire speech on the example of a small town in Colorado. She recounted in detail how the residents stimulated community interest in literature, theater, and painting, and the resourceful means they used to bring an occasional artist and writer with national standing to their town.

In the following quotation from an address by Oscar E. Ewing, "What Health Insurance Would Mean to You," all the examples are hypothetical. Not one actual case is cited. All are introduced by *suppose* or *if*.

> Good evening. I want to talk to you tonight, not about the nation's health, but about your own health. Suppose that tomorrow morning, you should become suddenly ill—seriously ill. Suppose you found that you needed an operation, with special medical care, and all kinds of x-rays and drugs. Suppose you had to stop working for months while you went through your operation and your convalescence. Suppose the doctor's bill, the hospital bill, the bills for special laboratory services and medicines, added up to hundreds of dollars—maybe even thousands. Would you be able to afford it? . . .
> If you have been lying in a hospital bed after an operation, worrying about where the money to pay the bills would come from, you know what I mean. If you have had to go to a loan company and borrow money to pay a hospital bill, you know what I mean. If you had ever received a note from your child's school, telling you that your little boy or your little girl needs adenoids or tonsils out, and wondered how you'd pay for it, you know what I mean. . . .[4]

Hypothetical examples are not always used this effectively, though, and most people prefer examples that are authentic. Listeners confronted by a plethora of contrived examples are likely to conclude that real examples do not exist or that the speaker cannot think of any. When used skillfully, hypothetical examples vividly dramatize reality and call up real examples in your listeners' minds.

[3] *Vital Speeches of the Day*, April 15, 1959, p. 414.
[4] *Vital Speeches of the Day*, May 15, 1952, p. 478.

DEVELOPMENT BY STATISTICS

An example is *one* case in point. Statistics are a shorthand method of summarizing a large number of examples.

BE ACCURATE IN HANDLING STATISTICS

Know the meaning of the unit you use. Statistics can be misleading unless you define your terms carefully. Suppose a university reports an enrollment of 5,000 students. Does that mean full-time students, or are part-time students included? If a student is registered in two different divisions, is he counted once or twice? In other words, the unit *student* must be defined before the statistics can be interpreted reliably.

Base your statistics on a fair sample. Offhand, it might seem that the records of a college health service should accurately reveal the incidence of common diseases among students. But if you investigate, you might find that commuting students seldom use the health service and that even resident students go to their family physicians when they are seriously sick. As a result, the health-service records alone do not give you an accurate picture. Statistics must be based on a sufficient number of representative cases if they are to be reliable.

Establish the stability of the unit in making statistical comparisons. Statistics compiled at one time and place may seem to be based on the same unit as those compiled at another time or place. A comparison of 1890 statistics on cancer with those compiled seventy years later might make it appear that the incidence of cancer is increasing. Actually it may mean merely that we now identify cancer more accurately. A fund raiser for a political campaign pointed out that the cost of Lincoln's campaign for the presidency in 1860 was $100,000. Today a half hour of TV time for political campaigning on a national network may cost this much. Granted, the cost of political campaigning has skyrocketed, but the comparison is misleading because the dollar has depreciated in value.

Be sure that your statistics measure what they say they measure. If you are reporting on the real income of wage-earners, statistics that give their income in dollars might be deceptive, since "real income" means dollars translated into things the worker buys. If women have fewer automobile accidents than men, can you conclude without question that women are better drivers? Or could it mean that women drive fewer miles than men and that they drive in places and at times when accidents are less likely to happen?

USE STATISTICS SPARINGLY AND SKILLFULLY

A blanket of statistics may smother your listeners, particularly if the statistics are highly complex. Translate statistics into concrete items that your audience can grasp. In the statement below, C. Langdon White reduces to human terms complicated data on the land-population ratio.

> Taking the world as a whole, there is only one acre of arable land available to each person and even in the United States only three acres per head. If the world population continues to increase at the present rate—that is, unchanged—in 600 years there will be only one square yard of land surface per capita. This "standing room" figure takes into account more than arable land; it includes all land—polar wastes, deserts, jungles, mountain tops, as well as available living space.[5]

Use round figures when you can compare them strikingly to make your point. For example, in 1800 there were 900 million people on the earth; by 1962 the figure had grown to over 3 billion; and the best estimates are that by 2050 the world's population will be between 9 and 13 billion. It may be more efficient and effective to convert figures in percentages. For example, saying that 20 percent of the students are commuters may be more effective than giving the actual number.

Use statistics dramatically if you can do so without distorting them. The following "stix" story (so called because it is designed to make statistics stick!) is an example.

> The first printing of the Revised Standard Version of the Holy Bible was 970,000 copies. These Bibles—each 1½ inches thick—stacked in one pile would tower 24 miles into the stratosphere—higher than 100 Empire State Buildings.[6]

Note the use of statistics in the following paragraphs to show the inflation in academic grades. Specific examples are cited and general conclusions drawn.

> In 1961, about half of the seniors at Harvard College graduated with honors; . . . when the class of '74 received their diplomas, degrees *cum laude* or better went to an astonishing 82 percent. The average University of Colorado student in 1964 maintained a grade-point average of 2.4 (out of a possible 4 points), but his counterpart today has a GPA of 2.82. Between 1962 and 1972, the University of North Carolina doubled the percentage of A's it handed out. The average grade at the University of Wisconsin has soared from C-plus to B-plus in just nine years. And the dean's list at the University of Virginia included 53 percent of the student body last year—compared with 21 per cent in 1965.
>
> "A few years ago, a C would put you in the middle," says Douglas Hobbes, a political-science professor at UCLA. "Today it puts you in the

[5] *Vital Speeches of the Day,* May 15, 1959, p. 462.
[6] Bernard Kalb, in *The Saturday Review,* December 20, 1952, p. 8.

bottom third of the class." Nationwide, in fact, B is now the average college grade, and a number of educators are voicing increasing concern over the rampant inflation of grades.[7]

DEVELOPMENT BY ILLUSTRATION

Although the word *illustration* is popularly used to cover many methods of developing ideas, we use it here to mean an extended comparison between two things drawn from quite different fields. An idea that is unfamiliar or doubtful is more likely to be accepted when it is compared with something your listener knows or feels confident about.

In one of his fireside chats, Franklin D. Roosevelt sought to interpret the nature of the New Deal at a time when it really was new, and to counter charges that it was revolutionary. He used an illustration to assure the people that the New Deal was wholly consistent with the American political tradition.

> While I am away from Washington this summer, a long-needed renovation of and addition to our White House office building is to be started. The architects have planned a few new rooms built into the present all too small one-story structure. We are going to include in this addition and in the renovation modern electric wiring and modern plumbing and modern means of keeping the offices cool in hot Washington summers. But the structural lines of the old Executive office building will remain. The artistic lines of the White House buildings were the creation of master builders when our Republic was young. The simplicity and the strength of the structure remain in the face of every modern test. But within this magnificent pattern, the necessities of modern government business require reorganization and rebuilding.
> If I were to listen to the arguments of some prophets of calamity who are talking these days, I should hesitate to make these alterations. I should fear that while I am away for a few weeks the architects might build some strange new Gothic tower or a factory building or perhaps a replica of the Kremlin or of the Potsdam palace. But I have no such fears. The architects and builders are men of common sense and of artistic American tastes. They know that the principles of harmony and of necessity itself require that the building of the new structure shall blend with the essential lines of the old. It is this combination of the old and the new that marks orderly peaceful progress, not only in building buildings but in building government itself.[8]

The value of an illustration lies in its suggestive power. It should never be offered or taken as a literal or complete demonstration of a point. Fresh illustrations illuminate points and indicate originality; hackneyed illustrations suggest a dull mind. As Dr. George Buttrick said, "The little

[7]*Newsweek,* July 1, 1974, pp. 49–50.
[8]Fireside chat, "Reviewing the Achievements of the Seventy-Third Congress," June 28, 1934.

boy who held his finger in the dike to avoid the flood is now an old man and should be sent home for a much needed rest."[9]

DEVELOPMENT BY STORIES

We recount anecdotes and tell stories for pleasure, and we use them to cinch points. Some of these stories we draw from personal experiences, literature, or history; others we create to point up some true-to-life situation. A well told story is one of the most effective means of kindling interest and dramatizing ideas. In a speech called "Awake the Dawn," Bishop Gerald Kennedy uses several well-placed stories to highlight ideas and strengthen points. Here is one example.

> The late Bishop Francis J. McConnell was once president of DePauw University. He always liked to be on the land, and after retirement he lived on a farm in Ohio. When he was at DePauw he had a small acreage where he raised chickens. He said that everything went all right except in the middle of the night the rooster would start to crow and wake everybody up. He could not understand this behavior so he stayed up one night to find out the trouble. He said that along about two o'clock in the morning, the interurban train coming out from Indianapolis would swing around a curve, and the headlight would shine into the chicken house. The rooster, thinking it was the sun, would begin to crow. And the bishop said, "It is not only roosters that mistake headlights for dawns." Indeed it is not! If men can sometimes bring the darkness, so sometimes in their pride and in their limited knowledge they can promise dawns which never come, and bring disillusionment.[10]

The value of a story, of course, may be more apparent than real. Be on guard against stories that oversimplify and that substitute a pleasant, facile explanation for rigor and accuracy. Unless you speak merely to entertain, your story must bear sharply on the point. You may have heard listeners remark, "I became so interested in his story that I missed the point he was trying to make."

DEVELOPMENT BY QUOTATIONS

Quotations may be drawn from anything in the vast reservoir of human expression—from history, literature, biography, technical reports, newspapers, speeches, conversations. Apt statements by somebody else may lend weight to your own views or may simply be more impressive, beautiful, or amusing than anything you can devise. A quotation loses its value, though, if it is laboriously dragged in or is too long. Make it clear that you are quoting and from whom you have taken your material.

[9]*New York Times,* September 29, 1937, p. L25
[10]A. Craig Baird, ed., *Representative American Speeches: 1956–1957* (New York: The H. W. Wilson Company, 1957), p. 185.

J. Martin Klotsche uses many short quotations in his speech, "On Being an Educated Person." Through these borrowed statements he sets forth with great economy a variety of views on education.

> A former distinguished professor of the faculty of the University of Wisconsin once defined an educated person as one "who tries to understand the whole of knowledge as well as one man can." Mark Van Doren held that the purpose of education is to see that "each man becomes more than he is," while William Whewell thought of education as the means "to connect a man's mind with the general mind of the human race."[11]

DEVELOPMENT BY MAXIMS, PROVERBS, AND SLOGANS

A *maxim* is a general statement of principle, advice, or counsel on human conduct and affairs expressed in tight, epigrammatic form. To be effective, a maxim must suggest its idea with memorable deftness. Here are a few examples.

> An Englishman is the unfittest person on earth to argue another Englishman into slavery. (*Edmund Burke*)
> Men may be sorely touched and deeply grieved in their privileges as well as in their purses. (*Edmund Burke*)
> Error of opinion may be tolerated where reason is left free to combat it.
> (*Thomas Jefferson*)
> It is better to work on institutions by the sun than by the wind.
> (*Ralph W. Emerson*)
> Only a people who can achieve the moral mastery of themselves can hope to win the moral leadership of others. (*Adlai Stevenson*)
> Self-criticism is the secret weapon of democracy, and candor and confession are good for the political soul. (*Adlai Stevenson*)
> It is my task to report the state of the Union; to improve it is the task of us all. (*John F. Kennedy*)

A *proverb* is a short, pithy saying that expresses a widely accepted truth based on common sense and practical experience. Proverbs are really a type of maxim that embody the folk-wisdom of a people. Benjamin Franklin's counsels, offered as the words of Poor Richard, are examples.

> He that falls in love with himself will have no rivals.
> 'Tis hard for an empty bag to stand upright.
> If you'd have it done, go; if not, send.

Many of the late President Kennedy's statements have the ring of proverb.

> A stern heritage is a good teacher.
> It takes two to make peace.

[11] *Vital Speeches of the Day,* August 1, 1957, p. 635.

Skillful speakers use proverbs and maxims sparingly. Overabundant use of these techniques sounds stuffy, and if a speaker's advice is premature or unwelcome, he may alienate his audience by this imprudence.

A *slogan* is a short, catchy statement used as a rallying point by a person, group, or party. Some slogans have undeniable social value, such as "The life you save may be your own" or "Help fight cancer with a check-up and a check." But slogans that boost products and services are often half-truths designed to beguile the unwary. However valid, a slogan soon becomes trite and loses its appeal.

DEVELOPMENT BY REPETITION

A reader has the advantage of being able to go back to an earlier page, to refresh his memory and review important points in the light of what followed. A speaker may provide much the same advantage for his audience by repeating in new ways what he has already said. By repeating an idea, a speaker underlines it and clarifies it for his listeners.

Theodore Roosevelt was a master of the art of *meaningful* repetition. On April 14, 1906, he spoke on "The Man with the Muck-Rake," in which he recalled the man in Bunyan's *Pilgrim's Progress* "who could look no way but downward, with the muck-rake in his hand; who was offered a celestial crown for his muck-rake, but who would neither look up or regard the crown he was offered, but continued to rake to himself the filth of the floor." From this allegory, Roosevelt drew his theme: that dishonest men in public and private life should be exposed, but indiscriminate muck-raking dulls the public conscience and benefits the scoundrels. In various ways, Roosevelt restates this theme, repeating it over and over again, dinning it into public consciousness.

Avoid needless repetition, of course. And when you do repeat a point, find new ways of putting it.

DEVELOPMENT BY VISUAL AND AUDITORY AIDS

Visual and auditory aids include charts, maps, graphs, diagrams, outlines, pictures, cartoons, posters, lantern slides, moving pictures, models, tape recorders, and objects used in demonstrations. These aids are particularly useful in teaching and in other types of informative speaking. A great deal of our conversation takes place in sight of the objects we are talking about. Television has an advantage over radio not only because the speakers can be seen as well as heard, but because they can use visual aids to supplement the spoken word. Here are suggestions for the use of aids.

LET THE AIDS SUPPLEMENT YOUR WORDS

Ask yourself, "Will visual and auditory aids help me achieve my purpose?" If so, use them. Fortunately, many ingenious devices are available. If you cannot find just what you want, homemade devices are well worth the time and effort spent in getting them together.

But don't drag in visual and auditory aids for their own sake. If your listeners conclude that you are simply parading a set of gimmicks, you will lose their respect as well as their interest. The best advice is this: Don't overload your speech with aids and never use them as mere "fill-in."

Make sure that your audience can see your visual aids without straining their eyes

An audience cannot be expected to take interest in an illustration that is too small or very minutely detailed or that is displayed in inadequate light. The thoughtful speaker will have clearly displayed aids, or, if that is not possible, will have small ones duplicated and distributed to his audience at the proper time.

Keep your aids simple and comprehensible

An "inventor" created a wonderful machine that would do the work of five men; but it took six men to operate it. If it takes more time and ingenuity for you to explain a chart than it would to explain the point you are trying to make, everyone will be happier if you skip the chart. The point of your exhibit must emerge quickly and easily, or else be lost.

Synchronize your aids with your remarks

To be effective, visual aids must become visible at exactly the moment they are needed. We have all seen lecturers who competed for attention with their own devices. They make the mistake of handing out charts, pictures, graphs, and the like before such aids are needed. As a result, the audience's attention is distracted from the speaker's words.

Have your aids in working order

Have you ever suffered along with a speaker who tried to use electrical gadgets that would not operate, lantern slides that were unnumbered or mixed up or upside down, maps that fell down, or demonstration kits that lacked an essential component? The strange thing is that some people seem not to learn very much from their own lack of preparation. Arrange things beforehand.

AXIOMS OF AMPLIFICATION

Why are definitions, examples, illustrations, visual aids, and all the other methods of amplification effective in speech? What are the sources of their strength and appeal? The axioms we offer here will throw light on these questions. In addition, they will serve as practical guides in selecting

material and developing it. In general, any technique of developing an idea
that makes use of the axioms that follow is likely to command interest.

SPECIFIC INSTANCES, ITEMS, AND CASES ARE USUALLY CLEARER AND MORE INTERESTING THAN GENERAL STATEMENTS

Specificity is particularly needed if your generalization falls outside
the immediate experiences of your listeners or if it is a tired one that needs
to be enlivened by the touch of reality. Without adequate attention to
details and applications, speech tends to become vague, loose and indefi-
nite.

CONCRETE THINGS—ACTUAL SUBSTANCES AND PERSONS—HOLD INTEREST BETTER THAN DO ABSTRACTIONS

Most generalizations are abstract, and specific instances may be. For
example, the law of supply and demand is a specific instance of economic
principles, and the law of excluded middle is a specific case of the so-called
laws of reasoning. But neither is concrete. If you want a concrete example
of the law of supply and demand, take your listener, figuratively speaking,
to a used car lot and let him see how this law works; and if you want a
concrete example of the law of excluded middle, draw a diagram of the sort
you can find in any elementary textbook on logic.

FAMILIAR REFERENCES BRING THE UNFAMILIAR WITHIN THE EXPERIENCE OF THE LISTENER

Rhetorical devices based on comparison and contrast are especially
useful here, but all methods of amplification draw on this axiom. A specific
case developed in concrete terms will usually be more effective if it deals
with familiar places, persons, and things.

THE NOVEL—THE RARE, THE UNUSUAL, AND THE DIFFERENT—ALSO ATTRACTS ATTENTION

A novel way of putting a familiar idea, an unusual experience, or any
method of amplification that contains an element of surprise relieves the
monotony of ordinary talk and enlivens formal speech. But precaution is
necessary: Bizarre materials that strain for novelty offend good taste and
place the speaker under a cloud of suspicion.

WHATEVER STRIKES A PERSON'S VITAL INTERESTS WILL INVOLVE HIM MOST QUICKLY AND DEEPLY

This story illustrates the point.

One evening in his club, a physician sat at the card table with three friends.
Word was brought to him that a child had suddenly become desperately ill.

As he rose to go, one of his friends remonstrated saying: "Don't rush off; the child's mother is probably unduly alarmed over the situation. Stay and finish the game before you go; that will be time enough."

"That's what you think I ought to do?" queried the doctor.

"Yes," answered his friend, "fussy, nervous people have no right to call a physician after office hours, anyway."

"Very well," said the doctor, "I'll take your advice this time because it is your child who is ill."[12]

Allusion to our vital interests immediately removes a matter from the realm of the casual and impersonal. Let an instructor say "The normal distribution curve is illustrated by the grades I gave on the quiz you took yesterday," and his students are likely to take a quick and keen interest in the curve.

PROXIMITY, RECENCY, AND IMMEDIACY LEND IMPACT

Illustrative materials that are remote from the listener's experiences are seldom so effective as those drawn from situations close at hand. If you can date your story "last night" or "today" and locate it "right here in this town" or "next door" or "in our sorority," you will see at once how quickly interest quickens.

CONFLICT—STRUGGLE, CLASH, AND CONTROVERSY—IMPLIES COMPETITIVENESS, ONE OF THE STRONGEST MOTIVATIONS IN OUR CULTURE

Who has not listened to comparisons between himself and others with mounting interest? The same kind of interest is evoked when a speaker compares one's town with a neighboring village or a local football team with its competitors. Interest in political conventions and TV debates is heightened by conflict. This device can be applied to any circumstances in which competing forces are at work.

ACTION AROUSES MORE INTEREST THAN DOES QUIESCENCE

Motion pictures and visual aids with moving parts put this principle to use. Narrative discourse is a popular oral method because it is lively. Personification of abstract qualities and animation of inanimate objects are other frequent applications of the motion axiom.

QUESTIONS FOR DISCUSSION

1. Chapter 12, "The Content of Speech," and chapter 13, "Developing Ideas," are closely related and complementary. Chapter 12 deals with the

[12]J. M. O'Neill and A. T. Weaver, *The Elements of Speech* (New York: David McKay Co., Inc., 1936), p. 257.

logical determinants of discourse; chapter 13 deals with psychological considerations—ways of accommodating logical content to persons and situations. As we have seen in earlier chapters, speakers typically face complementary responsibilities—the logical responsibilities inherent in purpose, and the psychological responsibilities imposed by audience and occasion. If they fail to meet their logical responsibilities, they are open to the charge of ignorance or sophistry or both; if they fail their psychological responsibilities, they risk surfeit, tedium, obscurity, and rejection.

This very basic duality exists in all discourse, written or spoken. The apparent dilemma it poses for writers and speakers has been the fulcrum for an enormous amount of bitter disagreement and misunderstanding.

   a. How can this dilemma be resolved? What are the speaker's options?

   b. Should a speaker place his logical responsibilities first in certain situations and psychological consideration first in others? Is this necessary?

2. Discuss the ways in which the methods for developing ideas set out in this chapter relate to and complement facts, expert opinions, and the modes of reasoning used in interpreting these data.

3. Comment on the following statement from Aristotle's *Rhetoric.* What does it mean? Do you agree or disagree?

> [When you wish to persuade] you must not begin the chain of reasoning too far back, or its length will render the argument obscure; and you must not put in every single link, or the statement of what is obvious will render it prolix. These are the reasons why uneducated men are more effective than the educated in speaking to the masses—as the poets say that the unlearned "have a finer charm ... for the ear of the mob." Educated men lay down abstract principles and draw general conclusions; the uneducated argue from their everyday knowledge and base their conclusions upon immediate facts.[13]

4. Discuss the applications of this chapter to speech that has inquiry as its primary purpose. Do all the methods of amplification apply? Do the "axioms" of amplification apply?

EXERCISES

1. Choose a term that not everyone understands. Define the term and clarify your definition by using examples, illustrations, visual aids, or other

---

[13]Lane Cooper, (tr.), *The Rhetoric of Aristotle* (New York: Appleton-Century-Crofts, Inc., 1932), pp. 155–56.

support. Terms such as *cubism, thermodynamics, agronomy, socialism, semantics, neurosis,* and *group dynamics* are good subjects.

2. Prepare a "master-example" speech by devoting half or more of your time to development of a single example to make a point. Do not merely cite an example, but build an entire speech about it.

3. Choose a subject that calls for a statistical development. Limit yourself to an aspect of some general problem such as membership in campus religious organizations today as compared with ten years ago, tuition charges, popular interest in TV programs, automobile sales, depletion of natural resources. Be mindful of all instructions for the preparation and use of statistics. A visual aid may help you present them.

4. Develop a speech around one or more auditory or visual aids. A talk on voting machines might employ a miniature model; one on jazz might benefit from recorded excerpts. Follow the advice given in this chapter.

5. Make a place, event, institution, or process come alive through skillful description and explanation. Make your listeners see vividly the Bingham Copper Mine, a session of the UN, the inside of a prison, or the stages in getting a cartoon from the drafting board into a newspaper.

6. There are three steps in this exercise: (a) open your talk with an example, story, or illustration that discloses your purpose; (b) develop each main point with one method listed in this chapter; (c) conclude with a maxim, proverb, slogan, or quotation.

14. Language and Style

Everyone has a speaking style, a characteristic way of patterning his words. But not all styles are born free and equal. Many people lack social, economic, and intellectual mobility because they are shackled by their own language habits. A command of language, oral and written, opens new worlds of thought, action, and human association. This chapter discusses common verbal impediments and suggests ways to improve language habits and develop an effective oral style.

MAKE YOURSELF UNDERSTOOD

Clarity is the first requirement of good style. Listeners must grasp what is being stated or asked before they can respond intelligently. Then they can take the next step—accept it, disagree with it, or disregard it, as they choose. Irwin Edman once said of Bertrand Russell, "He has the gift or the achievement of a style unfailingly lucid so that even when one disagrees with him, one knows exactly what it is with which one is disagreeing."

To establish clear lines of communication, (1) treat words as symbols, not "things,"; (2) anchor your words to valid facts and thoughts; (3) practice good usage and strengthen your vocabulary; and (4) avoid saying things the hard way.

TREAT WORDS AS SYMBOLS

Words are merely sound waves that vibrate membranes of our ears, or light waves that excite sensitive parts in our eyes. Words are symbols that we endow with meaning. We should not confuse the symbol with the "thing" nor should we act toward the symbol as if meaning were inherent in it.

Words vary in the stability of the meaning we assign them. Technical words used by specialists tend to be more restricted in their meaning and therefore more stable than words used in ordinary parlance. With time, most words acquire a greater range and variety of meaning. As Charles C. Fries, a distinguished language scholar, points out: the *Oxford English Dictionary* records and illustrates from our literature 14,070 separate meanings for the 500 most commonly used words in the English language.[1]

Misunderstandings may arise when a speaker uses a word or when a listener responds to it as if it held exactly the same meaning for everyone. To say that a person is or is not a Christian invites as many interpretations as there are denominations and sects. "You call yourself a liberal, but you're antilabor." "You bet I'm a liberal, and I'm telling you that labor is the most reactionary group in the country." As the conversation warms up, we become heated champions of our labels rather than cool-headed investigators of the meaning they carry for other people.

Come to an early understanding with your listeners on ambiguous terms. Be particularly careful when you use words that are abstract, that are unfamiliar, or that arouse emotions, such as *the common man, socialism, big business, radical, reactionary, love,* and *existentialism.* Avoid trouble by saying at the outset, "Now when I talk about academic freedom, I mean limited and specific things. I have in mind these privileges, these responsibilities, for these people."

Since you can't always anticipate what words will spawn misunderstanding, be alert to signals of confusion, perplexity, or hostility from your listeners. Then pause to find out if they are reacting adversely to your language as such, or to what you are really talking about. You can often find out by asking, "Do I make myself clear?" Or, "I notice you seem to disagree. I wonder why?" Or, "Let me put it another way and see whether we understand each other."

Of course you may discover that your listeners are perfectly clear about what you mean but that they simply disagree with you. Then you must either accept these differences or work them out by recourse to facts and reasoning. But be sure that you differ on a *real* issue, not simply on what the words mean.

ANCHOR YOUR WORDS TO REALITY

Communication becomes an illusion whenever a speaker and his listeners cut loose from their moorings and drift off together in a cloudland of words.

[1]Quoted in Irving J. Lee, *How to Talk With People* (New York: Harper & Row, Publishers, Inc., 1952), p. 15.

Verbomania is a virulent disease to which many people have low resistance. Our world of talk is infested with empty words, platitudes, and clichés. They pass from individual to individual, from group to group, until, through social osmosis, they get into our nervous systems; we respond to them as a dog does to a whistle.

The epidemic of verbomania once inspired A. Parker Nevin to write "A Speech for Any Occasion," a minor classic of satire on speechmaking. Job E. Hedges said of it, "You can call it 'The Crisis,' 'Justice,' 'Solution,' 'Destiny,' or anything you want. It covers the whole range of human thought and is unanswerable." Here it is.

Mr. Chairman, Ladies and Gentlemen:

It is indeed a great and undeserved privilege to address such an audience as I see before me. At no previous time in the history of human civilization have greater problems confronted and challenged the ingenuity of man's intellect than now. Let us look around us. What do we see on the horizon? What forces are at work? Whither are we drifting? Under what mist of clouds does the future stand obscured? My friends, casting aside the raiment of all human speech, the crucial test for the solution of all these intricate problems to which I have just alluded is the sheer and forceful application of those immutable laws which down the corridor of Time have always guided the hand of man, groping, as it were, for some faint beacon light for his hopes and aspirations. Without these great vital principles, we are but puppets responding to whim and fancy, failing entirely to grasp the hidden meaning of it all. We must re-address ourselves to these questions which press for answer and solution. The issues cannot be avoided. There they stand. It is upon you—and you—and yet even upon me that the yoke of responsibility falls.

What, then, is our duty? Shall we continue to drift? No! With all the emphasis of my being I hurl back the message *No!* Drifting must stop. We must press onward and upward toward the ultimate good to which all must aspire. But I cannot conclude my remarks, dear friends, without briefly touching upon a subject which I know is steeped in your very consciousness. I refer to that spirit which gleams from the eyes of a newborn babe, that animates the toiling masses, that sways all the hosts of humanity past and present. Without this energizing principle all commerce, trade and industry are hushed and will perish from this earth as surely as the crimson sunset follows the golden sunshine. Mark you, I do not seek to unduly alarm or distress the mothers, fathers, sons and daughters gathered before me in this vast assemblage, but I would indeed be recreant to a high resolve which I made as a youth if I did not at this time and in this place, and with the full realizing sense of responsibility which I assume, publicly declare and affirm my dedication and my consecration to the eternal principles and receipts of simple, ordinary, commonplace *JUSTICE*.

For what, in the last analysis, is justice? Whence does it come from? Where does to go? Is it tangible? It is not. Is it ponderable? It is not. Justice is none of these, and yet, on the other hand, in a sense it is all of these things combined. While I cannot tell you what justice is, this much I can tell you: That without the encircling arms of justice, without her shield, without her guardianship, the ship of state will sail through unchartered seas, narrowly avoiding rocks and shoals, headed inevitably to the harbor of calamity.

Justice! Justice! Justice! To thee we pay homage. To thee we dedicate our laurels of hope. Before thee we kneel in adoration, mindful of thy great power, mute before thy inscrutable destiny![2]

Nevin's speech was once read to a class of twenty adults, who were then asked to summarize the message and evaluate the talk. No two could agree completely on what it was all about, but most of the class seemed to think it was a fine speech. One person acknowledged that he hadn't the foggiest notion of what the speaker was driving at. None recognized the speech as satire, for all had been listening to "speeches for any and all occasions" most of their lives.

You may delude some of your listeners by tossing unanchored words about. You may also delude yourself. It is poor praise to be complimented for your ability to sling the King's English. It is high praise to be assured that you talked sense and to know that your listeners carried away a clear idea of what you wanted to get across.

Listeners have the choice of surrendering to the spell of language or critically inspecting the speaker's ideas and words to see whether they are firmly anchored to reality. Critical listening is the best defense against verbomania, and how you react as a listener is likely to influence how you yourself behave as a speaker.

PRACTICE GOOD USAGE AND STRENGTHEN YOUR VOCABULARY

When you talk extemporaneously, you are privileged to take more liberties with language than when you write. By means of vocal inflection, change of pace, and emphasis, you are able to give force and clarity to a sentence that would not pass muster in writing. This liberty, however, does not give you license to disregard the accepted rules of good usage and syntax. Mangled sentences such as "I crossed in an airplane the distance of the continent that took my grandfather a week to ten days in eight hours" impose a considerable strain on listeners, who must reconstruct the sentence to extract the meaning.

All bad language habits can be corrected. Familiarity with the basic rules given in grammars, books on good usage, and dictionaries is a requirement that nobody can ignore without victimizing himself and his listeners. An effective speaker will supplement his study with practice sessions in which he experiments with various ways of expressing an idea until it emerges with clarity and economy.

[2]Robert H. Davis, "Bob Davis Recalls," *New York Sun,* March 22, 1927. Reprinted by permission.

To transmit our meanings accurately, we need an adequate vocabulary. We can recognize and identify many more words in our reading and listening than we use in our writing and speaking. To develop an effective working vocabulary, you will need (1) to add words to your recognition vocabulary from your reading and listening and (2) to recruit new words for speaking from your recognition vocabulary. Some people resort to word lists compiled by somebody else. It is more profitable to build your own list, drawing on the synonyms and highly expressive words that already constitute your recognition vocabulary.

Learn the meaning of new words and check your understanding of familiar ones. Pronounce them out loud and fix their spelling in your mind. Often the origin and derivation of a word will help to establish it in your vocabulary. Put each word into sentences and practice using it in private. Finally, assimilate each word by introducing it into your conversation and speeches. If you make a habit of following this procedure, you will begin to build a larger speaking vocabulary.

Many people, even college students, use barbarisms like *irregardless* and *irrevelant*—words that have limited status. Betrayed by superficial resemblances between words, they reach out at random and grab whatever comes to mind. "My opponent flaunts public opinion," the politician charges. He means *flouts*. "This building is inexhaustible," declares a travel guide; he means *indestructible*. "Our education takes up a great part of our formidable years," says a student, who means *formative*. "You excelled the speed limit," insists the traffic cop, meaning *exceeded*. A speaker who confuses *noisy* and *noisome* describes an attractive residential neighborhood as noisome because it falls within the traffic pattern of a metropolitan airport.

Our language is filled with words that have almost, but not quite, the same meaning: *amiable* and *amicable; comprehensive* and *comprehensible; impassive* and *impassible* (*impassable* means something different from either); *bellicose* and *belligerent; glance* and *glimpse; intrude* and *obtrude; minute* and *moment; rigid* and *rigorous.* Verbal acuity enables you to sense the distinctions between such words in various contexts. A good, standard dictionary is indispensable, and a useful adjunct is *A Dictionary of Contemporary Usage* by Bergen and Cornelia Evans. You will discover that the Evanses' *Dictionary* makes word study not only informative but fascinating as well.

AVOID SAYING THINGS THE HARD WAY

A plumber once wrote to a government agency, saying he found that hydrochloric acid quickly opened drain pipes. He wanted to know whether this was a good thing to use. A scientist at the agency replied that "the efficacy of hydrochloric acid is indisputable, but the corrosive residue is incompatible with metallic permanence." The plumber wrote back, thanking him.for his assurance that hydrochloric acid was all right. Disturbed by this turn of affairs, the scientist showed the letter to his boss—another scientist—who then wrote to the plumber, "We cannot assume responsibility for the production of toxic and noxious residue with hydrochloric acid and suggest you use an alternative procedure." The plumber wrote back that he agreed—hydrochloric acid worked fine. Now greatly disturbed by these misunderstandings, the scientists took their problem to their chief. He broke through the jargon and wrote to the plumber: "Don't use hydrochloric acid. It eats holes in the pipes."

Be as economical as you can without impoverishing your thought. Choose a simple, direct way of expression or, at least, when there are several ways of saying the same thing, choose the simplest way. Simple speech is not to be confused with speech for the simpleton. Simple speech is unencumbered speech. As Dr. George Buttrick once remarked, "Great diction is not the linking of unusual words, but the unusual linking of usual words."[3]

USE VIVID AND ENERGETIC LANGUAGE

SPECIFIC LANGUAGE ETCHES IMPRESSIONS

Specific words and phrases focus attention and etch sharp mental images. Sentences made up of nonspecific language hint at vagueness and leave a blurred impression. Compare these examples.

> Somebody told me that a good many people in this general area are down with an ailment of some sort.
>
> Dr. Hewitt reports that there are thirty-two cases of bronchitis in Belleville.

CONCRETE WORDS RECREATE EXPERIENCE

Walt Whitman once said, "Language, be it remember'd, is not an abstract construction of the learned, or of dictionary-makers, but is something arising out of the work, needs, ties, joys, affection, tastes, of long generations of humanity, and has its bases broad and low, close to the ground."

Concrete words are linked in our minds with the things we hear, see, smell, tough, taste, and feel—so closely, in fact, that when we hear concrete words spoken our nervous system reproduces vicariously the sensory experience itself. When you hear somebody tell of a crackling fire, you can almost hear the crackle of a bonfire, campfire, or burning building.

Compare these two descriptions:

[3]*New York Times,* September 29, 1937, p. L25.

In autumn the leaves display diversity in color.
In October the leaves go wild with color—purple and green, red and gold,
all running into each other.

The first statement is clear and precise, to be sure; the second is just as clear
and just as precise but, in addition, it is "close to the ground." Its language
stirs associations and stimulates us to feel the tangy air and see the riot of
color.

GOOD FIGURES OF SPEECH DRAMATIZE RELATIONSHIPS

Simile and metaphor point up the resemblance between two seemingly dissimilar things. They help us to understand something unfamiliar,
abstract, or complex by comparing it with something familiar or simple.
If the simile or metaphor is particularly deft, we are surprised by a resemblance we have never perceived before; if it is pertinent and fresh, it may
also give us aesthetic pleasure or amusement.

The *simile* is a short statement in which the comparison is spelled out.
Words such as *like, as,* and *as if* usually provide clues to a simile. For
example: "She plays the piano as if she were wearing boxing gloves."
"Talking is like playing on the harp; there is as much in laying the hands
on the strings to stop their vibrations as in twanging them to bring out their
music" (Oliver Wendell Holmes). Lincoln likened the thinness of Douglas'
arguments on popular sovereignty to soup made from boiling the shadow
of a starved chicken. "Once one knows which Communist line a Communist leader is using," declared Richard Rovere, "listening to him becomes
almost as unendurable as hearing someone count to fifty thousand."

The simile calls attention to the fact that a comparison is being
drawn. The *metaphor* merely *implies* a comparison. For example, a secretary
of state, trying to show that the objectives of a certain country remain the
same despite appearances to the contrary, once declared that "The switch
is simply from hob-nail boots to carpet slippers." The implication is that
only the tactics of the country have changed, not its objectives. Winston
Churchill brought home a complex problem in international relations with
a metaphor: "From Stettin in the Baltic to Trieste in the Adriatic, an iron
curtain has descended across the continent." In his tribute to Mrs. Roosevelt, Adlai Stevenson said movingly, "She would rather light candles than
curse the darkness and her glow warmed the world."

Our everyday talk abounds with similes, metaphors, and variations
on these basic forms. Many of the figures we use are no longer novel and
no longer catch our ear, but we go on using them out of habit and because
they possess universal applicability. We say a person is a tower of strength,
straight as a ramrod, a bundle of energy, has nerves of steel, is dirty as a

pig. But these and hundreds of other familiar figures of speech are over-worked and tired. If we rely only on the old expressions, discriminating listeners will conclude that our speech is trite and our minds dull. Fresh, vivid figures inject life and color into our speech.

Relaxed, competent speakers are vivid without straining to be original. Poorly devised and mixed-up figures are good vehicles for low comedy, but make a serious speaker appear ludicrous. For example, a young teacher groped for a figure to convey his impressions of teaching and said, "You carry all thirty of the students on your back, and just when you're ready to throw in the towel, you strike gold." Use metaphors intelligently.

PERSONAL FORMS ARE NATURAL TO SPEECH

We all like dialogue. We are familiar with its patterns, and we enjoy its intimacy and movement. Real and hypothetical illustrations used in informal and formal talk can often be couched in the form of dialogue. Notice how R. W. Jepson makes you a party to dialogue in a speech called "Potted Thinking: The Necessity of Going Deeper than the Headlines."

> Have you ever come across the man who buttonholes you and poses you with a question and insists on your answering, "Yes" or "No"? He will say to you: "Now then, are you a Free Trader, or aren't you?" And you might reply: "Well, the removal of all restrictions and barriers on international trade would be an ideal thing to my mind. But as things are—" Then he will burst in and say: "Come along now, I asked you a plain question. Give me a plain answer." Once again you will probably stammer out a few "buts." Then he will tell you you are hedging. "Either you are, or you aren't," he will say. "Which is it? 'Yes' or 'No'?" You know the kind of person: the real whole-hogger.[4]

In public speaking, rhetorical questions help bring the listener in as an active partner in communication. Observe how Franklin D. Roosevelt created the sense of dialogue between himself and his listeners even though he didn't really expect them to answer back.

> But the simplest way for you to judge recovery lies in the plain facts of your own individual situation. Are you better off than you were last year? Are you debts less burdensome? Is your bank account more secure? Are your working conditions better? Is your faith in your own individual future more grounded?

Use personal pronouns in formal talks much as you do in everyday speech. Remember, you are talking with people, not to mannequins. The

[4] *Vital Speeches of the Day*, December 15, 1937, pp. 135–36.

personal pronouns *I, you,* and *we* are natural, simple expressions of sincere speech. They help establish rapport. Impersonal substitutes for real persons are stilted and affected. It is less wooden and more direct to say "I think that . . ." than it is to say "In the estimation of this speaker, it is not an unjustifiable assumption to say. . . ." Of course, the personal pronoun may be conspicuously overworked.

STURDY SENTENCES ADD STRENGTH TO SPEECH

Make your sentences stand on their legs and march. Flabby sentences start off with a limp and end in a crumpled heap. They begin, "And then there's another thing . . . And then there's something else . . . and incidentally, there's still this that I might mention. . . ." They end, " . . . and things like that," " . . . and so forth," or " . . . several other miscellaneous matters."

Avoid overloading your sentences with so many phrases and clauses that they jostle each other.

> Now my friends, we all believe in the purposes of public education, the great bulwark of our free country, our greatest heritage, but we also must be realistic and inquire closely into the financial feasibility of expanding our school plant at this moment when we contemplate an augmentation of salaries for the instructional staff, whose members are charged with shaping our childrens' futures.

Because of the clumsy composition of the passage, it is difficult to form a sharp, clear conception of what the speaker is saying. Now note how easily the sense comes across when put into sturdy sentences that step along briskly.

> We all want the best in plant, equipment, and staff for our public schools. We agree on this. But let's ask, "Can we afford to build a new gymnasium this year and at the same time improve salaries for teachers?"

Sturdy sentences feature nouns and verbs. Excessive use of clamorous words like *very, great, colossal, stupendous,* and *terrific* drowns out the essential ones.

Clinch your main ideas with climaxes. Before leaving an important point to go on to the next, drive home the sense and significance of what you have just said. For example, one speaker capped a key point on the threat of communism by saying, "The greatest danger communism presents to America is not by arms but by invitation." A series of strong, climactic sentences is particularly suited for the conclusion of speeches of advocacy and evocation.

USE LANGUAGE WITH PROPRIETY

SUIT YOUR LANGUAGE TO THE OCCASION

Ordinary speech is colloquial. We don't prepare our words when we are bargaining over the counter, asking someone to pass the butter, or exchanging the news of the day. But we all know there are times when our handy, everyday words are inadequate. Some occasions demand that we sort out our words and compose speech with distinction.

Compare the snatch of conversation below with a short passage suitable to a formal speech on the same subject. First the conversation.

> A university is not out to please customers. It's more of a busybody than a business. Its job is to poke around, sniff out facts, air them—no matter whether people like 'em or not. It ought to puncture prejudices and platitudes. Let the bigots howl. A university is a people's hairshirt.

Now the formal speech.

> A university that does not lead is a university only in name. A true university diligently pursues facts amid appearances. It is a critic of what is, and standard-bearer for what ought to be. Often it must speak as a solitary voice, championing truth against the clamor of outraged opinion and prejudice.

The language in the first passage is colloquial and suggests the informality of a living room or office conversation. Most of the words in the second passage are colloquial too, and the sentences are simple. But it is evident that the style has been refined and elevated for the public platform. It is not a question of which style is better—the formal or informal. Each is suited to its setting. In general, audiences expect the language of public speech to have tone and distinction that lifts it above the level of casual, off-the-cuff conversation.

AVOID WORDS THAT VIOLATE GOOD TASTE

Some words are plainly taboo. Public disapproval of such words is spelled out, for example, in radio and television codes. These are not the decrees of self-appointed censors; they are reflections of our social mores. It is risky to skirt the boundaries of good taste, and it is suicidal to flout public standards.

Slang should be used cautiously and sparingly. When it is picturesque and earthy, it spices conversation and public address. But slang quickly loses its freshness and appeal. It is seldom appropriate for formal occasions, and a slangy tone debases style on any occasion.

QUESTIONS FOR DISCUSSION

1. What are the differences, if any, between good style in speaking and good style in writing?

2. Comment on the following:

> The first rule, then, for a good style is that the author should have something to say; nay, this is in itself almost all that is necessary. . . . Such an author, just because he really has something to say, will never fail to express himself in the simplest and most straightforward manner; because his object is to awake the same thought in the reader that he has in himself, and no other.
> (*Arthur Schopenhauer*)

> Some writers always avoid a positive assertion wherever they can possibly do so in order to leave a loophole for escape in case of need. Hence they never fail to choose the more *abstract* way of expressing themselves; whereas intelligent people use the more *concrete*, because the latter brings things more within the range of actual demonstration, which is the source of all evidence.
> (*Arthur Schopenhauer*)

> An obscure and vague manner of expression is always and everywhere a very bad sign. In ninety-nine cases out of a hundred it comes from vagueness of thought; and this again almost always means that there is something radically wrong and incongruous about the thought itself—in a word that it is incorrect. (*Arthur Schopenhauer*)

> The necessity of labor and conversation with many men and things to the scholar is rarely well remembered; steady labor with the hands, which engrosses the attention also, is unquestionably the best method of removing palaver and sentimentality out of one's style, both of speaking and writing. . . . Surely the writer [or speaker] is to address a world of laborers, and such therefore must be his own discipline. . . . The scholar may be sure that he writes [or speaks] the tougher truth for the callouses on his palms.
> (*Henry David Thoreau*)

> Regarding language as an apparatus of symbols for the conveyance of thought, we may say that, as in a mechanical apparatus, the more simple and the better arranged its parts, the greater will be the effect produced. In either case, whatever force is absorbed by the machine is deducted from the result. A reader or listener has at each moment but a limited amount of mental power available. To recognize and interpret the symbols presented to him, requires part of this power; to arrange and combine the images suggested requires a further part; and only that part which remains can be used for realizing the thought conveyed. Hence, the more time and attention it takes to receive and understand each sentence, the less time and attention can be given to the contained idea; and the less vividly will that idea be conceived.
> (*Herbert Spencer*)

EXERCISES

1. Choose a concept that is unfamiliar to your listeners or about which they have imprecise ideas. Examples are: humanism, existentialism, nationalism, the poetic attitude, the American way of life, psychosomatic medicine. Make your concept the subject of a report. Develop your talk with specificity and concreteness.

2. Take a stand on a controversial issue. Be as precise as you can in outlining your position. As you speak, keep checking on the reactions of your audience. Respond to signs of disagreement or misunderstanding by putting your thoughts in other words. If the signs keep coming, don't hesitate to stop and clear up possible misunderstandings. Determine whether the disagreement is verbal or substantive. The object here is not "smooth talk" but to experiment in reaching a meeting of minds on what is being said.

3. Prepare a two-minute descriptive talk on a topic such as one of these: a sunset, an airplane ride through a thunderstorm, a horse race, landing a salmon, the Golden Gate Bridge, the New York skyline, Niagara Falls, a quaint village, an impressive monument or painting, Main Street on Saturday night, sailing a boat, a locker room between halves. Through vivid language recreate the scene or event for your listeners.

4. Rework a speech you have given before. Clarify and brighten your language and style in ways that will win a new interest for your subject.

5. Select a short speech that has appeared in print—one that falls short of the standards of good speech style. Revise it. Read portions of the original speech and of your revision to the class.

6. Arrange a group discussion on a controversial question. Most of the class will take part in the discussion, but appoint four or five members as observers to take notes on the language behavior of the speakers. Have the observers look especially for these things.

   a. Instances of remarkably clear and precise statements of a point.
   b. Instances when the discussion bogged down because of cloudy or rambling "contributions."
   c. Language that blocked or sidetracked the discussion.
   d. Instances when members spotted and clarified misunderstandings; instances when misunderstanding went unchecked.
   e. Differences that sprang directly from opposing convictions rather than from confusions in language.

7. Prepare a speech on a subject of your own choice that is designed to report, to advocate, or to evoke. Write this out from beginning to end in your best oral style. Read the speech aloud in class. The class will then compare the style of this speech with your earlier extemporaneous efforts.

8. Select a passage from a speech to read aloud—one that exemplifies the language and style recommended in this chapter.

15. Motivated Listening

In this chapter and the next we use the term "listening" to include *attention* to both verbal and nonverbal speech stimuli. Attention is a normal prerequisite to perception and reaction. We are concerned here, then, with the role of the speaker in attracting and sustaining attention, and the role of the listener in granting attention.

KINDS OF LISTENING

As you gain experience as a speaker—in public speech and in conversation —you will discover that audiences listen in different ways. Although any listening may be better than none at all, certain kinds of listening get the best results.

VOLUNTARY VS. INVOLUNTARY LISTENING

Some sounds we listen to by choice; others we hear whether we want to or not. Involuntary listeners seldom make a good audience. You may win an initial hearing from listeners simply by talking loudly enough for them to hear. They listen at first without really choosing to listen. But unless you succeed very quickly in capturing their interest and in making them *want* to listen, chances are they will tune you out.

CASUAL VS. PURPOSEFUL LISTENING

A casual listener is one who gives offhand, careless, or irregular attention to what you say. He is likely to drift off unless you provide him with some good purpose for hearing you out. A purposeful listener may soon become a casual listener if you fail to recognize his purpose and help him carry it out. Casual listening is a very short step from no listening at all.

DISCIPLINED VS. MOTIVATED LISTENING

Fortunately for dull speakers, some people force themselves to listen out of courtesy, or habit, or in the hope that they may get something worthwhile if they work hard enough at it. And sometimes these self-disciplined listeners reap a fine harvest, because poor speakers may be able men. But much more comes through to listeners when they listen because they want to and when they find pleasure in doing so. Motivated listening takes place when the promise of reward is great enough to command the listener's attention without his having to exercise great self-discipline.

CRITICAL VS. UNCRITICAL LISTENING

The critical listener follows the speaker's ideas carefully and thoughtfully and tries to evalute them objectively. He is alert and keeps all his mental faculties at work. A critical audience is the best kind of audience for a speaker who knows what he is talking about and who is willing to enter his ideas in a free, competitive market where they must stand or fall on their own merits. Speakers with less confidence may be better off with less discerning listeners. In fact, some speakers even try to create an atmosphere that invites uncritical acceptance of their ideas. The motives of such speakers may be either good or bad, but the listener who yields to their efforts does so at his own risk. Uncritical acceptance may imply indifference or poor critical acumen.

COOPERATIVE VS. HOSTILE LISTENING

The cooperative listener hopes for the best from the speaker and gives him friendly attention; the hostile listener dislikes the speaker or his ideas, and will not cooperate with him.

THE RESPONSIBILITY FOR LISTENING

A quick review of the kinds of listening will show that people are more likely to give close attention to a speaker when they *want* to hear what he has to say—when they believe he has a message of value to them. This simple fact provides a very practical criterion for determining who is responsible for good listening. If a person has some information you want very badly, you will listen when he speaks and gladly assume the responsibility for doing so. On the other hand, if the speaker is very anxious to get something across in which you are not especially interested, the burden of commanding your attention rests on him. In other words, the primary responsibility for good listening lies with the party to communication— the speaker or the listener—who stands to reap the greater gain.

Fortunately, there are many situations in which the speaker and his audience have a mutual interest in the outcome—where *both* stand to gain. Here the responsibility of good listening is shared. The speaker does his best to maintain interest, and the listener does his best to follow what is being said. Mutal interest and shared responsibility are desirable goals in all communication.

PRINCIPLES OF GOOD LISTENING

What are the principles of good listening? Perhaps the best way of getting at these principles is to examine several situations that invite good communication. As you read the following examples, imagine yourself first as the speaker and then as the listener.

1. The day before a final examination, the professor summarizes for his class what he regards as the highlights of the course.
2. A successful writer of mystery stories explains to a group of hopeful writers how to plot a marketable "whodunit."
3. A judge gives final instructions to conscientious jurymen who are about to bring in a verdict in a case where a man's life hinges on their decision.
4. A technician reports to other technicians the phenomenal results of an experiment that has made old methods obsolete and that will determine future procedure.
5. Alert, intelligent parents attend a popular lecture given by a professor who has favorably altered the course of their sons' or daughters' lives.
6. Men in the club car of a train pull their chairs closer as one man says, "I just heard a good one."
7. A builder explains to his carpenters a new construction method he expects to use in several homes under contract.
8. A doctor explains to a cardiac patient the adjustments he must make in order to prolong his years of usefulness.
9. Following a disastrous flood that has stripped the topsoil from miles of farmland, an engineer suggests to the owners methods of restoring fertility, and of preventing another flood.
10. In a strike-threatened factory, the manager calls in a respected foreman and asks him to explain and interpret the causes of the workers' grievances as he understands them.
11. A month before an important election, the candidate of a major party speaks for the first time in your home town.

The three principles of good listening implicit in these examples are (1) the more rewarding the outcome promises to be, the higher the quality of the listening will be; (2) listening is best when both speaker and audience have a stake in the communication; and (3) the person who stands to make the greater gain from the communication has the primary responsibility for promoting good listening.

Review the eleven examples with these three principles in mind. Answer the following questions in each case. What opportunities for a useful or pleasurable experience are there? What does the listener stand to gain? What does the speaker stand to gain? Who is likely to have the greater interest? What might the speaker and listeners do to improve communication? The following pages will help you answer the last question.

WHAT CAN THE SPEAKER DO TO ACHIEVE GOOD LISTENING?

No one is going to listen for long unless he starts out with a good reason for listening, or unless the speaker is skillful enough to provide him with such a reason. This means that the speaker must know his audience and must accommodate his remarks to it. In short, analyzing the audience and adapting to it are the speaker's best approach to good listening.

ANALYZE YOUR AUDIENCE

The same group of people may behave as an entirely different audience from day to day. When the President of the United States delivers his State of the Union message, the public's reaction will depend in part on what the state of the nation really is. Although the same congressmen may be present day after day, their attitudes toward speeches and the quality of their listening will vary with the topic, with domestic and international moods and circumstances, as well as with the speaker's ability. What seems to be the same audience will react quite differently to different subjects and occasions.

Outside your speech class—now and in the years ahead—you will encounter an almost infinite variety of audiences. No two audiences are exactly alike. And the characteristics of the particular audience you happen to be addressing will guide you in adapting your speech to your listeners. Audiences differ in five important characteristics: *composition, information, attitude, participation,* and *homogeneity. Composition* refers to the membership of your audience. How large is it—one, two, or a hundred people? What age? What sex? What is the educational level, religion, occupation, economic status, political outlook? In any given situation, you will be interested in those factors that appear to affect the receptivity of your listeners. The economic status of your audience, for example, need not even enter into your thinking if you are discussing what we know about the moon. But it would be critically important if you were proposing a hike in corporation income taxes. The political attitudes of your listeners would obviously be important if you were campaigning for public office but would be of little significance if you were describing the plight of our migratory waterfowl.

How much *information* do your listeners have about your subject, about you, and about the occasion? A member of a research team investigating a problem will not report his findings to his colleagues as he would address a group of people who know little or nothing about the subject. A speaker has a major advantage if he knows in advance whether his audience is informed, uninformed, or misinformed about his subject matter.

What is the *attitude* of your audience? How do your listeners regard you as a person? How do they feel toward one another? What interest do they have in what you plan to talk about? And what is their attitude toward your purpose and your stand on this subject? The attitude of your listeners may range from deep respect for you, strong group cohesiveness, keen interest in your subject, and complete acceptance of your ideas, to open hostility, rejection, disinterest, and complete disagreement.

How much opportunity does your audience have for *participation* in the proceedings? Audience participation may be overt or covert, but the audience must participate if there is to be any kind of listening at all. If the physical setting makes it difficult or impossible for your audience to see or hear you, there will be little or no participation—and little or no communication. Most of the remedies for this barrier to communication are within the power of the speaker to control. But audience participation may go well beyond silent responses. It may reveal itself in the form of applause, expressions of disapproval, or questions, replies, and remarks that place a member of the audience at least temporarily in the role of speaker. This kind of overt behavior may seem disruptive at the moment, but it may also lead to a dramatic improvement in the quality of listening.

Is your audience composed of people who are essentially alike or of people who have almost nothing in common? An audience of like composition, information, and attitude and with equal opportunities for participation is known as a *homogeneous* group. Such an audience may or may not be a good audience, but at least its members are likely to respond in a fairly similar way to what you say.

A *mixed* audience presents special problems, however. Should you try to appeal to what appears to be the majority? Should you give special attention to a minority? Should you diversify your approach in an attempt to hold the entire group? The answers depend mostly on your purpose and the occasion. But the wise speaker makes some decisions at the outset and sets some goals. Otherwise he will find himself appealing to no one at all.

ADAPT TO THE AUDIENCE

Almost everything you say and do as a speaker can be adapted to your audience—your choice of subject, your purpose, the structure and materials of your speech, your language and style, your manner of speaking, and sometimes even the time and place of your speech. These and many other choices are usually the speaker's. But how can you know what the best choice will be in each case? We know that the best listening takes place when an audience thinks it is going to get something of value out of what is said. The speaker's job, then, is to make the audience want to listen. This is where analysis of the audience comes into play. The better you know your audience and the circumstances under which you are going to talk to them, the easier it is to command their interest and attention. The basic purpose of audience adaptation is to develop motivated listening. There are, of course, other obvious accommodations—speaking loud enough to be heard, using language that can be understood, providing necessary information, and so forth—but the subtlety of achieving audience adaptation consists in making an audience feel that it has an important stake in the proceedings.

We all act in response to needs, wants, desires, drives, or urges. And we listen in response to the same basic motivations, because listening is a kind of action. True, we respond to different motives in different situations, and certain motives operate more strongly in some of us than in others. That is why knowing your listeners helps you to enlist their interest. But a working knowledge of the more basic motives that affect human behavior—listening included—is part of the equipment of every effective speaker.

Other things being equal, audiences are more likely to listen if their *security, status, ambitions, affections,* and *pleasures* are related or appear to be related to the speaker's purpose.

SECURITY

Some of the most powerful motives are those that spring from our desire to preserve and perpetuate ourselves. These involve both physical and psychic security—health, comfort, and freedom from danger, care, and fear. Most people identify their happiness and well-being with security. Anything that threatens their security is a matter of concern, and anything that promises them greater security is a matter of interest. By capitalizing on these concerns and interests, effective speakers command the attention of their listeners.

STATUS

Many of our real and fancied needs spring from our desire for social approval. What others think of us is often more important to us than we care to admit. We strive for a reputation that will give us satisfaction, compete with others for social recognition, and conform to custom in order not to lose caste. Even the nonconformist is lonesome if his aberrant behavior goes unnoticed. Many of the beliefs we profess and many of the things we want have their greatest value to us as status symbols. A pat on the back, an approving comment, or any token of recognition sincerely given will help you enlist the interest of the people to whom you speak.

AMBITIONS

Most people have goals, objectives, and values that they seek as a means to self-realization and personal growth. These goals represent what we want to be and what we want to accomplish with our lives. They may be low and crass, but they may also be high and worthy. The desire to realize one's potentialities, to make something out of oneself, continues to be a strong drive in our culture. Our hopes, dreams, and ambitions may be dulled by cynicism or frustration, but the skillful speaker can energize them into powerful motives for listening.

AFFECTIONS

Strong emotional attachments control our behavior in many situations. We develop these emotional bonds with people, institutions, traditions, ideals, and even with some of our material possessions. These affections explain many of our loyalties and many of our defensive and protective attitudes. They are usually rooted in long associations, familiar conditions and circumstances, and often are surrounded by nostalgic memories. Whenever the speaker's message impinges on the strong affective ties of his listeners, he will soon discover that he has to work with these ties or work around them. Our affections seldom yield to a frontal attack.

PLEASURE

The desire for pleasure—relaxation, release, escape—is a primary reason for listening in many situations. We often listen to be entertained, and we are held by speakers whose recommendations give promise of pleasurable rewards.

You have probably noticed that motives never exist in pure form but are always modified and affected by countless influences. Most of the things you want for yourself are things that you also want for others—for your family, your friends, your church, your school, or your town, state, or country. These group-centered motives are often even stronger than self-centered motives. A father will risk his life to save his child, people will make sacrifices to build a new church or synagogue, and fanatical loyalties grow up around group symbols.

To add to the complication, motives are usually *mixed*—compounded of several of the motivations we have discussed. And these mixed motives often contain competing elements that pull in different directions. The expression "I have mixed feelings about that" is usually an indiction that conflicting motives are at work.

In many cases, the motives for listening are already present in your audience. Your job is to recognize the interests at work and to make the most of them. If these interests do not exist, your job is to discover the motives that can best be enlisted in your cause and to involve them in the development of your subject. In either case, you face a task that must be handled subtly and adroitly. Any obvious or overly contrived attempt to capitalize on the motives of your listeners is likely to alienate them rather than win favorable attention.

Ask yourself this question: Why should this audience want to listen to me discuss this subject? If there is no good answer, you had better look for another audience or another subject. If you find the answer, you have found the motives that will serve you best.

Always remember, though, that adapting your speech to your listeners is not the same as capitulating to them. The customer is *not* always right, and you may need to tell him so point-blank at times. A speaker who sacrifices his integrity for the sake of expediency betrays both himself and his listeners.

WHAT CAN THE AUDIENCE DO TO ACHIEVE GOOD LISTENING?

The final decision on all listening is necessarily made by the listener. We can resist the best efforts of any speaker if we choose to do so. We face two questions as potential listeners: *When* should we listen? And what are the *best ways* to listen if we decide to listen at all?

WHEN SHOULD YOU LISTEN?

Almost every waking minute of every day someone is demanding that you listen to him. You should, and usually will, give your attention to the speakers who seem to have the most to offer. Apart from observing common courtesies, you are under no obligation to listen to every speaker in search of an audience. Choose wisely, for much of the wisdom and pleasure of life is transmitted through the spoken word. And remember that in many cases good listening is much more important to you than it is to the speaker. You may have more to gain than he has.

You will be exposed to many speeches in your course in speech. You will be the listener today and the speaker tomorrow. If you want the attention of your classmates when you speak, they have a right to expect the same of you. Not all good speakers are good listeners and not all good listeners are good speakers. Use your speech class as a means of improving both your speaking and listening skills.

HOW SHOULD YOU LISTEN?

There are two answers to this question. First, listen in ways that will encourage the speaker to give you his best. Second, listen in ways that will enable you to profit by the best the speaker gives you. Both efforts contribute to the same result—the best communication possible, no matter how effective or ineffective the speaker may be.

An attentive audience is an incentive to any speaker. Under most circumstances, if a speaker is worth listening to at all, it will pay you to give him a fair hearing. This does not mean that you have to make serious compromises with your own values and convictions; nor does it mean that you have to put up with incompetence. If and when your best listening efforts fail to bring rewards, then is the time to direct your attention elsewhere.

In listening to a speaker for the first time, try to gauge him as a person and assess his ideas carefully. Guard against being deceived by a superficially attractive manner, but keep in mind the possibility that a speaker whose manner does not immediately appeal to you may have valuable counsel.

Critical listening also demands skill in analysis—the ability to perceive a speaker's purpose, his main points, and how he develops them. Here is the first test of critical listening: do you know *what* has been said? Then ask yourself this question: does it *make sense?* This second test involves judgment, interpretation, and evaluation. Whatever leads to proficiency in speaking also develops competency in listening. If you know what makes good speech, you will be a far more intelligent consumer of speech.

Listening to speech is much like reading a book or article. The principal difference is in the immediacy of the spoken word. Unless speech is recorded, you have to get it here and now or it may be gone forever. You can put a book aside and come back to it at your leisure. As a reader you have an opportunity to study and ponder a matter and return to the writer's words for further reference. The speaker's message must be received and, very often, interpretated and reacted to without benefit of long reflection. A good speaker accommodates his remarks to these exigencies of oral communication, but opportunities for misunderstanding, misinterpretation, and even exploitation are undeniably present. Their presence imposes a responsibility on the audience to listen carefully and sometimes even cautiously. The next chapter analyzes a few of the stratagems that overzealous speakers may use with unwary listeners.

QUESTIONS FOR DISCUSSION

1. Discuss the three principles of good listening in relation to the eleven examples cited on page 163. Answer the questions about these examples cited on the next page.

2. Discuss the relative strength of the basic motives that affect human behavior—security, status, ambitions, affections, pleasures.

3. Is this a complete list of motives? What would you add or subtract?

4. How are these motives related to logical and emotional response? Is a motivated appeal the same as an emotional appeal? Do motivated appeals necessarily compromise logical structure?

5. Discuss the logic and motivation of the following:

    a. Don't drink that stuff; it is poison!

    b. Take your feet off the table; what will people think?

    c. Take the job; it will give you a parking place next to the boss.

    d. Be careful; the life you save may be your own.

    e. Early to bed and early to rise makes a man healthy, wealthy, and wise.

    f. Go to college; you may find a husband.

EXERCISES

1. Plan a group discussion on a question that has evoked great public interest: a trial, a strike, a prison riot, a crime, a legislative proposal. Find out all you can about the event beforehand. But in the discussion concentrate on the *people* who are involved in it. Try to see through their eyes what happened. Try to find out all you can about the backgrounds and conditions that motivated them. Your purpose here is not to evaluate their motives but to understand them.

2. Bring to class two or three "human interest" news items—stories about people who caught the public eye for a moment because they did something unusually kind, amusing, stupid, or bizarre. Tell or read the stories and analyze *why* the behavior of these people attracted attention. Can you find any clues to the motives that led the people to act as they did?

3. Select two speeches directed to a nationwide audience by a public official. Have all members of the class analyze them. What did the speaker try to accomplish? What motives did he appeal to? Did he appeal to them directly or obliquely? Did he choose the right appeals for his purpose? Organize a class discussion based on the analyses.

4. Prepare a five-minute speech explaining a complicated process. Try to teach the class to master the process. When you finish, question the audience to see how well they grasp what you have said.

5. Think of an audience that you know well. Prepare a speech for this audience that will impose heavy demands on you if you are to capture its interest and win it over to your point of view. Deliver your talk to the class;

but before you speak, ask the class members to "become" the audience you have in mind. Describe your hypothetical listeners in detail. Let members of the class ask you further questions so that they will have a clear idea of the audience you are aiming at. After you have given your talk, have the class members discuss how well they think you have succeeded.

16. Critical Listening

Critical listening is analytical listening: the speaker presents his analysis and the listener examines the analysis. This is the best kind of listening when problems of some consequence are being discussed, reported, or debated. If the speaker's position will stand close scrutiny, as it should, critical listening is best for him; and if the listener hopes to understand, as he should, it is also best for him. The critical listener wants to know *what* the speaker has said and *why* he has said it. Such perception invites dialogue that offers the best hope of mutual understanding.

Our purpose in this chapter is to discuss some of the more common fallacies, stratagems, and obstacles that lead to distortion and deception in communication. If they are unintentional on the part of the speaker, he suffers his own mistakes; if they are deliberate, he risks exposure and deserves it. In either case, the listener is a potential victim. The sensible listener will remember the old marketplace warning *caveat emptor* (let the buyer beware) when he is invited to accept another man's ideas.

PERSON AND MANNER

We all know that the person and manner of the speaker affect our acceptance of his ideas. Although ideas should be able to stand on their own two feet, the means for assessing these ideas are not always immediately available, and we necessarily rely on our impression of the competence and honesty of the speaker.

PRETENSIONS

The best credentials a speaker can submit to his listeners are those he reveals by competent treatment of his subject. A speaker who finds it necessary to resort to adventitious claims in his own behalf is at least suspect. It is notorious that persons introducing speakers to an audience will often embarrass everyone, including the speaker, with exaggerated accounts of the speaker's achievements. Few speakers are tactless enough to parade their own credentials blatantly, but many resort to devices designed to build their reputation. Listeners should be aware of these devices and wary of speakers who abuse them.

Most of us have encountered the *name-dropper.* He sprinkles his speech with apparently casual references to famous people—authors, artists, executives, politicians, and the like—in an attempt to suggest familiarity with these people and thereby enhance his own prestige. The names dropped may be familiar to the audience: "The last time I talked with the president . . . ," "The boss dropped in to get my advice on . . . ;" or the names may be completely unfamiliar to the audience (and not much more familiar to the speaker). But who wants to admit he does not know the world-renowned Mr. X or Madame Y or the Right Reverend Mr. Z?

Technical or pseudotechnical jargon may be applied to impress, to confound, or to cover up one's own inadequacies. Some discussions demand a specialized vocabulary; even so, the speaker should make every effort to make himself clear. If you suspect that the speaker's "professional" vocabulary is impeding communication unnecessarily, you may wish to withdraw your attention or to force him to make himself understood.

Nothing is more disarming to the pretentious speaker than utter frankness and honesty on the part of the listener. You may say very frankly that you never heard of Mr. X, that you haven't the slightest idea what the speaker is talking about, or that you have a few questions for him. If you have misjudged the speaker's pretensions, he will set you right in a hurry. If your suspicion was well founded, communication may be considerably improved.

SIMULATION

We place confidence in speakers whose personal qualifications we respect. A speaker may pretend to be something he is not, to win favor with the audience. If the suggestions in Chapter 7 for improving the speaker's relations with his listeners are misapplied, one of two things is likely to happen: If the speaker succeeds in passing himself off as someone to be trusted and respected, his listeners may be seriously misled; if he fails, he is discredited as a person, and the cause he is pleading suffers, sometimes undeservedly.

What protection do you have against imposters? Fortunately, bad currency has a false ring. Even the cleverest actor usually gives himself away. It is hard for a speaker to feign intellectual, emotional, moral, and social qualities. Critical listeners—who must have considerable sophistication in human relations—are an imposter's severest enemies. A speech course affords experience for both speakers and listeners; both learn that their stake in communication is shared and their efforts are reciprocal.

CONTRIVED MOTIVATION

If a speaker praises his listeners, they may impute to him insight, sympathy, and understanding that may not exist. It is heartwarming to find someone who appreciates us and who appears to see in us what we would like to be, but it pays to be objective in assessing flattery. A speaker has every right to present his cause in terms of the wants, desires, and needs of his listeners as he perceives them, but this kind of motivation is dangerously contrived when the listener is regarded as a potential victim to be taken in by exploitation of his personal weaknesses and vanities.

Ask yourself these questions as a listener: What is the speaker's motivation? Does he stand to gain more than I do? Does the praise he accords me have anything to do with the decision he is asking me to make? Has he made a sound case for his proposal, quite apart from any personal involvements I may have in the matter?

DIVERSION AND DISTRACTION

In decorating a room when you suffer from limited resources, it is a common practice to place the most worthy furnishing or *objet d'art* where it will attract attention to itself and accord relative inconspicuousness to more vulnerable objects. Speakers are not above this kind of arrangement in presenting their ideas.

SLANTING

A slanted speech mingles truths, half-truths, and falsehoods in a subtle mosaic that attempts to pass for the whole truth and nothing but the truth. All of the techniques of slanting may be reduced to *selection* and *arrangement*. The speaker goes as far as he thinks he can in selecting just those materials that appear to support his position, and adroitly sidesteps damaging facts and interpretations. He then arranges these materials in ways that emphasize his strengths and conceal his weaknesses. The careless or gullible listener is thus diverted from objective analysis.

Slanted discourse results from censorship exercised by the speaker to achieve specious plausibility. The unwary listener is led astray by errors of omission and commission infiltrated into a speech that seems honest and authentic. Truth and falsehood seldom come in wholly separate packages. A completely false report is much easier to spot than one that stretches the truth, tells only part of the story, or glosses over sticky facts. The listener who wants to believe, who is predisposed toward the speaker, is especially vulnerable to this kind of concealment.

EXTENSION

Setting up straw men and knocking them down is the essence of diversion by extension. Vulnerable statements may be cleverly substituted for defensible or relatively defensible statements to which they bear some resemblance, in an attempt to shift the discussion to the speaker's advantage. Who has not had the experience of taking a reasonable position only to have it seriously misrepresented and then attacked in its distorted form?

There are variations of diversion by extension. The strategy may be used against a speaker by an opponent who deliberately misinterprets his views; or it may be used positively by a speaker who substitutes a more defensible position for the relatively weak motion he is trying to win approval for. The subtlety of the technique lies in a superficial resemblance among statements that may range from sense to nonsense. Thus, a man who does not like cats because he is allergic to them may find himself attacked as an animal hater who in all probability is unkind to his children. Or an advocate of some modest social reform of limited usefulness may lay claim to the larger values of more substantial action that he surreptitiously identifies with his own proposal.

The obvious remedy in all such cases is to identify the proposition under discussion and insist as best you can that the speaker stay with it.

SIDE ISSUES AND IRRELEVANCIES

This kind of diversion is caused by unsound analysis, intentional or otherwise. The speaker concentrates on some minor point and presses the matter in an attempt to sidetrack the discussion. The result may be a victory on the side issue with the appearance of victory on the real issues. In any case, the vital points on which the question should be settled are obscured and may go unchallenged. Any resolution so determined can hardly be expected to yield good results.

MANIPULATION

All of the stratagems of diversion discussed above attempt to draw attention away from the real issues. It often happens, however, that a speaker will stay with the issues but argue in ways that obstruct sound reasoning. We call these tactics *manipulation.*

BLACK-AND-WHITE REASONING

The most pervasive of the manipulative stratagems arises from failure to understand that most of the phenomena we talk about are variable and difficult to classify without making arbitrary distinctions. Scientists can sometimes devise rigid categories for the things they wish to describe. But in ordinary conversation, whatever we wish to describe probably falls into a *continuum* or group of things that share a fundamental characteristic yet differ in degree from one another. A continuum exists between black and white; if an object is gray, are we justified in classifying it as black or white? Black-and-white reasoning attempts to categorize things in just that way, and may achieve specious plausibility by using classifications and definitions that ignore degrees of difference.

The essential fallacy involved in black-and-white reasoning is *hasty generalization,* imputing to all members of a given species, class, or category what may be true of only some or even of most members, or what may be true of all but only to a certain degree. Discussion of racial distinctions among mankind is frequently hampered by hasty generalization that results in black-and-white thinking. What generalizations can we safely and honestly make about any group without doing an injustice to individuals? Yet, when action is required and policies must be determined, some distinctions must be made. Any speaker may find himself in a dilemma: If he offers no hard and fast definitions and classifications, he may be charged with confused thinking; if he does attempt to make distinctions for purposes of clarity and precision, he may be accused of dogmatism.

What we might call the *gray thinker* can be just as perverse as his black-and-white comrade. This man decries any attempt at classification and orderly arrangement and complains about generalizations of any kind no matter how carefully qualified.

Both the black-and-white speaker and the gray speaker are guilty of manipulation when they deploy their reasoning to gain strategic advantage by promoting a cause of their own or defeating a motion proposed by someone else.

The mean between two extremes

This variety of manipulation attempts to exploit a preference most of us have for moderation. A speaker may show that his position occupies mid-ground between two extremes—not too cautious or conservative and not too radical, daring, or different—to suggest that his proposal is moderate and reasonable.

There is nothing wrong in claiming moderation as one of the virtues of a proposal, but such a claim is *not* established by merely suggesting that the recommendation in question is neatly in the middle of two more extreme positions. The fact of the matter is that any conceivable proposal can be presented as a mean between two extremes by simply constructing the so-called extremes. An expenditure of a thousand dollars is comfortably in the middle between the extravagance of fifteen hundred dollars and the penuriousness of five hundred, but this fact in and of itself proves nothing. If this means moderation, then any amount can be shown to be moderate by resort to the same expedient.

A careful listener will insist that any proposition be argued on its own merits. If moderation is claimed, then it should be established by a reasoned analysis of the problem in relation to the available means of dealing with it.

THE LOGICAL NEXT STEP

If a man were to build a house and stop short of putting a roof on it, it could be argued with considerable cogency that a roof of some kind would be the logical next step. In any given situation, there are almost always further steps that might and perhaps should be taken. This line of argument carried to its logical conclusion, however, would mean that we are always committed to future action by the very fact that certain steps have already been taken. You buy a new car and then you are pressed to buy innumerable extra gadgets with the argument that since you have spent four thousand dollars already you might as well throw in another five hundred to make the car presentable.

You may already have recognized that we often use this "logical next step" thinking to rationalize our own desires. It is not at all surprising, therefore, that speakers try to exploit this weakness by encouraging us to take steps to which we are in no way committed, by the simple stratagem of suggesting that these additional steps merely complement action already taken.

Any action may or may not be a logical next step. A careful listener will insist that these further commitments be argued on their own merits. And it is sometimes worth considering that a so-called logical next step may mean putting good money after bad. If you have made a mistake, certainly nothing is gained by taking steps that compound it.

QUESTIONS FOR DISCUSSION

1. Discuss the list of stratagems and specious reasoning presented in this chapter. Try your hand at adding to it. (You will get help in Chapters 7, 12, and 14 in this book.)

2. Discuss ways of handling speakers who practice these distortions and deceptions—inadvertently or intentionally. One way, of course, is to stop listening and keep still. If suffering in silence is unfair to others, how can you get speech back on the track without using disruptive disciplinary measures?

3. An entertaining talk, even on a serious subject, sometimes involves a kind of playful gamesmanship in which skillful speakers and listeners spar with each other for the fun of it. How should you conduct yourself in this arena?

EXERCISES

1. Discuss in class the following questions about acting (playing a role in a drama) and speechmaking.

   a. What are important differences between acting and speaking to an audience?

   b. Do you think that training in acting is helpful or harmful to a public speaker? Why?

   c. Is role playing ever proper and useful in public speaking? What are the advantages and disadvantages?

2. Discuss in class the following questions about definition.

   a. Is it ever possible to define a term or a concept so that the definition admits no exceptions? Give examples.

   b. Can you distinguish: *work* and *play; sane* and *insane; black* and *white; friends* and *enemies; kind* and *unkind; like* and *dislike; now* and *later; old* and *new; good* and *bad?*

   c. What is meant by a *continuum?* How does this concept enter into definition and classification?

3. Bring to class two or three examples of *slanted reporting.* Examine the news columns of newspapers for these examples. Be prepared to demonstrate that the reporting you select is slanted and to show how this slanting was accomplished. Consider these questions in relation to your examples: Can a reporter ever achieve complete objectivity in reporting? How objective should a report be?

4. Try your hand at slanted writing by producing two or three paragraphs on some controversial issue. Then rewrite these paragraphs to avoid slanting. Compare the two compositions.

5. Test your understanding of the stratagems discussed in this chapter by preparing and presenting a short speech on a controversial subject about which you feel deeply. Take a stand and make strong recommendations; so far as possible get into areas where you might expect to encounter these stratagems, but do *not* employ them.

   Listen to these speeches carefully and critically. Discuss both delivery and composition.

6. You can have fun with this exercise: Prepare and present a speech that employs as many of the stratagems discussed in this chapter as possible; don't be too obvious; use them subtly. Then give members of the class a chance to test their listening by exposing and identifying the stratagems.

17. The Values of Silence

In a society as complex as ours we are almost constantly bombarded by sounds from countless sources, including human speech. Ecologists are properly concerned with the kind of environmental pollution that develops from uncontrolled noise. It invades business and industry, public meetings, and even our homes and vacation retreats. Psychiatrists might have fewer patients if we devised ways of escaping this continuous clamor.

Some people are compulsive talkers. They begin in the morning and continue through the day far into the night. And if their beleaguered listeners finally escape, the talkers can always turn to the telephone, or participate vicariously in the canned talk provided by radio and television. Such people can be social boors and public nuisances.

One of the basic principles of good speech is *timeliness.* It is last on our list in Chapter 2 and we have referred to it only obliquely here and there in the text. But this chapter—the shortest in the book—is dedicated to the men and women who know *when* to talk and *when* to keep still!

Quality is a better criterion of good speech than quantity; and timeliness is a significant factor in quality. Many an otherwise good speech has been devastated because it was poorly timed—too long, or launched at the wrong time, or both.

Silence has its own rewards—the opportunity to ingest and digest what has been heard and read; the opportunity to give attention to one's own thoughts rather than somebody else's; and, at the very least, the opportunity to relax without the intrusion of unwanted garrulity.

Certain religious sects, notably the Quakers, make conscious use of silence to achieve these values and others. Many churches provide time in their services for silent prayer. To an increasing extent, the planners of conferences and meetings arrange agenda to include time for silence and regeneration.

Throughout this book, we have tried to point out the productive uses and methods of good speech. And we would be remiss here not to note that silence has its price as well as its rewards. We think that the price is too high when we withdraw from communication because of cynicism or fear; it is too high when we sit mute in a meeting where our ideas might help; and it is too high when self-consciousness denies us a share in rewarding social conversation.

There are times when we ought to stand up and be counted. These are the times when the confidence and the ability to speak in ways that do your best self full justice will pay their greatest personal and social dividends.

QUESTIONS FOR DISCUSSION

1. We have added *timeliness* as the thirteenth basic principle of good speech: Discuss the applications of this principle.

2. What values, if any, do you see in planned periods of silence in meetings and conferences?

3. "Overkill" is an expression frequently used to describe excesses in the manufacture and storage of weaponry: Does this concept have useful applications in communication? Does too much talk risk "killing" a good idea? Do you risk alienation in pressing a point too long and too hard? Might a matter too ardently pursued suffer an undeserved fate? When have you said enough?

EXERCISES

1. Listen to a speech or read an essay or editorial on a controversial subject—one to which you respond strongly: Jot down your immediate reactions, intemperate as they may be; then give yourself a little quiet time, and record your reactions again. "Cooling off" periods frequently temper reactions helpfully.

2. Work out an agendum for a two-day conference or retreat in which serious matters are to be discussed and resolutions adopted. Include strategically placed breaks where the conferees are left to their own resources.

18. Inquiry

We now begin four chapters dealing with the special methods associated with the four primary purposes of speech—inquiry, reporting, advocacy, and evocation. We identified these purposes in Chapter 8 and have referred to them repeatedly throughout the book. There are unquestionably special methods best adapted to achieve each of these purposes, but it is unrealistic to categorize these methods in any way that ignores the complementary roles they play in communication. Although one of the primary purposes should be controlling in any communication, one or more of the others typically enter in as secondary. For this reason, flexibility is preferable to rigidity in applying these special methods in any given situation.

THE ROLE OF INQUIRY

Inquiry is a search for meaning, understanding, and guidance. In this respect it is unique among the purposes and methods of speech. In our other capacities as speakers we make use of insights and understandings, but first we must discover them. Speech performs one of its most important services in aiding in this search and discovery.

We are impelled toward inquiry by the problems we face in our daily lives and the larger problems of the society in which we live. But sensitive, thoughtful people raise questions in all areas of human experience, even to the nature of man and his ultimate destiny. The will and the capacity to explore these questions reflectively and creatively are among the highest marks of maturity.

THE NATURE OF INQUIRY

Inquiry may be a solitary venture, or it may take place when two or more people meet to think together. There is no such thing as "group thinking," of course, except in a metaphorical sense. Only individuals think. But individuals within a group do think, and often they think more gainfully than they would if each were by himself. By sharing information, exchanging views, and trying out ideas, we find our way to new vantage points and to a higher level of creative thinking.

An everyday conversation with a friend may contain some, most, or all of the elements of organized inquiry. You tell him about a problem that is worrying you. He responds with interest. He draws you out. He asks questions that focus on aspects of the problem you haven't considered. Together you ponder various answers, discard some, and ultimately settle on the one that seems to fit the case. This is inquiry in its simplest form.

The most favorable setting for inquiry is a small group of interested, congenial people. Even large conferences and legislative assemblies refer most questions to committees for preliminary study. In small groups, everyone has a chance to participate. Roles shift from speaker to listener and back again. In large meetings, this kind of give and take usually yields to public speeches of inquiry followed by an open forum. Even in small groups, though, it is often wise to let a person talk himself out on a point without interrupting him. Such miniature speeches contribute most when they fit the spirit and pattern of inquiry.

THE PATTERN OF INQUIRY

Inquiry is both an analytical and a creative process. At its best, it combines rigor and freedom. Sometimes it resembles loosely organized chaos but there is much to be said for letting ideas tumble forth before trying to sort them out. Inquiry should be relatively uninhibited, but must not degenerate to aimless conversation.

What pattern of thinking leads most readily to the answers to a problem? People who have studied this question have identified six steps in *reflective thinking.* Used flexibly and imaginatively, these steps provide a sound guide for inquiry.

1. IDENTIFY THE PROBLEM

Reflective thinking is triggered by a problem. Begin by stating and describing the problem as specifically as you can.

Phrase the problem as an open question that will invite a variety of answers. It is better to ask "How should I invest my savings?" than "Should I buy Goods, Inc.?" The second question tends to limit answers to a simple "Yes" or "No." Put your question objectively. "How may we get rid of our worthless physical education requirement?" is a loaded question that is likely to block discussion at the outset. "How may we best insure a student's physical fitness?" opens the question objectively.

Explain the problem so that others can identify it. Then get them to share your concern so they will seek the answer as eagerly as you do.

2. ANALYZE THE CAUSES

Most important problems have numerous and complex causes, some close at hand and others deep-seated and obscure. The reflective thinker must detect those causes that seem most vulnerable to attack and most intimately related to an ultimate solution of the problem.

Product analysis may indicate that one reason for an item's failure to sell is its unappealing package design. This might be the root of the problem. But before jumping to such a conclusion a marketing executive would probably ask whether the firm's advertising campaign was appropriate, whether some deficiency was inherent in the product, and other questions to determine possible further causes for the problem.

3. CLARIFY YOUR VALUES

Before you consider various solutions to the problem, you must establish standards by which to judge them. These standards or criteria are your values—what you want the solution to do, the specifications that it must meet. Faced with the question "How may we improve our college newspaper?" students might agree that any forthcoming suggestions will have to fit within the fixed budget, be consistent with a balanced coverage of college news, and not make excessive time demands on the student staff.

4. SUGGEST SOLUTIONS

Try to develop one or more solutions and then judge each proposal on its merits. Spare no effort at this stage to draw forth as many suggestions as possible. Even seemingly farfetched ideas should be welcomed and given a hearing, for no one can be sure in advance that a novel approach might not turn out to be the best.

5. WEIGH THE ALTERNATIVES

Treat each proposal as a working hypothesis, as a guide to further exploration. Discuss its pros and cons, but avoid committing yourself prematurely. Superficially attractive answers may not stand up under exposure. Ask questions such as these: Does this proposal get to the root of the problem? Does it fit our criteria? Can it be made to work? Will it cost too much? If it solves the problem at hand, will it introduce new problems in the future? The solution that you ultimately agree on may be one of the suggested solutions, an integration of two or more of them, or a compromise.

6. TEST THE SOLUTION

Once you reach consensus, recheck your thinking before you make the decision binding. This is imperative if the decision is to be irrevocable. Often it is wise to keep the decision tentative until everyone has had a chance to ponder it or to talk it over with others. Or you may decide to experiment with the proposal on a limited scale.

INQUIRY THROUGH GROUP DISCUSSION

PREPARING YOURSELF

Nothing is gained by pooling ignorance and misinformation. Most of the suggestions given in Chapter 10 will help you explore your subject in preparation for a discussion. Following the six steps in reflective thinking, work up a discussion outline that records your information, organizes your thinking, and directs your questions. You may or may not refer to your outline during the discussion. Under no circumstances should you try to force the discussion to follow the outline. Good discussion combines the thinking of all. Your outline should merely sharpen your own preparation and enable you to apply your best efforts.

The sample discussion outline that follows does not record the facts and expert opinions that you would consult and use, but it does trace out the lines of thought in each phase of the reflective thinking process. The facts, quotations, and examples that undergird your thinking may be included in your outline, recorded on file cards, or stored away in your head.

How Should Our Colleges Handle Financial Aid to Students?

  I. What is the problem?
    A. What is meant by financial aid?
      1. Are scholarships included?
      2. Are student loans included?
      3. Are grants-in-aid without specific grade requirements included?
      4. How about tuition rebates?
      5. Should board, jobs, and the like, provided by the college, be regarded as a form of financial aid?
    B. What are the present provisions for financial aid to college students?
      1. How much aid is given?
      2. What kinds of aid are given?
      3. Who gets this aid?
      4. On what basis is it granted?
      5. What are the sources of the funds?

    C. How adequate are the present provisions for financial aid to students?
       1. Are worthy students denied a college education because they cannot afford it?
       2. Are needy students in our colleges forced to give too much time to jobs in order to stay in college?
       3. Are colleges using financial aid funds to best advantage?
II. What are the principal causes of the problem?
    A. Do the colleges face increasing demands for financial aid? From what sources? Why?
    B. Is financial aid more easily obtained in certain educational fields than others?
    C. Are the budgetary provisions for financial aid too limited?
III. What should our objectives be in granting financial aid?
    A. A college education for every worthy student regardless of financial resources?
    B. An equitable distribution of the available funds?
IV. How can this problem be solved?
    A. Should colleges appropriate larger sums for student aid in their operating budgets from the sources now available to them?
    B. Should colleges seek aid from outside sources: private foundations; the federal government; industry?
    C. On what bases should aid be given: scholastic ability; need; service to the college?
V. What are the merits of these proposals?
    A. Is it wise for colleges to appropriate more money for student aid?
       1. Do they have the money to use for this purpose?
       2. How would an increase in funds for student aid affect other items in the budget?
    B. Should colleges seek student-aid funds from outside sources?
       1. How available are funds from these outside sources?
       2. Is there any danger that these outside agencies would exercise objectionable control over these funds?
       3. Will student-aid funds from outside sources force the colleges to pay hidden costs not covered by these funds?
    C. Should student-aid funds be granted on the basis of scholarship, need, or service?
       1. Should good students be denied scholarships because their parents can pay the bills?
       2. Whose need should determine the assistance: the student's need; society's needs? And what constitutes need?
       3. Should students work for the financial assistance they receive from the college?

VI.   How sound is the proposed solution to the problem?
    A. Does it attack the causes of the problem?
    B. How well does it achieve the objectives?
    C. Is it workable?

TAKING PART IN GROUP DISCUSSION

Inquiry at its best is "thinking out loud." You submit your ideas in a spirit that encourages others to assess their merits, to agree or disagree, and to point out why they agree or disagree. Sometimes you are not at all certain just where you inquiry will lead you. Other times, you will have formulated a tentative conclusion and will invite others to examine the thinking that has led you to it. You ask your listeners questions such as these: How do you react to this idea? Am I right? Where have I gone wrong? Your listeners may answer you with an account of their own thinking. Out of these exchanges emerge a clarification of the problem and new insights that enable you to progress.

The spirit of inquiry is essential to the success of inquiry. You are engaged in a cooperative undertaking to find the best answer. If special interests come into play, or if participants become more concerned with private gain than with group purpose, the level of inquiry quickly sinks. Inquiry demands *cooperation among people* and *competition among ideas.* Ideas need to stand on their merits—not on the personality or prestige of their defenders.

Inquiry, then, calls for ideal attitudes—attitudes that are seldom perfectly realized. People have special interests and prejudices but they can learn to act maturely. Those who do are able to engage profitably in group discussion.

In an informal discussion of your college's plan to increase the mathematics requirement from one to two years, you might favor the new policy by stating your real reasons or by giving reasons that simply sound good, or you might assert your opinion without giving reasons. If you realize during the discussion that your enthusiasm for mathematics is due mainly to your success in the subject, your opinion might waver when you consider that not everyone has had the same happy experience. But if you reverse your opinion, you fear that you will be suspected of retreating under fire. So you continue to defend an opinion you no longer whole-heartedly believe. This behavior denies you the full benefit of discussion. If you persist in such behavior, you may find yourself unwelcome in serious conversation.

An objective attitude toward people and their ideas leads to the most rewarding inquiry. People with an objective attitude show a lively interest in ideas; they are willing to suspend judgment until they have heard the whole case for the other side; they can accept fair criticism of their ideas without taking it as a personal affront; they are willing to give up or modify ideas that have proved untenable; they can criticize poor ideas without attacking the person who proposed them; they assume that others are acting in good faith until they prove otherwise; they try to make it easy for people to back down from weak positions.

HOW TO LEAD DISCUSSION

The leader of a discussion may be someone who is formally appointed or elected, or someone who assumes the job with the approval of the group. In fact, leadership often shifts as one person after another temporarily assumes the responsibility.

The essential duties of the leader are to stimulate, guide, and integrate the group. He *stimulates* the members of the group by arousing their interest, by focusing their attention on relevant matters, and by encouraging them to contribute their ideas. He *guides* the members of the group by helping them think through the problem together, but without forcing them to follow any preconceived pattern. And he *integrates* the group by helping members resolve differences, recognize areas of agreement, and come to some kind of understanding. These duties are best performed by a democratic leader who helps each participant to make his greatest contribution.

The two most useful skills in leading discussion are the ability to ask good questions and the capacity to summarize matters clearly and succinctly. Skillfully worded questions, asked at the right time and directed to the right people, are the leader's first responsibility. He builds his questions around the words *what, why,* and *how.* What is the problem? Why is it a problem? How can it be solved? Such questions help the group to identify the problem, to discover its causes and effects, and to work out a solution.

If you are leading a discussion, try to ask questions that will draw out the members of the group. What is your position? Why do you feel that way? How would you handle the matter? Keep the discussion moving along by raising a new question as soon as each successive point has been handled adequately. Use questions to probe into important aspects of the problem, to introduce phases of the problem that might otherwise be overlooked, and to explore the bases of agreement and disagreement.

Questions evoke discussion, and summaries pull together what has been said. Make short, tentative summaries when agreements have been reached and when disagreements have been fully explored. Use summaries to rephrase a position that needs clarification, to state the points at issue, to remind the group of the ground that has been covered, and to pin down conclusions. If your summary is acceptable, the group can move on to new ground; if it is not, it will open the way to further discussions of a controversial point.

INQUIRY THROUGH PUBLIC SPEECH

PUBLIC SPEECH AS A VEHICLE OF INQUIRY

Public speeches of inquiry are *open-ended,* and in this respect they differ from other forms of public address. A report transmits information. A speech of advocacy urges acceptance of a predetermined conclusion. An evocative talk inspires or entertains. But in an inquiry the speaker remains a seeker whose goal is to find a solution to a problem by enlisting others to join in the search. If circumstances permit, his audience may enter into the discussion after he has finished his talk. Otherwise, the most he can do is to send his listeners away intent on continuing the search he has initiated. But whether or not the audience has an opportunity to think aloud, the speaker achieves his purpose only if he can induce his listeners to think with him.

Here are typical examples. A president confronts his board of directors with the unhappy news that the company's business is slipping. Why? He explains the reasons as he sees them. Then he goes on to suggest alternative ways of recovering the lost business. His speech sets the stage for a general discussion by members of the board of directors. At a chapter meeting, a sorority girl analyzes rush methods, raises doubts about the efficacy of present practices, and stirs other members to consider new ones. An instructor in philosophy analyzes the moral issues of war, discloses various ethical theories that come to grips with these issues, and challenges the class to assess the merits of the theories.

Speeches of inquiry don't make their way into anthologies much oftener than pictures of a house under construction are placed among photographs of model homes. Such speeches are thought in process rather than the product of thought. And they should always be judged by standards appropriate to their unique purpose.

DEVELOPING A SPEECH OF INQUIRY

The six steps in reflective thinking offer a natural sequence for a speech of inquiry. Just how many of the steps you should try to take depends on the situation. Under some circumstances, it is enough to establish the validity and urgency of the problem itself. Here is an actual instance in which most of the speeches were properly limited to problem analysis.

A community grew up around an airbase that was originally planned for small military training planes and later was converted into a base for jet planes. Many residents felt threatened by the switchover and called a mass meeting. Anyone who wanted to speak was given the opportunity. Some speeches called for immediate action, but most were exploratory. The speakers addressed themselves to questions such as these: Does the conversion to jet planes threaten lives and property? What is the magnitude of the threat? Do we have a problem that is serious enough to investigate further? Out of such probing, consensus was reached that a problem did exist and that a committee of citizens should plan an extended study of all possible ways to deal with it.

Whether you choose to develop your talk through some or all of the steps in reflective thinking depends upon the nature of the problem, your present knowledge and insights, the time at your disposal, and the background of your listeners. Student speakers often are challenged by topics that are too big and complicated to be carried through all the six steps in reflective thinking. They may perform a distinct service, however, simply by creating an awareness of the topic *as a problem* and by stimulating thinking where there has been none before.

Private inquiry may lead you to a tentative conclusion. When you speak, invite your audience to examine the steps that led you to your conclusion. This should not be an *ex post facto* report of your private struggles with a problem. Remain open-minded and be prepared to modify or abandon your conclusion if the thinking you provoke in others justifies a revision in your own thinking. The sample outline on financial aid for students is applicable to a six-step speech of inquiry as well as to group discussion. If you have tentatively concluded that federal funds provide the best source for extending aid to worthy college students and you know that this conclusion is highly controversial, you will wish to share the thinking that led you to this conclusion—the same thinking you would introduce if this were a group discussion. Such a speech might then become the basis for an open forum or group discussion.

The skeletal outline below suggests the general framework for a speech of inquiry on the question, "How can scientists communicate with the public?"

The Scientist and the Public

INTRODUCTION

I. Dr. Albert H. Crews, Director of the Argonne National Laboratory, warns that unless scientists learn to communicate with the public, the country is in danger of splitting into two cultures—one of *science,* the other of *magic.* He puts it this way: "Those who practice science will be able to communicate effectively only with other scientists. The rest of the population will live in a world of magic—a world of devices, gadgets, appliances, and structures that are not understood by them and that are provided by the other culture. . . ."

II. If Dr. Crews is correct in his view, it is useful to ask: How can we establish better communication between the scientists and the public?

BODY

 I. How wide is the gap between the scientist and the general public?
     A. Have scientists lost touch with the general public?
     B. How literate is the public in the realm of science?
 II. What factors are operating to produce this schism?
     A. How communicable are modern scientific data and their applications?
     B. Is our educational system at fault?
         1. Is our scientific education too specialized?
         2. Is the exposure of nonscientists to scientific training too limited?
III. Would our society gain by closer communication between the scientific community and the public?
     A. To what extent do policy decisions in our society require scientific knowledge?
     B. Who should make these decisions: the scientists; our elected representatives?
IV. How might communication between scientists and the public be improved?
     A. Should we provide scientific training for all?
     B. Should the education of scientists be strengthened in the humanities and the social sciences?
     C. At what level of scientific sophistication should this communication take place?
     D. Should we look to the scientists for more social leadership?

CONCLUSION

 I. Communication is a two-way street. If we are to close the gap between the scientific community and Dr. Crews's "world of magic," it would seem essential that some common ground be established where the people who populate these two worlds can meet and talk together.
 II. I invite your consideration of ways and means of achieving this common ground.

QUESTIONS FOR DISCUSSION

1. The piece below is not a speech, but it might have been; it qualifies as an open-ended comment designed to raise questions and invite further study and discussion. It is an invitation to inquiry. Most speeches of inquiry are planned to serve this purpose.

   "Land use" is one of the national questions, with state and local applications, that is being studied and discussed by the League of Women Voters the country over. If you wish to use this question for class speeches and discussions, source materials, including bibliographies and related League publications can be obtained at modest prices by addressing the League of Women Voters of the U.S., 1730 M Street, N.W. Washington, D.C. 20036.

Land Use—The Growing Edge

A wide range of problems fight for our immediate attention and concern, as citizens form battle lines from the Tennessee-Tombigbee Waterway to the Alaska Pipeline. Conflicting passions rise as interstate highways are built around business districts or through parklands, wetlands are filled for construction sites or drained for farming, vacation resorts are planned along windswept beaches. Central to such environmental, as well as economic and social issues, is land use. How shall we plan for the future use of our land?

Competing demands for land are increasing every day—for housing, community development recreation, agriculture, commerce, industry, mining, and open space. But the immutable fact remains: while our population grows, our supply of land remains constant.

In 1973, the United States had a population of over 210 million, and the most modest of census projections predicts 40 million more people by the year 2000. Where will they live and work?

The Commission on Population Growth and the American Future estimates that the total land area encompassed by urban regions will double between 1960 and 1980 and grow at a slower rate after that. By the year 2000, as much as 5/6 of our nation's people may be living in urban regions covering 1/6 of coterminous U.S. land. If these projections are true, the land we occupy in the year 2000 is largely being settled now. The Commission observes that if we settle our land badly *now*, we shall endure the consequences *then*.

How can we guide future growth? How can we assure that our varied use of land is harmoniously related, efficient, and beneficial to people and the environment?[1]

2. In the quotation below, the term "constructive reasoning" is used to characterize what we have called "reflective thinking," and the term "intentional reasoning" is used to describe the reasoning of the advocate.

Read the quotation and discuss the "aspects and peculiarities" of reasoning in discussion as compared with that in debate.

In constructive reasoning it is the object of the reasoner to discover truths yet unknown, that is to say, new derivations of one group of phenomena from another. . . .

In such reasoning, the reasoner has at the outset no intention or desire to maintain certain points at the expense of certain others. He wishes only to discover *the truth,* whatever it may be. The "intentional" reasoner, on the other hand, starts reasoning in order to try to demonstrate the accuracy of

[1]League of Women Voters Education Fund (Current Focus, 1973), p. 1.

definite assertions in which he has a particular interest. In one case the reasoner does not know in advance the final result of the new series of imagined experiments any more than the experimentalist knows the result of certain experiments which he sets out to perform for the first time. The second, on the other hand, always knows the results of his reasoning *because he desires it.* . . . It is clear that such "intentional" reasoning must, on account of this very different function, present aspects and peculiarities very different from "constructive" reasoning.[2]

EXERCISES

1. Adopt a question worthy of discussion during two or more class meetings. Develop discussion outlines and come to class prepared to work through the six steps in reflective thinking. Take up each step systematically and carefully. Your main purpose here is to gain mastery of the reflective thinking process and experience in applying the process in discussion.

2. Use the subject you selected for Exercise 1, or some other problem of your own choice, for a speech of inquiry.

3. Plan a discussion in which each member of the class comes prepared to act as leader. Appoint someone to begin as leader and then pass this responsibility around to others as the discussion progresses. Be prepared to ask questions that evoke discussion and to provide short, terse summaries that pull the discussion together.

4. Divide the class into groups of five or six, adopt questions for discussion, appoint a leader for each group, and prepare discussion outlines. Then seat the panel in front of the class. The audience may be invited to present questions at the conclusion of the panel discussion. The leader of the panel may preside over this question period.

5. One way of conducting an inquiry is through interviews. Choose a person you would like to interview, select a problem, and prepare questions that follow the six steps of inquiry. Conduct your interview on the basis of these questions.

[2]Eugenio Rignano, *The Psychology of Reasoning* (New York: Harcourt, Brace and Company, 1927), pp. 209–10.

19. Reporting

The reporter's job is to find relevant information, to communicate it with maximum accuracy, clarity, and economy, and to do this in ways that invite the interest of listeners. Most of us do not expect to become professional reporters, yet hardly a day passes without our making or hearing reports. As our life experiences broaden, more and more we are cast into the role of reporter. How well we acquit ourselves depends primarily on how well we understand the job.

KINDS OF REPORTS

Perhaps the most useful way to classify reports is on the basis of the audience to whom you are reporting: learning groups, policy-determining groups, the general public, your friends and associates, or people to whom you want to give directions or other instruction.

The oral report is a familiar aid to learning. A teacher gives such reports when he lectures to his class. And you, as a student, may be asked to report on your own studies, a special investigation, or on research that you have conducted. When you give such a report your purpose is basically the same as that of the teacher: to increase your listeners' knowledge and understanding of the subject.

Many reports are given to policy-determining groups such as boards of directors, councils, and legislative bodies. Such groups usually have standing committees to make reports at regular intervals and special committees to make reports on problems as they arise. In either case, your job as a reporter is to provide dependable information on which decision and action may be based. At a later date, you may be called on to survey the results of a policy thus determined and report your findings back to the group for review. If you make a career as a consulting engineer, a legal investigator, an auditor, or a diagnostician, reports of this kind will be an important part of your professional duties.

Other reports are made to the general public by news reporters and commentators. Most people who listen to radio and television have their favorite reporters, men and women who can be depended on to report reliably, clearly, and interestingly. Any report designed for the general public must necessarily take into account the broader interests of this audience and the many other sources of information competing for their time and attention.

Much of the reporting you do consists of conversation with friends, neighbors, and other close associates. You report experiences, give explanations and directions, and pass along news. There is no reason why this informal reporting should not be entertaining. But if your primary purpose is to inform rather than entertain, your first responsibility is to meet your obligations as a reporter.

QUALITIES OF A GOOD REPORT

RELEVANCE

"Who does not know fellows," asks Oliver Wendell Holmes, the Autocrat of the Breakfast Table, "that always have an ill-conditioned fact or two which they lead after them into decent company like so many bulldogs . . . ?" Holmes' quarrel is not with facts as such, the hard core of knowledge, but with people who turn their minds into almanacs and then proceed to abuse the privileges of discourse. They use facts to intimidate others or kill off the free play of minds; they grab or create openings and unload everything they know about hi-fi apparatus, the intricacies of missile construction gained from *Popular Science,* the relative merits of various types of lawn fertilizers, and other ill-assorted items. Such people are bores—if not boors—utterly insensitive to the possibilities of satisfying conversation and oblivious to the truth that information is seldom welcomed if it is not really wanted.

Since formal reports are usually commissioned in advance, their relevance may be presumed. Even so, formal reports often fail because they are burdened with unnecessary materials that obscure essential information and tire the listeners. We respond affirmatively to information when we need it and to speakers who stay on the track. Always ask yourself: "Have I properly analyzed the informational needs of my listeners? Does my report stick to the point? Are all details pertinent? Is my report well within the time limits?" The speaker who flounders in a sea of irrelevancies is likely to be dismayed when he sees listeners furtively looking for some inconspicuous exit.

CLARITY

Clarity is dependent upon a number of things. The speaker must have a good grasp of his materials, have a purpose and plan, and make adaptations to his audience. Audience adaptations are particularly important; it is a common failing among reporters to concentrate exclusively on their subjects.

Granted, not every subject can be made intelligible to everyone who happens to be within earshot. If you must talk of highly technical matters in technical language, then you are bound to overshoot the uninitiated. More typically, though, you are likely to be called upon to report about matters of mutual concern to people with different backgrounds, interests, and capacities. Somehow you must link what you have to say with listeners as you find them.

Begin where your listeners are, and relate the new to the old. Learning proceeds from the known to the unknown, from the perceived to the unperceived, from the understood to the less well understood. Some of the best adaptive devices are examples, comparisons and contrasts, illustrations, and stories. Such devices translate the general into the specific, the abstract into the concrete. They serve as bridges from the familiar to the unfamiliar. In reports that involve statistical analyses, you will discover that charts, diagrams, graphs, maps, and pictures are invaluable aids to clarity.

A speaker should be full of his subject, but clarity demands that we think through our subjects imaginatively in relation to the particular audience we shall face.

DEPENDABILITY

A report stands or falls on the dependability of its information. It is completely useless if it misleads because of insufficient, inaccurate, or misinterpreted data, and sometimes its consequences prove downright vicious. The point hardly needs to be labored for anyone who has wandered aimlessly in a strange city because he was given incorrect or inadequate directions on how to find a particular address. You want assurances that the insulation for your house is as good as the claims that are made for it, that the milk you drink is pure, that the ice is safe for skating, and that the legislator's record justifies your vote.

Since the ostensible purpose of many reports is to lay the basis for belief and perhaps action, the reporter is under obligation to render a true and faithful account of his investigations. He may take it for granted, therefore, that in any matter of serious interest to his listeners, his report will be subjected to scrutiny, that its credibility will be judged by its concurrence with information listeners have on hand and by verification they may undertake later. Inevitably, too, the audience will judge the dependability of the report by what they already know about the reporter's reputation for competence and integrity and by impressions they gain about him while he speaks.

INTEREST

Oral reports seem particularly susceptible to dullness. Even people with a keen and vested interest in the information often complain bitterly of being bored. Speakers are often so completely dominated by their material that they neglect the normal, human requirements that must be satisfied to sustain good listening. Conventions of learned and professional societies offer many examples of speakers who assume that all they need to do is dish up facts for listeners eager to lap them up. Not so. And at least one group, the American Chemical Society, has felt impelled to issue injunctions against the more common of the dreary faults, urging speakers to use short sentences, refrain from using a manuscript, and keep up their interest in what they are saying as a way of sustaining the interest of the audience. Oversimplified and insufficient as are these bits of advice, they underscore the problem that provokes these admonitions. Many of the suggestions we offered in behalf of clarity will also enliven your report.

If in effect you dismiss your listeners *as listeners,* then it is well not to impose on them as a speaker. It will be far better for everyone if you simply write up your report, have it duplicated, and distribute it for people to read at their leisure. But if you choose to report orally, then a vivid sense of your listening audience should manifest itself in attributes of oral style and in the expressiveness of your delivery.

REQUISITES OF A GOOD REPORTER

HEALTHY SKEPTICISM

Facts seldom lie exposed like driftwood on a beach. They are often hard to discover, identify, and isolate. Because things are not always what they seem to be or what they are represented to be, the reporter must dig facts from a world of appearances.

Our legal system demonstrates the difficulty of distinguishing between facts and nonfacts, between truths and half-truths when people's interests are in conflict and must be adjudicated. Advertisements may conceal more than they reveal. Claims made for a drug say nothing about the possibility of harmful side effects. Travel advertisements that tempt us with exotic palm trees near blue, blue water never caution against insects, infectious fungi, or high pollen counts. Exceptions to the protective provisions of a contract are often written in print so fine that it requires a reading glass.

Healthy skepticism cautions the reporter in search of facts to evaluate sources and to distinguish between verifiable data and special pleading. He knows that anyone with a commitment to a point of view may present only those facts that support it.

Healthy skepticism is the *sine qua non* of the good investigator.

OBJECTIVITY

Objectivity comes hard, for we are human beings first, reporters second. All of us carry around preconceived notions that guide our perception of things. Each of us is forever threatened by his gullibility and by his private herd of sacred cows. But a good reporter has a cultivated awareness of these susceptibilities that is his first line of protection against them.

It is easy, of course, to be objective about matters that seem remote from our immediate interests. We can be coolheaded about the bookbinding business, tariff schedules, the tide tables for Hong Kong, and the history of the dye industry in Germany, so long as they do not significantly touch our lives. But objectivity is more difficult when we deal with topics that involve our personal interests—topics, possibly, such as federal aid to schools, the pesticide and pollution controversy, civil rights, real estate taxes, the population explosion, and divorce laws.

Even though he may be tempted to do so, the reporter who is worthy of his craft does not grind axes. He tries honestly to see the facts for what they are and to present them as he finds them, not as he or anyone else wishes they were. He resists short cuts, doctored information, and slanted statements. The reporter with integrity seeks the truth and reports it with dispassionate accuracy, letting the chips fall where they may.

PERSPECTIVE

Perspective involves discriminating awareness of what is important, what is of lesser importance, and what is unimportant. It expresses itself in focus and proportion. Without perspective we may be accurate in everything we say without saying anything of consequence. For example, a reporter who pretends to cover a musical event actually commits a travesty if all that he offers are tidbits taken from program notes, interspersed with social notes on celebrities in the audience. What about the success of the music itself?

METHODS FOR COMPOSING YOUR REPORT

Exposition, description, and narration are your principal tools in reporting. Exposition gives an explanation, description paints a picture, and narration tells a story. You will find that most of your reports are primarily expository, with description and narration playing supporting roles.

Exposition classifies the data you wish to report and then identifies the more significant items in each category. For example, you might report the operations of a corporation by explaining the several departments of the corporation and the essential activities of each. The short exposition below reduces the principles of elephant stalking to a few simple steps and then tells you how to perform each of these steps—at your own peril.

> As an expert elephant stalker of 72 hours' experience, I now elucidate to you the principles of elephant stalking.
>
> First you must do it in a motor vehicle of instantaneous acceleration. You will find no difficulty in stalking by automobile, for the elephants like to walk on roads and frequently stay on or near them.
>
> Next you spot your elephant, knocking down trees or dallying in a water hole. You find which way the wind is blowing by throwing a handful of dust into the air. You want to approach him in such direction that the wind blows from him to you. For if it is the opposite, it will carry your obnoxious odor to him and he will either charge you or run away in nausea.
>
> The next thing to know is that the elephant has very bad eyesight. There is a legend that bull elephants sometimes show off in front of large boulders for hours on the mistaken assumption that the latter are potential mates. If you remain stock still, an elephant cannot see you at thirty yards distance. Even when you are moving, he loses sight of you at fifty yards distance.
>
> Now . . . you spot your elephant, get the wind on the right side of you, then you back your vehicle up to the pachyderm slowly, the cameraman on the back shooting pictures. This is so that when he gets sight of you and charges, you can move forward, away from him, at top speed. Since he becomes blind to you at fifty yards distance, when you have put that space between you and him, you are safe, and the elephant will thrash around in the bush blindly and never find you.[1]

Description gives your listeners a picture of your subject by dividing it *spatially* and then listing the qualities—size, shape, color, texture, smell, feel, taste—of the significant items in this division. When you focus your camera on a landscape, you can capture the entire picture with one click of the shutter. But if you want to describe the same scene in words, you have to begin with the cottage in the foreground, or the hills that form the

---

[1]Reproduced by permission from a CBS broadcast made by Howard K. Smith on November 17, 1954.

backdrop, or the sunset, or the sheep grazing on the slopes. These spatial relations give your listeners perspective and provide you with topics for description that you can put into clear, vivid word pictures.

Narration tells how something happened, usually by giving the details of the event in chronological order. Here, *time* rather than *space* is the guiding principle in organizing your report. Description stops the clock and takes a still picture; narration keeps the clock running and takes a motion picture. For example, one speaker used narration in making a report on shipping by freight. He gave a narrative account of the travels of a freight car in a single month—where it was loaded, the freight it carried, the switching terminals it passed through, the tracks it traveled, and the stops it made. He told a story, but in telling it he gave an informative report on the car pool maintained by American railroads and the purposeful wanderings of freight cars from one line to another.

ORGANIZING YOUR REPORT

The topical pattern is best suited to reporting because it is a process of analysis and synthesis. It breaks a subject into its parts and exhibits the relationships between the *whole* and its *parts.* These parts or components might be steps in a process or operation, in an explanation of how to make out your income tax, how to treat the common cold, or how to use the library; they might be the working parts of a machine you are trying to explain, a classification of the parking regulations in your community, the formations most commonly used in professional football, the leading characters in a play; or they might be a list of trends, causes, historical periods, or basic principles. Actually, you may divide your subject into its parts on any conceivable basis or principle, so long as the division provides a useful organization for your report.

In a report on the accident problem in masonry construction, for example, the speaker began by discussing the most dangerous operations in masonry construction. Next he considered the most common types of injury; then he explained the incidence of accidents among workers of different age and experience; and he concluded with an explanation of a three-step plan of attack to reduce accidents. He discussed each of these topics in terms of the "parts" provided by the division: the *operations,* the *types,* the *incidences,* and the *steps.* [2]

No matter how you organize your report, always work for accurate, concise, sharp divisions. Mixed lists, long, unclassified lists, overlapping

---

[2] A report by Howard H. Warzyn, Senior Engineer, Construction section, National Safety Council.

topics, fuzzy distinctions, and intrusions of unrelated items are signs of faulty analysis.

The sample outline that follows is an example of topical organization suitable for reporting. Such outlines may be tight and rigorous or relatively relaxed and informal, depending on the subject and needs of the occasion.

The Woman Voter

INTRODUCTION

I. The woman voter is important in this election year.
   A. Over 110 million people in the United States are eligible to vote.
   B. Over 63 per cent of the eligible voters cast ballots in the last presidential election year.
   C. More than half (approximately 56 million) of the eligible voters are women.
II. I wish to analyze the woman's use of the vote, factors influencing the woman's vote, and some of the effects of the woman's vote.

BODY

I. To what extent do women value the franchise?
   A. Voting records show that women are becoming increasingly active in political life.
   B. What women vote?
      1. A larger percentage in upper-income brackets vote.
      2. There are more voters in the upper educational brackets.
      3. A larger percentage vote in metropolitan areas than in rural areas.
II. These factors influence the woman's vote.
   A. Women vote more according to their interests than men do, and with more of an awareness of issues.
   B. There is greater conservatism among women voters.
   C. Family influences affect their vote.
      1. In one case in twenty, the husband and wife vote for different political parties.
      2. Parents and children vote differently in one case out of ten.
      3. The proportion of disagreement among in-laws is one in five.
III. What are the effects of the woman's vote?
   A. What is its impact on political parties?
      1. Control remains in hands of men.
      2. Women are active on the precinct level.
      3. Women are given modest positions in party organizations.
   B. Women have greater influence on local elections and local issues than at the national level.

C. There is enough difference between distribution of men's votes and women's votes to make women's votes crucial in close elections.

CONCLUSION

I. Women are making progress in using the franchise.
   A. They were given the ballot in 1920.
   B. The percentage of women casting the ballot is increasing.
   C. The development of organizations such as the League of Women Voters tends to increase their influence.
II. Parties and candidates cannot afford to neglect the woman voter.

QUESTIONS FOR DISCUSSION

The Carnegie Commission on Higher Education has issued a comprehensive report on its findings. We present here an outline of a report on their report. Read this outline as a sample and consider the possibility of adopting the Carnegie Report as a *common source* for class discussions, reports, debates, and perhaps even speeches to entertain or inspire.

Priorities for Action in Higher Education

INTRODUCTION

I. What the Carnegie Report is:
   A. The report of a six-year, $6.5 billion dollar study of higher education by a nineteen-member commission of educators and laymen.
   B. Established by the Carnegie Foundation for the Advancement of Teaching in 1967.
   C. Commissioned to make recommendations about higher education for the 1970s and beyond.
II. Two statements in the report characterize the general tenor of its findings:
   A. Survival, with memories of past glories, is not enough of a program for higher education as it approaches the year 2000.
   B. We end our six years of study of higher education, in the time of its greatest trauma of self-doubt, with faith in its potential continued vitality and with a deepened belief in its essential value to American society.
III. I shall report in summary fashion on several recommendations which are alleged to "merit special attention."

BODY

I. Listed first is "clarification of purposes and re-creation of a great new sense of purpose." It calls for:

      A. Adoption of codes of conduct for members of the campus community that reflect these purposes;

      B. Reaffirmation for faculty members of their responsibility to provide inspired teaching;

      C. Development of guidelines for the exercise of public authority that will guarantee the essential independence of institutions of higher education.

  II. The Commission recognized the financial bind in which many colleges and universities find themselves:

      A. Declares in favor of state financial support for private colleges and universities; and

      B. More attention at all levels to the most effective use of resources.

  III. The Commission does not overlook the students. Listen to these recommendations.

      A. Greater participation of students in the decision-making process of the colleges and universities;

      B. Introduction of variable time options for students, especially a three-year degree program for the A.B. degree;

      C. The strengthening of general education requirements;

      D. The extension and improvement of educational channels beyond high school other than the conventional colleges and universities.

CONCLUSION

  I. The recommendations reported here affect the clarification of purpose in higher education, financial support, and new programs.

  II. Some of these recommendations are obviously controversial, but I suggest you hold your fire until you have the opportunity to read the report for yourself.

  III. You can get it in your library, or at the Book Store for $1.95. I am sure most of you have spent more for less.

EXERCISES

1. Make a report on some process—how something is made, how something operates, how something is marketed, how you use a product. Try to reduce the process to a series of steps. These will be your main points. Amplify each main point with specific, concrete materials. Make your report interesting as well as informative. In preparing this report, be certain to draw up a careful topical outline as a basis for your speech. Discuss this kind of outline in class until you are sure you understand it.

2. Plan a short biographical report on a historical figure, a contemporary person, or an interesting fictional character. Make the subject of your report come alive for your listeners. Deal with two or three of the most interesting facets of the man's life. Here is a chance to use vivid description and narration.

3. Choose an important event that genuinely interests you—either a recent event or one that took place long ago. Steep yourself in information about it. Report it to your audience so that the event will live for them. Give your report the color and life and suspense that marked the event itself.

4. Plan a review of a book you have read or a play or movie that you have attended. Your primary purpose here is to report rather than evaluate. Make the review interesting and vivid, but remain impartial and objective. We are interested here in *learning about* the book, play, or motion picture, rather than in your opinion of its merits.

20. Advocacy

The president of the Student Council is speaking to the student body: "As you know, the Council has voted to uphold the Board of Publications in their decision to replace Jim Meyers as editor of the *Daily Reporter.* Several of us sat in on the Board's discussion of the case. Later we took it up in Council meetings. Professor Smith, who has been chairman of the Board of Publications for years, gave us an unbaised report on the whole incident leading to Meyers' dismissal. Now, we've got nothing against Jim. We like him, and we respect his position. At the same time we're convinced that the Board's decision is right. We think you should support the action of the Board and Council because. . . . "

Here is an introduction to a speech of advocacy. The president of the Council has made an inquiry into a problem and has studied a report on it. He has reached a conclusion. He has committed himself to a position, and he now speaks to win support for it. This is advocacy in action.

KINDS OF ADVOCACY

Some people are professional advocates—lawyers, salesmen, and public relations men, to name a few. Men and women in many other occupations—clergymen, executives, and legislators, for example—often speak as advocates. But advocacy is not limited to these occupations. All of us speak to convince and persuade in family councils, community meetings, and even in the most informal social gatherings.

Advocacy may be presented in public speech or in conversation. And, in either case, other speakers may or may not be moved to express opposing views. If such opposition does develop, we have all the necessary ingredients of debate, no matter how public or private, formal or informal the occasion may be.

THE METHODS OF ADVOCACY

An understanding of the methods of advocacy will enable you to present your views convincingly and persuasively. Basically, these methods consist of five clear-cut steps. But how closely you follow these steps in any particular situation will depend on your specific purpose, the nature of the occasion, and the presence or absence of others who argue against your views.

1. DETERMINE WHAT IT IS YOU ARE PROPOSING OR ATTACKING

In the parlance of the debater, your proposal is your *proposition.* But whether you call it a proposition, a motion, a bill, or simply a statement of position, both you and your listeners need to know what it is. You should always be able to state your proposition in clear, concise, unambiguous terms.

The matters you propose or attack will appear as statements of *fact, value,* or *policy.* Your proposition may be a *factual* judgment: "Air travel is the safest means of transportation." "Television reduces attendance at sports events." Or a *value* judgment: "The new Plymouth is the best buy in the low-priced field." "Alaska is the land of opportunity." Or a *policy* judgment: "State University should build a guest house for parents." "Smoking should be prohibited in all public places."

2. DETERMINE THE ISSUES

Once you have phrased your proposition, you are faced with this question: What do I have to do to get my proposal accepted, endorsed, or favorably acted on? Or, if you are on the other side of the fence: What do I have to do to defeat the proposal? Whenever you are under some obligation to *prove* your proposition, you must look to the issues for the answer to this question. And you will always be on safer grounds if you know what the issues are. Otherwise you may deceive yourself as well as your audience.

The issues are the *inherent* and *vital* points on which the truth or falsity of a proposition hinges. The words *inherent* and *vital* are the keys to the matter.

The issues are *inherent* because they exist or inhere in the proposition quite apart from anyone's personal wishes or predilections. You discover issues. You don't invent them or make them up. Two or more persons analyzing a proposition independently should discover the same issues. If they do not, either their analysis is faulty or else the proposition is ambigious.

The issues are *vital* because the life of the proposition depends upon them. If any one of them is opposed successfully, the proposition is lost, just as death results when a single vital organ is destroyed. No point may be regarded as an issue simply because it is interesting, or even because it is important. To qualify as an issue it must be vital.

Suppose we say that the Jones farm, now up for sale, is a good investment. Here is a proposition of value. How do you know the farm is a good investment? In other words, what are the issues? First, is the farm *a good value*—in terms of agricultural production, future subdivision, or any other uses to which it might be put? Second, is the asking price *a fair price* on the current market? And third, are *real estate prices likely to rise* so that the investment will yield a significant inflationary increment?

Let's take our example one step further. Suppose a real estate agent offers the Jones farm to Mr. Davis as an investment. Now we have gone beyond a proposition of value—we have a proposition of policy. In addition to the first three issues, we now have three new ones: Does Davis have *the financial resources* to swing this deal? Will he get *a fair return* for his time and trouble in making the transaction? Is this the *best investment* he can make?

The problem of finding the issues may be simple or complex. In many propositions the issues are fairly obvious; in others, considerable study and analysis is required. The following steps may help to direct your search: (1) Be certain that you know exactly what your proposition means (define all terms); (2) study both sides of the question; (3) array the leading arguments pro and con; and (4) test the points believed to be issues.

By an "array" we mean a written list of the arguments for and against the proposition arranged in parallel columns. After you have prepared such a list, consolidate the arguments in each list under main headings. Then compare the affirmative and negative lists and note where the main affirmative and negative arguments clash. These points of clash are likely to be the issues—or, at least, a close approximation of the issues.

After the issues have been phrased tentatively, the following tests should be applied: (1) Is *each* proposed issue vital to the proposition? (2) Do the proposed issues include *all* the vital points necessary to establish the proposition? (3) Are the issues as proposed *mutually exclusive?* Does each issue operate as a single, independent factor or variable; (4) Are the issues so phrased that the affirmative answers "Yes" to each issue and the negative answers "No"?

3. PLAN YOUR CASE

Your case is the sum of the arguments, evidence, and any other inducements you offer to secure acceptance of your proposition. You stand or fall on how your case is regarded by the people you are trying to get to accept your proposition. You may present your case in a public speech. You may develop it in conversations with other interested parties. In any event, whenever circumstances permit, it is wise to plan your case carefully.

THE MAIN POINTS

These are the principal divisions or lines of argument in your case. They may or may not coincide with the issues.

Let's say that a village council is discussing the advisability of drilling a well to provide a central water supply. Up to now the villagers have had to secure their own water by means of private wells, cisterns, or rain barrels.

There appear to be four issues involved here: (1) Will the proposed well reduce significantly *the inconveniences* imposed by the present arrangement? (2) Will the new well produce water in *sufficient quantity* to meet the needs of the village? (3) Will the new well deliver water of *good quality?* (4) Are *the costs* of this project reasonable?

Assuming these to be the issues, the case *for* the new well might be organized around four main points—convenience, quantity, quality, and cost. And the case *against* the well might be organized around these same points. In both cases, the main points would coincide exactly with the issues.

There is no compelling reason, however, for organizing either case in just this way. A speaker favoring the new well, for example, might decide to break the issue of inconvenience down into two main points, then handle the issues of quantity and quality under a single main point, and conclude with a final point based on the issue of cost. Or he might omit one or more of the issues completely, if they do not appear to be contested.

Any advocate, whether he is for or against a proposition, should build his case with full knowledge of the issues. But how he *plans* his case —how he *uses* the issues—will depend on his analysis of his listeners and the known or potential opposition. The issues are impersonal logical considerations. The main points of the case represent the speaker's appraisal of the issues in terms of the occasion. A contention does not become an issue simply because some speaker chooses to make it one of the main points in his argument.

THE BURDEN OF PROOF

The burden of proof in any argument always lies with the advocate who is dissatisfied with things as they are. For example, if you propose a new high-school building for your community, you have the burden of proof. This simply means that you must initiate the argument and make a convincing case for your proposal before you can expect action on your proposal. Let's say your next-door neighbor is perfectly happy with the present high-school building. In these circumstances, there is no reason for him to offer a defense of the present building until you have made a case for a new building. And even then, it may be sufficient for him merely to refute your arguments.

Any proposition you choose to discuss, whether it is a proposition of fact, value, or policy, will fall into one of two categories: It will propose some *new* idea, policy, or way of looking at things—some *change* in the status quo. Or it will argue for the preservation of the status quo—for things *as they are now,* for our *present* institutions, values, and convictions. The burden of proof always rests on the speaker who is advocating change. He is the dissatisfied party. He is the one who stands to lose if nothing is done.

In advocacy of any kind, it always pays to know whether you have the burden of proof. This burden imposes two responsibilities: that of initiating the argument, and that of making a case that supports the issues. If you advocate any proposition that involves a change in existing policies, attitudes, and beliefs, these responsibilities are yours. On the other hand, if you support existing policies or attitudes and beliefs generally held, you have no reason to make a case for them until they are effectively challenged. And when you do make your stand, it is sufficient, if you choose, to defeat your opponent on any *one* issue—on any matter that is vital to his proposal.

This doctrine is simple common sense. Our example of the village council illustrates all its points. When the council is in session, quite obviously the people who want the new well will have to present their proposition and defend it. If they say nothing—make no motion and no case—the meeting will adjourn without even considering the matter. Certainly the people who oppose the new well aren't going to mention it. Why should they? They are satisfied with the present water facilities.

But let's say a motion is made that the new well be approved and a strong case is made in its behalf. Such a case, of course, calls for an answer from those who oppose the new well, because it threatens their position. They can no longer remain silent. They must counter this threat with a case that defeats the proposal on at least one vital count, at least one issue. The issues involved here, as we have seen, appear to be convenience, quantity, quality, and cost. The attack would be completely devastating if all issues were opposed successfully. Here the opposition would contend that the present water facilities are adequate, that the proposed well would not deliver enough water anyway, that what water it did produce would be of poor quality, and finally that the costs were prohibitive.

Actually any one of these points would logically defeat the motion.

Why seek a new water supply if the present supply is fully adequate? Why drill a new well if it won't produce enough water? Why turn to a well that will deliver water of such poor quality that no one wants to use it? Or why give serious consideration to a proposal that you can't pay for?

The point is simply this: Wherever and whenever you speak as an advocate, you either have the burden of proof or you don't have it. If you understand the duties and the privileges that are yours in these different circumstances, you are in a position to behave much more persuasively and much more strategically than you would otherwise be able to do. The issues and the burden of proof prescribe your *logical* responsibilities in planning a case. You *may* win an argument without discharging these responsibilities, but critical listeners and informed opponents are likely to hold you to them.

REFUTATION

When you are planning a case, try to take care of arguments that may be used against you or that may exist in the minds of your listeners. This is what *refutation* means—replying to arguments that oppose your position. You may include a scheme for refutation as part of your planned case, or you may devise it to be used in replying to another speaker.

Your refutation may take the form of an *objection*—you may point out flaws in the other speaker's argument. Or it may take the form of a *counterargument*—you may present an argument of your own to support a conclusion that is inconsistent with the one you are trying to refute. For example, your opponent declares that Latin should be a required subject because a knowledge of Latin enables students to speak and write English more competently. You might offer the *objection* that he has presented no convincing evidence for his proposition. Or you might *counter* by showing that if the time given to Latin were spent on the study of English, better results would be achieved in the students' use of English.

There are four ways of dealing with arguments that are raised in opposition to your position:

1. Ignore them if they are unimportant.
2. Admit them if you can show that they do not damage your case.
3. Show that they are irrelevant.
4. Refute them: first state them clearly and correctly; then show why they won't hold up.

4. PREPARE A CASE OUTLINE

The outline you prepare for a speech of advocacy should reveal the structure of your case. It gives you a chance to organize all the materials —facts, expert opinions, and inferences—that you plan to present.

The logical outline (see Chapter 11) is ideally suited for speeches of advocacy, for here you present your main points as reasons in support of your proposition. You buttress your main points, in turn, with subpoints that serve as reasons to support the main points. You can carry this reasoning process down to points that can be supported directly by evidence (facts and expert opinions) or to points you believe will be accepted without further support.

This kind of rigorous, logical organization is useful in close argument, but you may find that it denies you the freedom to develop your case persuasively. And it is true that this organization, methodical and logical though it is, may be heavy-footed and dull if it is not brightened by description, narration, and exposition. Consequently the most skillful advocate often combines logical and topical outlining in whatever pattern best serves his purpose.

Here is a tightly drawn logical outline. Notice that complete sentences are used and that all subpoints, except those in the introduction, serve as direct support for the points under which they appear.

A Hedge Against Inflation

INTRODUCTION

I. I should like to propose that now is the time to invest in common stocks.
   A. If you have any surplus funds to invest, I am convinced that common stocks are your best investment at this time.
   B. If you don't have funds to invest, you may know somebody who does.
II. The distinction between stocks and bonds is essential to an understanding of my argument.
   A. A stock certificate is evidence of ownership of one or more shares in a corporation.
   B. A bond is a certificate of ownership of a specified portion of the *debt* of a corporation.

BODY

I. We face an inflationary period in the years immediately ahead, because
   A. Strong inflationary forces are at work, because
      1. There are heavy consumer demands, because
         a. There is a shortage of residential units.
         b. We are not keeping up with the demand in many commodity lines.
      2. Heavy expansion of manufacturing plants and equipment is in prospect.

      3. Government spending is increasing, because
        a. The international situation calls for heavy military expenditures.
        b. The philosophy of the present administration favors large governmental expenditures.
    B. The evidences of inflation are already at hand, for
      1. Prices have started up again.
      2. We have strong demands from labor.
  II. Common stocks increase in value during periods of inflation, because
    A. The tangible assets of the corporation increase in value, because
      1. Plant and equipment are worth more.
      2. Commodity inventories on hand increase in price.
    B. The corporations are able to pay larger dividends out of increased profits.
 III. The real value of bonds decreases during inflation, because
    A. They are paid off in cheaper dollars.
    B. The interest rate is fixed.

CONCLUSION

  I. Investments with fixed returns suffer in an inflationary period.
  II. Common stocks are your best hedge against inflation.

This next sample is another example of a logical outline. Here the speaker is urging action, and he develops his case with this purpose in view. Notice that he also includes some refutation.

Vote for the City Manager Plan

INTRODUCTION

  I. I should like to open this meeting with a message from Mayor Brown.
  II. I join the mayor in urging you to go to the polls tomorrow and vote for the city manager plan.

BODY

  I. The old mayor-council form of city government has outlived its usefulness, because
    A. The system can't handle the growing complexities of city government.
    B. It makes a political football out of city government.
    C. The argument that the mayor-council system is more responsive to the will of the people is a myth.
  II. More progressive cities everywhere are adopting the city manager plan—over a thousand of them—because

    A. It streamlines city government—it is more efficient, because
      1. It places a professional manager in charge.
      2. It fixes responsibility.
      3. It reduces the size of the council.
    B. It takes corruption out of city government.
    C. The contention that we will be unable to get a good city manager for the salary we propose is groundless, because
      1. We already have two applicants.
      2. We know where we can go for a man with an established record as a city manager.

III. Now is the time for us to act, because
    A. Mayor Brown, the best mayor we have had in decades, is retiring.
    B. Mayor Brown supports the new plan.
    C. With few exceptions, our community leaders are behind the plan.

CONCLUSION

  I. I am not going to promise you that your taxes will be reduced, but I think I can promise more for your tax dollar.
    A. We'll get our garbage collected on time!
    B. We'll get the snow cleaned off the streets!
    C. We'll get better fire and police protection!
    D. And last, but not least, we'll let a little fresh air blow through the city hall!
 II. These things are worth voting for!

5. DEVELOP YOUR CASE PERSUASIVELY

Persuasion rests squarely on four basic concepts: attention, motivation, suggestion, and implication.

ATTENTION

Listeners respond favorably to speakers who capture their attention and hold it at a high level. An audience that listens only grudgingly and halfheartedly is unlikely to be stirred into action or into acceptance of a proposition. In giving speeches of advocacy, put to work what you learned about developing your ideas in Chapter 13 and what you learned about motivated listening in Chapter 15.

Plan an exciting opening. Make your listeners feel that you are talking to each of them as an individual. State your proposition arrestingly. Make abundant use of illustrative materials so that the bony structure of your case will be endowed with flesh and blood. Fresh language ignites interest; tired language snuffs it out. Show directness and vitality in your delivery. It is easy to accept the conclusions of an interesting speaker and just as easy to reject the conclusions of a dull one.

MOTIVATION

Make your listeners feel that their needs or desires will be satisfied by what you are recommending. Offer them a reward for buying your proposition. Some people respond most readily when the rewards are concrete and immediate. As they listen to you, they are asking, "What's in it for me?" But don't assume that everyone acts only for selfish purposes. Every day people are moved by calls to greatness. Every day they make personal sacrifices for the sake of justice, compassion, and the common good.

Effective motivation is not accomplished by working a few purple patches into your speech or by making a few isolated appeals. It must be part of the warp and woof of your argument. The reasons you use to prove your case should motivate your listeners to accept your conclusion. Ask yourself *two* questions about each reason before you use it in developing your case: Does it advance my argument logically and convincingly? And does it offer an incentive to my listeners to believe or act as I want them to believe or act?

In short, the key to effective motivation is first to identify the needs, interests, wants, and desires of your listeners and then to show them how your proposition will help satisfy those needs.

SUGGESTION

Sometimes you can persuade listeners by dropping hints rather than by giving them a developed argument. You let them come around to your conclusion in their own way. In short, you don't spell everything out, although you should be able to do so if you have to. Present your listeners with an attitude, a word, an example, a story, or a gesture, and then let them interpret it for themselves.

A speaker who was urging a bond issue for a new school once said, "I'm going to vote for this bond issue even though I'm a taxpayer and haven't any children in school. And I'm not wholly altruistic in doing so either." He didn't have to spin out his argument. He simply suggested that if he was willing to pay higher taxes even though he didn't have children, those who had children should be much more interested. He merely hinted at the benefits the new school would bring to the community and the general increase in property values that would accompany it.

Another speaker, confronted with an incredibly stupid argument, simply shook his head slowly and said, "I pass." This action was more tactful and perhaps more eloquent than an extended reply would have been. It simply suggested that the silly argument had refuted itself. In effect, the speaker said, "Why go into it? We all see its weakness. Let's get on with the business."

IMPLICATION

In using implication, you lead your audience to draw the conclusion that you want them to draw by explaining a matter to them, by describing a situation, or by telling a story. You use description, narration, and exposition—the tools of the reporter—to present a picture that implies your conclusion. The argument is implicit in your explanation, but you don't state it outright.

Let's say you want to persuade a friend to accompany you on a short vacation to New Hampshire. You describe the brilliant foliage, the hills, the "Old Man of the Mountain," inviting trails, streams and lakes teeming with fish. You tell him about a lodge off the beaten path where interesting people sit around a huge fireplace on cool evenings. You have certainly used this technique at one time or another, whether or not you called it development by implication.

The outline below is for a speech that is persuasive in purpose and implicative in development. The talk is designed to involve the audience psychologically and stimulate the "vagabond spirit." The topical outline is appropriate since the talk proceeds along descriptive, narrative, and expository lines, and key phrases are sufficient because of the highly personal and informal nature of the material and occasion.

A Summer on Tiptoe

INTRODUCTION

I. Traveling to Europe in a vagabond spirit
    A. The high adventure of planning the trip
    B. Joining the green passport club
II. Watching the New York skyline recede from the deck of the Queen Mary

BODY

I. First stop is Britain
    A. Glimpses of the countryside from the window of a boat train
    B. This is London
        1. City of medieval towns
        2. Excellent transportation plus the courtesy of the people make it easy to get around
        3. Queuing up for a day in Parliament

C. Short journeys out of London
   1. The spires of Oxford
   2. On the banks of the River Cam
   3. The swans of Avon
D. The moors of Scotland
II. From Dunkirk to the Riviera
   A. Making your fractured French work in the provinces
   B. Left Bank—Right Bank
      1. The live-and-let-live attitudes of the Parisians
      2. A city of art, superb cuisine, and gaiety
   C. A week end at Villefranche
III. The trek north from Rome to Amsterdam
   A. Crisis on the crest of the Apennines
   B. The tinkle of cow bells at St. Gotthard Pass
   C. Twilight specters in the historic city of Worms
   D. The land of green canals
      1. From the terrace of the Hotel Grand Gooiland
      2. Rembrandt's "Night Watch"
      3. The Peace Palace of the Hague
IV. Some quick glimpses of Belgium

CONCLUSION

I. Goodbye to the White Cliffs
II. Europe is within your reach

QUESTIONS FOR DISCUSSION

1. In the last section of Chapter 8 we noted a continuity of purpose from inquiry to reporting to advocacy to evocation. Our chapters on special methods associated with these primary purposes appear in the order in which these methods typically come into play in attacking a problem: an *inquiry* into the problem comes first; then the findings of this inquiry may be *reported;* the information given by these reports provides the basis for *advocacy* and—if there are differing conclusions—for debate; *evocative* speaking runs concurrently or follows a final resolution.

   a. Relate this sequential development to scientific inquiry and subsequent technological applications.

   b. If your community or college or university were planning a campaign to raise funds for a worthy project, might the planning and execution of this campaign be developed in this sequence?

    c. Might a single meeting or conference embrace all these purposes and methods?

    d. How about a single speech of advocacy? Might it be developed on this sequential plan, with inquiry, reporting, and evocation in supporting roles?

2. Ethical questions affecting communication enter into all purposes, but probably have their most direct bearing in advocatory speech. Do you agree? Why might this be the case?

3. Is a speaker ever justified:

    a. In withholding information affecting the proposition he is advocating?

    b. In disguising weaknesses in his case?

    c. In short-circuiting logical processes by subtle suggestion?

    d. In concealing personal motives and private interests?

    e. In warping judgment by arousing listeners to anger, jealousy, or compassion?

    f. In evading the issues through plausible arguments?

    g. In employing stratagems to gain an advantage?

4. Discuss the following defense of deliberative speech as a means of preventing "the triumph of fraud and injustice."

> It is valuable, first, because truth and justice are by nature more powerful than their opposites; so that, when decisions are not made as they should be, the speakers with the right on their side have only themselves to thank for the outcome. Their neglect of the art needs correction.[3]

Apply this doctrine to advocacy in the *courts,* in *legislative assemblies,* in *private deliberation.*

5. Here is a definition and analysis of the nature of *propaganda:*

> A satisfactory psychological definition of propaganda is the following: *Propaganda is an organized attempt to influence public opinion in behalf of some special interest by means of suggestion.* This definition has three parts. Propaganda must attempt to influence *public* opinion (which means the opinion of many people). . . . Secondly, some *special interest* always motivates propaganda. Usually it is a selfish financial or political interest held by the propagandist himself. But the special interest may be altruistic in character as in a safety campaign or in propaganda for peace. Nevertheless, it is a special interest in the sense that it represents an emotional goal of great personal importance to protagonists of the cause. Lastly, and most significant for psychology,

[3]Lane Cooper (tr.), *The Rhetoric of Aristotle* (New York: D. Appleton and Company, 1932), p. 5.

propaganda always depends upon the use of *suggestion*. Open argument and presentation of all the facts of the case are not propaganda. A conclusion reached in the light of all available evidence on both sides of a question is not the product of suggestion. Suggestion, rather, is the process of reaching a conclusion with only part of our mental equipment. . . . In short, suggestion is the absence of complete self-determination.[4]

a. Discuss the nature and social role of propaganda.

b. How is propaganda affected if free competition exists and equal opportunity for exposure is provided for all attempting to propagandize?

c. Does such free competition and free access to the mass media exist in our society now?

EXERCISES

1. Phrase five propositions of policy that you would like to defend or oppose in speeches of advocacy. State the issues in each proposition and be prepared to defend your analysis.

2. Plan a speech of advocacy on any one of the propositions you devised in Exercise 1. Make this a tight, logical speech in which your main points coincide exactly with the issues. Give special attention to cogency of argument and adequacy of evidence.

3. Plan a persuasive speech in which you urge your listeners to take a specific action. Make sure that the action is reasonable and that they are capable of taking it. For instance: Join an organization; read a particular book; eat at a certain restaurant; buy something. Give your speech with conviction and sincerity.

4. Divide the class into groups of five. Let each group adopt a proposition of policy that lends itself to debate. Two people will defend the proposition and two will oppose it. The fifth person will act as chairman and moderator. Then conduct a debate in which the positions of the several speakers are developed through conversation. Do *not* work as teams. Each speaker is on his own and it is up to him to get his ideas accepted as best he can. The moderator's job is to hold the reins on the debate, to draw speakers out, to give each speaker a fair chance, and to invite questions and comments from the class when the debate is concluded.

[4]Gordon Allport, "Social Control Through Language" (unpublished lecture, Symposium in Public Speaking, Northwestern University, June 1938), p. 12.

21. Evocation

The purpose of evocative speaking is to inspire or entertain. It rewards listeners with emotional satisfactions ranging from the sublime to the ridiculous. Mind and emotions combine in all speech, but evocative talk gives *priority* to man's emotional needs.

Inspirational talk engenders a feeling of fulfillment, energizes hopes, reaffirms loyalties, stirs sympathy, stimulates appreciation. Its purpose is to awaken, quicken, and excite us. Entertaining speech, on the other hand, diverts and relaxes us. Listening to a pun, a joke, or a bizarre experience releases us from tension and tedium.

Although evocative speaking is commonly associated with sermons, lectures, ceremonial talks, and after-dinner speeches, it is by no means limited to public occasions. We seek diversion and fellowship through informal conversation with our friends. Inspiration and entertainment find their way into interviews, conferences and all sorts of group meetings. The term *evocative speaking,* then, applies to all situations in which either emotional stimulation or relaxation is appropriate.

ELEMENTS COMMON TO EVOCATIVE SPEAKING

A HIGH DEGREE OF SPEAKER SENSITIVITY

All good speaking calls for sensitivity, but evocative speaking requires a particularly fine awareness of what is appropriate. A report or a logical demonstration of a proposition invities objectivity. Evocative speaking, on the other hand, ventures into intimate areas of personal experience around which we ordinarily throw a protective cloak—our fears, hopes, failures, whims, ideals, and caprices. Our guards are up until the speaker satisfies us that he is a sensitive and perceptive person. We need to feel confident of his sense of taste and propriety. We want assurance that he knows the difference between sentiment and sentimentality, between wry humor and boorish jokes.

To say that evocative speaking calls for high sensitivity is not to suggest that only a few, rare mortal beings are endowed with this capacity. Everyone, as he grows up, learns to draw upon his accumulated experiences and make judgments of what is fitting. You learn when to stifle an impulse to laugh, and when to let go. If you're talking to someone who is in a panic over his grades, you withold the joke about the fellow who was booted out of school. You don't make sport out of your interest in the obituary columns in the local newspaper when talking with someone who has recently lost a close relative. You choose the friends with whom you are willing to share your deepest personal feelings involving love, ambition, and fears.

The point is this: In evocative speaking, you must make full use of your sensitivities. No two situations are identical. Factors such as age, sex, and religion may be critical. Moods are evanescent. Never assume that a joke or appeal that was successful in one situation will be suitable to the next.

A HIGH DEGREE OF AUDIENCE INVOLVEMENT

You want your listeners to do more than agree with you. You want them to empathize with you and what you are saying. You must create or recreate *specific experiences* with which your listeners can identify their own emotions.

Our minds assent to praise for Albert Schweitzer, the great humanitarian, but the winsome story of a boy's admiration for Schweitzer *moved* thousands to follow his lead. When thirteen-year-old Robert Hill, son of an army sergeant stationed in Italy, read of Schweitzer's hospital in Africa and its continuing need for medical supplies, he wanted to help out. He bought a bottle of aspirins and then asked an Allied Air Force Commander if he would drop it off when he flew over the hospital. By chance an Italian radio station carried the story. It caught on, and donations of $400,000 poured in. Subsequently, Robert and four and a half tons of medical supplies were flown to Africa in planes provided by the Italian and French governments. Said a grateful and astonished Dr. Schweitzer, "I never thought a child could do so much for my hospital." The point here is that someone at the Italian radio station discerned the evocative elements implicit in this human interest story and recognized its possibilities for creating audience sympathy and empathy. No doubt, though, the results exceeded his expectations.

A HIGH DEGREE OF CREATIVE IMAGINATION

Do you cringe a little when you hear the word *inspiration?* You have been drenched with corn-soaked exhortations to "buck up, old boy" and to strive upwards and onwards. Does "speaking to entertain" seem fatuous to you? You're probably still groaning at musty after-dinner jokes of the

Pat and Mike variety. We all borrow ideas and materials, of course, but we should never be tempted by embalmed platitudes and decayed jokes. Some approaches have been worked to death. "When I was a boy, I walked five miles through snowdrifts to get an education"—however honest and sincere the speaker is, this opening probably leaves you a bit cold too.

Avoid hackneyed formulas. Inject fresh insights and your own individuality into what you say. Nobody else has had exactly the same experiences as you. No matter how ancient your theme, your listeners will find new inspiration and new delight if you endow it with authentic freshness and individuality. And match the freshness of your approach with freshness of language. Use words that are rich in associations, words that conjure up images. Observe how Carl Sandburg evokes appreciation for the character of Lincoln through images that suggest antithetical qualities he embodied and held in tension.

> Not often in the story of mankind does a man arrive on earth who is both steel and velvet, who is as hard as rock and soft as drifting fog, who holds in his heart and mind the paradox of terrible storm and peace unspeakable and perfect.[1]

SPEAKING TO INSPIRE

Although there is no single, all-purpose method for you to follow in speaking to inspire, you will find that you can choose one of four master-plans, and perhaps use one or more of the others in subsidiary ways.

THE IMPLICATIVE METHOD

To understand and appreciate the essential characteristic of the implicative approach, we suggest you first read Eric Sevareid's radio talk entitled "The Dark of the Moon."

> Good evening ... This is not only Friday night, thank goodness, but the first warm and balmy night of the year in these parts; the first frogs are singing; altogether this is hardly the night for whispering sweet sentiments about the reciprocal trade act, the extension thereof. But since we are confined, by tradition to the contemplation of public themes and issues, let us contemplate the moon. The lovely and luminous moon has become a public issue; for quite a few thousand years it was a private issue; it figured in purely bilateral negotiations between lovers; in the incantations of jungle witchdoctors and Indian corn planters; poets from attic windows issued the statements

[1]Carl Sandburg's tribute to Lincoln before a joint session of Congress, February 12, 1959. *Vital Speeches of the Day,* March 1, 1959, p. 293.

about the moon, and they made better reading than the mimeographed handouts now being issued by assistant secretaries of defense.

The moon was always measured in terms of hope and reassurance and the heart pangs of youth on such a night as this; it is now measured in terms of mileage and foot-pounds of rocket thrust; children sent sharp, sweet wishes to the moon; now they dream of blunt nosed missiles.

There must come a time, in every generation, when those who are older secretly get off the train of progress, willing to walk back to where they came from, if they can find the way. We're afraid we're getting off now. Cheer, if you wish, the first general or Ph.D. who splatters something on the kindly face of the moon. We shall grieve for him, for ourself, for the young lovers and poets and dreamers to come, for the ancient moon will never be the same again. Therefore, we suspect, the heart of man will never be the same.

We find it very easy to wait for the first photographs of the other side of the moon; for we have not yet seen the other side of Lake Louise or the Blue Ridge peak that shows through the cabin window.

We find ourself quite undisturbed about the front page talk of "controlling the earth from the moon," because we do not believe it. If neither men nor gadgets nor both combined can control the earth from the earth, we fail to see how they will do so from the moon.

It is exciting talk, indeed, the talk of man's advance toward space. But one little step in man's advance toward man—that, we think, would be truly exciting; let those who wish try to discover the composition of a lunar crater; we would settle for discovering the true mind of a Russian commissar or the inner heart of a delinquent child.

There is, after all, another side, a dark side to the human spirit, too. Men have hardly begun to explore these regions; and it is going to be a very great pity, if we advance upon the bright side of the moon with the dark side of ourselves, if the cargo in the first rockets to reach there consists of fear and chauvinism and suspicion. Surely, we ought to have our credentials in order, our hands very clean and perhaps a prayer for forgiveness on our lips as we prepare to open the ancient vault of the shining moon.[2]

What elements emerge from your reading of Sevareid's remarks that are common to the implicative development? Thematically, the speech focuses upon values by which people live. Symbolical in tone rather than literal, the talk is developed by means of hints and suggestion rather than by argument or didactic exposition.

Quietly speculative, the talk unfolds through juxtaposition of ideas that provide new insight and by a succession of subtle images that stimulate the listener's imagination. It affords an example of what Lew Sarett called the discovery of poetic implications in the prose facts of life. In short, the success of the implicative method as applied to evocative discourse turns on some problem in human values, on originality in the juxtaposition of ideas, and on stylistic deftness.

[2]CBS News broadcast presented over the CBS Radio Network, March 28, 1958. Reprinted by permission.

THE METHOD OF COMPARISON AND CONTRAST

You can create a mood and heighten appreciation by pointing out dramatic similarities and differences between ideas, events, people. You might spark a new response to our rich, diversified heritage, for example, by contrasting the stark, crude frontier life suggested by the restoration of New Salem, Illinois, with the gentility and elegance of Mount Vernon, Virginia. In his speech "The New South," given in 1886, Henry Grady developed his theme by unfolding a succession of comparisons and contrasts. He opened with, "There is a South of slavery and secession—that South is dead. There is a South of union and freedom—that South, thank God, is living, breathing, growing every hour." As Grady continued, he used contrast and comparison to soften the bitterness between the sections and to emphasize their common culture and common ideals.

THE CHRONOLOGICAL METHOD

Carrying your audience through successive periods of time is particularly appropriate on occasions that call for tribute, dedication, and commemoration—speeches in which you evaluate human experience. A notable example is the Gettysburg Address. Lincoln opened with a reference to the past ("Fourscore and seven years ago . . ."), moved on to the immediate occasion ("We are met on a great battlefield of that war. We have come to dedicate . . ."), and ended by holding up the goals of the future (". . . that this nation, under God, shall have a new birth of freedom —and that government of the people, by the people, and for the people, shall not perish from the earth").

Naturally you don't have to stick slavishly to one order of events. You might want to open with the present, look ahead to the future, or flash back to the past.

THE METHOD OF CUMULATIVE DEVELOPMENT

You give an idea impact by restating it in new contexts. You impress the idea on your audience by weaving together example after example, illustration after illustration, quotation after quotation.

Suppose you speak to affirm some principle drawn from human experience, such as "The only thing constant is change itself" or "Imagination is the power behind all creative effort." You might open by stating your theme and then give examples and illustrations that reveal the range of its truth and applications. But your speech will be even more arresting if you open with a well-chosen example that suggests the theme, and then offer additional instances that carry your thought forward into ever widening circles of human experience. Note this emerging pattern in the introductory passage of a sermon by Ernest Fremont Tittle:

Opening
example
suggesting
the
universal
principle
to be
developed

Once there was a young man in Anathoth, a small town not far from Jerusalem, who was called of God to be a preacher. He began his ministry in his home town and was not well received. Quite the contrary. A group of influential people, taking umbrage at the things he was saying, determined to get rid of him. In fact, they went even so far as to plot against his life. When the young preacher learned of this, not unnaturally he was upset. In his anxiety he turned to God for some word of encouragement, and the word that came was this: "If you have run with men on foot, and they have tired you out, then how will you keep up with horses?" Strange comfort! Like the whimsical admonition: "Cheer up, the worst is yet to come." Yet in Jeremiah's case it availed. Life for him did become more strenuous, more difficult and dangerous. But learning to run with men on foot and not get all tired out, he won the power to keep up with horses.

Application
of
principle
to a
variety of
personal
situations

That life's demands increase with the years is a fact of human experience. In high school you may think the assignments are pretty stiff, and so they are; but how relatively easy in comparison with what is required of you if and when you get into college! When the first baby comes, you may think: Oh my! What would I do if I had two or more to care for? And presently you may find out. When you try to get started in business or in a professional career, you may take comfort from the belief that the first years are the hardest. You will, however, be mistaken. The first will presently appear easy in comparison with what you are now up against. You may even look back upon them with a feeling of nostalgia, wishing that life were now as relatively simple and undemanding as it then was. It is indeed a fact that burdens and responsibilities increase with the years.

This holds true of human history as well as of the individual life. Life for us is easier in some ways than it was for those who came before us. Streets are lighted and paved. Houses have bathrooms, electric lighting, central heating. . . .

Extension
of
principle
to wider
areas of
human
experience

But technological advance, if it in some respects made life easier, has at the same time created new problems and dangers. Those who came before us knew the meaning of privation and hardship but not the meaning of mass unemployment or of widespread want in the midst of plenty. They were confronted with the problem of winning fundamental freedoms from reluctant kings, emperors, and *czars,* but knew nothing of the problem of how to *preserve* freedom in a world situation become so complex as to make necessary an increasing measure of government control. They knew the meaning of war but not of total war waged with absolute weapons against whole populations.

Science and technology have brought it to pass that, whereas those who came before us ran with men on foot, we have got to keep up with horses.[3]

OUTLINING INSPIRATIONAL SPEECH

In working up an inspirational speech, use the topical outline. Organize and state your points with finesse lest you blunt the fine edge of your purpose. The following outline is drawn from a speech by Raymond Fosdick, "The Challenge to Knowledge," delivered at the dedication of the giant telescope on Mount Palomar, California.[4]

INTRODUCTION

I. In 1843, John Quincy Adams helped dedicate the Cincinnati Astronomical Observatory.
  A. He deplored the neglect of science in the United States.
  B. His speech did not foreshadow today's gap between advancing science and social control of it.
II. Today, knowledge and destruction have joined in a Grand Alliance.

BODY

I. Our dilemma is that we can't foresee the uses to which knowledge will be put.
  A. Knowledge itself can't be classified into safe and unsafe categories.
  B. We can't predict how the instruments of knowledge will be used.
    1. The University of California's cyclotron, which was used to further the atomic bomb, was originally conceived of as an instrument of pure research.
    2. Who knows to what purposes this telescope may be converted?
  C. We may elect to use any segment of knowledge for destructive purposes.
II. How should we deal with our modern dilemma?
  A. We can't fix the boundaries of intellectual adventure.
    1. This would certainly lead to retrogression.
    2. We can't suppress man's innate and insatiable desire to know things.
  B. We need to anchor knowledge to sound moral purposes.
    1. Man's towering enemy is his own moral inadequacy.

[3]*A Mighty Fortress* (New York: Harper & Row, Publishers, 1950), pp. 19–21. Reprinted by permission.
[4]See *Vital Speeches of the Day,* July 15, 1948, pp. 586–87.

2. Man's survival hinges on the moral use he makes of his new knowledge.
III. Modern man may well face his final choice.
   A. He can use his knowledge to build a rational world.
   B. Or he can put his knowledge at the disposal of his untamed passions.

CONCLUSION

I. This telescope holds the promise of a healing perspective.
   A. Through it man confronts the order and beauty of the universe.
   B. It will dramatize the unsolved mysteries of his universe and existence.
   C. It will help man to see himself in proportion.
II. There is a real sense in which Mount Palomar is Mount Everest.

SPEAKING TO ENTERTAIN

The range of topics suitable for an entertaining talk is almost unlimited. The subjects grow out of your experiences, interests, observations, and imagination. On the surface, this statement may not strike you as very helpful. But there are no categories of entertaining talk as such. Almost anything can be treated entertainingly if you have an intimate acquaintance with it, look at it from a fresh point of view, and present it engagingly.

Call to mind experiences and interests your listeners might consider unusual. Recall out-of-the-way places where you have lived or visited, extraordinary events you have witnessed, a novel hobby you pursue, a curious institution you know about, a cult you have studied, a celebrity you have met, a harrowing experience. Here are some examples of novel subjects that students have used successfully for entertaining talks.

Life in a ghost town
My fractured French in Quebec
Face-to-face with a bear in the woods
My interview with the vice president
My summer as a ballet dancer
A restaurant where you pay what you think the meal is worth
Working my way through Europe
Fighting a forest fire
Outwitting a thief
A parrot that talked too much
Playing in a bagpipe band
Hurricane panic
I was there when my father was married

A summer on a sheep ranch
The deepfreeze I won

But novelty is not a requisite. You know from your own listening that people talk engagingly on ordinary, prosaic matters. They give these everyday occurrences a unique twist, a wry interpretation, a comic slant, or a suspenseful development. Remember too that a subject may seem ordinary to one audience and extraordinary to another. These subjects, for example, have yielded delightful speeches.

A night on a day coach
An acre of tri-levels
Pets that have known me
Mannerisms of teachers
A TV commentator who speaks as the Voice of Destiny
Frantic behavior during exam week
Traffic snarls
The ideal parent
My thirty seconds of play in a football game
A broken fiddle string
Summer brings poison ivy and Aunt Maud
Profile of a Good Humor man
Blind dates
A fifty-year-old teen-ager

KEYS TO EFFECTIVE ENTERTAINING TALK

1. RE-CREATION

As you plan your talk, re-create it in your imagination so vividly that once again you hear, see, touch, taste; so realistically that once again you feel fear, panic, rhythm, or whatever sensation you wish to convey.

2. SEQUENCE

Line up your steps or points so that you won't stumble or backtrack. Avoid interrupting yourself with, "Oh, I forgot to mention. . . ." True, you need to keep your material flexible enough for easy adaptation to your audience. But you can plan without putting your speech into a straitjacket.

3. SUSPENSE

An element of suspense and surprise picks up interest. Don't model every speech after a whodunit, but keep your audience guessing whenever you can. This calls for close attention to details that build toward your punch line or climax. Suspense depends on subtle blending of composition and delivery.

4. VIVIDNESS

Give enough detail to establish mood and action—but don't use a dump truck. Let concrete language and images work for you. "The man dressed oddly" doesn't help us to see him. But suppose you say he wore a Homburg hat, a rumpled plaid shirt, a dinner jacket, gray flannel slacks, and a pair of sneakers. Now we see what you mean.

5. DRAMATIZATION

If it is conversation you are recounting, let the participants speak for themselves. Use actual dialogue. If you have a knack for mimicry, go right ahead. Suggest mood and action through posture, gestures, and pantomime.

6. TIMING

This is tricky. Droll incidents can be annihilated by machine-gun delivery. On the other hand, action-loaded material needs to be presented at a good tempo. Fit the pace to the nature of the materials and the mood of the occasion. Bear in mind too that subtle touches are conveyed by well-placed pauses and skillful phrasing.

HUMOR

Humor is useful (1) in helping you to get on good terms with your audience quickly, (2) in making serious points painlessly, (3) in providing comic relief from concentrated mental effort and tension, and (4) in affording mutual delight by uttering and hearing nonsense.

Humor arises out of a spirit of play and out of a surprising or incongruous turn of events.

CHARACTERISTIC FORMS OF HUMOR

1. PLAYS ON WORDS

These include boners, slips-of-the-tongue, misused words leading to confusion, and puns. A lawyer is questioning a witness in police court. "Will you testify to the driver's sobriety?" asks the lawyer. "Well, now I dunno," replies the witness, "but my guess is that he ain't so bright."

A pun is more likely to be intentional. If it is perfectly timed and turned to the situation, it will get the laugh it deserves. Two men driving along barely miss a collision when a Cadillac cuts sharply into their traffic lane. One of the men says, "You never know how a cad'll act." Whether or not you find this pun funny, remember that it takes its humor from the event and emotions of the moment. But a pun can never be quite sure of itself. One man's pun may be another man's punishment.

2. OVERSTATEMENT AND UNDERSTATEMENT

Overstatement leads to a broad, open kind of humor. Work in some element of plausibility, though, unless you can put your story across with such dexterity that your listeners will delight in your ingenuity. Usually exaggeration succeeds best when your manner underplays your words. The comic effect of Will Rogers' outrageous comments was heightened by his dry, mischievous manner. Mark Twain perfected a deadpan delivery.

Understatement is a more sophisticated form of humor. "Waiting to be whipped," said Josh Billings, "is the most uninteresting period of boyhood life." *Uninteresting,* as any boy who knows will testify, is hardly the word. It surprises by saying too little. Mark Twain was a master at combining overstatement and understatement. Note the abrupt switch in this passage from a speech on widespread property damage, injuries, and death caused by Fourth of July celebrations.

> I have suffered in that way myself. I have had a relative killed in that way. One was in Chicago years ago—an uncle of mine, just as good an uncle as I have ever had, and I had lots of them—yes, uncles to burn, uncles to spare. This poor uncle, full of patriotism, opened his mouth to hurrah, and a rocket went down his throat. Before that man could ask for a drink of water to quench that thing, it blew up and scattered him all over the forty-five states, and—really, now this is true. I know about it myself—twenty-four hours after that it was raining buttons, recognizable as his, on the Atlantic seaboard. A person cannot have a disaster like that and be entirely cheerful the rest of his life.[5]

3. CARICATURE

This is humor through distortion. A ridiculous subject is treated with mock seriousness; a serious subject becomes absurd. Under suitable circumstances, almost anything may be caricatured—individuals, events, groups, manners, and customs. As one of America's most popular lecturers, John Mason Brown knows well the types of people who live to be heard.

> ... Before the hall has been cleared and the chairman has asked for any questions, their full lungs have ballooned them to their feet. When they do leap up, they do so with the vigor of salmon headed upstream.
>
> "Mr. Chairman!" they call, their eyes rolling with frenzy, their voices a cross between Daniel Webster's and Willie Stevens', and their notes tucked behind their backs. "Mr. Chairman!"
>
> But the chairman, knowing them all too well from previous sessions, looks the other way. To him they seem not men and women but dreaded ectoplasms. He no more sees them than Macbeth's guests spied Banquo at the banquet. "Mr. Chairman," they continue, eyeing the audience as Danton must have surveyed the Convention. The audience mutters, sometime going

so far in its forgetfulness of Emily Post and the Bill of Rights as to cry, "Sit down," "Throw him out," "Shut up."

"Mr. Chairman, is this the United States of America or is it not?"

The chairman, well aware of his Rand McNally, is sorrowfully compelled to admit it is.

"Oh, you, Mr. Ventrelibre," he says, much as a judge might recognize an old offender. His tones would have chilled anyone else, but not Mr. Ventrelibre.

"Mr. Chairman," continues Mr. Ventrelibre, whose name is legion, "as an American citizen I demand the right to be heard."

And heard he is, while you and the chairman get so tired of standing that finally you have to sit down, and while those in the audience who have remained for the question period begin to run, not walk, to the nearest exits.[6]

4. SATIRE AND IRONY

Although not identical, these two forms of humor are closely related. *Satire,* which often bears a trace of irony, is trenchant wit laced with a spirit of ridicule. Commonly this ridicule is directed against specific human blunders, stupidities, vanities, and vices. In *irony,* we say one thing and mean another. We poke fun by intimating meanings that are in opposition to or at least at variance with the literal sense of our statements if taken at face value.

Both satire and irony backfire if their barbs are so sharp that they puncture the spirit of play and create sympathy for the victims. After long suffering at the hands of maladroit program chairmen, Stephen Leacock had won the right to satirize them:

When any lecturer goes across to England from this side of the water there is naturally a tendency on the part of the chairman to play upon this fact. This is especially true in the case of a Canadian like myself. The chairman feels that the moment is fitting for one of those great imperial thoughts that bind the British Empire together. But sometimes the expression of the thought falls short of the full glory of the conception.

Witness this (word for word) introduction that was used against me by a clerical chairman in a quiet spot in the south of England.

"Not so long ago, ladies and gentlemen," said the vicar, "we used to send out to Canada various classes of our community to help build up that country. We sent out our laborers, we sent out our scholars and professors. Indeed, we even sent out our criminals. And now," with a wave of his hand towards me, "they are coming back."

There was no laughter. An English audience is nothing if not literal; and they are as polite as they are literal. They understood that I was a reformed criminal and as such, they gave me a hearty burst of applause.[7]

---

[6] *Accustomed As I Am* (New York: W. W. Norton & Company, 1942), pp. 52–54. Reprinted by permission.

[7] Reprinted by permission of Dodd, Mead & Company from *Laugh With Leacock.* Copyright 1930 by Dodd, Mead & Company, Inc.

Note the vein of irony in this passage from a speech by Mark Twain. After commenting on the great number of people killed in railroad accidents, he added:

> ... But, thank Heaven, the railway companies are generally disposed to do the right and kindly thing without compulsion. I know of an instance which greatly touched me at the time. After an accident, the company sent home the remains of a dear distant relative of mine in a basket, with the remark, "Please state what figure you hold him at—and return the basket." Now there couldn't be anything friendlier than that.[8]

SUGGESTIONS ON YOUR OWN USE OF HUMOR

1. ORIGINAL HUMOR IS BEST

Don't hesitate to try your own brand. You may have more ability than you have yet discovered. Given a mellow mood, listeners enjoy the sly comment, the quick comeback, banter, raillery, a play on words. Remember, you don't always have to work for the big laugh. There are many states of amusement short of the guffaw.

2. BE SURE THE HUMOR IS APPROPRIATE

Adapt your humor to the sophistication of your listeners and the tone of the occasion. Humor may be too subtle or not subtle enough. Low humor is dubious.

3. PLAN HUMOR WHEN IT IS INTEGRAL TO YOUR SPEECH

Good humor may be spontaneous or it may only appear to be so. If you are forewarned that your audience will be expecting you to talk with a light touch, you will want to make careful preparation just as you do for any other type of speaking. Experienced humorists seldom depend on the inspiration of the moment.

4. HANDLE HUMOR EFFORTLESSLY

You can't drive an audience to laughter. You have to lead it. It's pretty painful to watch a speaker struggling with his audience to make them laugh.

5. DON'T ADVERTISE YOUR HUMOR

Avoid comments such as "You'll die laughing at this one," or "Let me tell you a very funny story." If it's funny, your listener will discover it for himself.

[8] *Mark Twain's Speeches* (New York: Harper & Row, Publishers, 1910), p. 415. Reprinted by permission.

OUTLINING ENTERTAINING SPEECH

In outlining a speech of entertainment, use the topical form. Your outline need not be so detailed or tightly drawn as outlines for other types of speaking. The example below is based on a speech Mark Twain gave to the students of Barnard College, called "Morals and Memory."[9] Though a casual speech with a light touch, it has a design and order of its own.

INTRODUCTION

I. Here are two things common to our human experience.
   A. Everyone has a memory, however capricious.
   B. Everyone has morals though I won't inquire into yours.
II. I want to tell you about some freaks of my own memory that may teach you some kind of a lesson.

BODY

I. I always considered myself a model boy.
   A. Oddly, I seemed to be alone in this opinion of myself.
      1. People around me seemed to think this estimate lacked something.
      2. Even my mother in her old age had forgotten everything about me except this youthful self-prejudice.
   B. There's a moral here if you search for it.
II. Once I "extracted" a watermelon from a farmer's wagon.
   A. I was overcome with remorse—when I discovered the melon was green.
      1. I returned it to the farmer and made him replace it with a ripe one.
      2. I also upbraided him for peddling green melons.
   B. My timely action helped to reform this farmer.
III. I learned something from another boyhood event I can vividly recall.
   A. This is what happened one day when I went fishing without my parents' knowledge or consent.
      1. A stranger in town was killed in a brawl.
      2. My father, who was the coroner, laid out the corpse in our living room.
   B. I came home after dark, not knowing what had happened.
      1. I decided to sleep on the sofa so I wouldn't disturb my parents.
      2. By stages I came to know who was in the living room with me.
      3. My exit was sudden.

[9] *Mark Twain's Speeches* (New York: Harper & Row, Publishers, 1923), pp. 224–37.

IV. A theatre date with "a peach" made a lasting impression on me.
    A. I slipped off my boots and couldn't get them on again.
    B. The trip home was miserable.
V. Once I rudely dismissed a "peddler of etchings" who called at our house.
    A. He turned out to be a friend of the family.
    B. I had to make amends.

CONCLUSION

I. I hope I taught you some inspiring lessons.
II. I know I enjoyed you more than I enjoyed that "peach" of fifty-three years ago.

QUESTIONS FOR DISCUSSION

1. What relationships do you see between *inspiration* and *entertainment* as objectives of speech? What common elements are involved in evoking these responses? How do they differ?

2. Entertaining has been defined as "holding attention agreeably, diverting, or amusing." Discuss the propriety of these objectives in inquiry, reporting, and advocacy.

3. Inspiration has been defined as "an animating, quickening, or exalting influence." Consider the role of these reactions in facilitating inquiry, reporting, and advocacy.

4. Does evocative speaking profit uniquely by the personal characteristics of the speaker? Of the listeners? Are the nonverbal stimuli—bodily action, appearance, and setting—of special importance?

5. Can any good speaker be a good entertainer? An inspirational spokesman? What special qualifications, if any, might be useful?

EXERCISES

1. Select a great speech or sermon whose ideas stir you. Consult the Bible, Shakespeare's plays, or anthologies of speeches. Open your talk by reading portions of your selection. Then in your own words carry forward the ideas expressed.

2. Use this speech to stimulate interest in and appreciation for some person who is unknown or little known to your audience, but whose life in some way has affected theirs. He may be a founder of your college or university, a donor, a teacher who is only a memory to the alumni, an alumnus who has conferred distinction on alma mater.

3. Prepare a "This I do believe" type of speech. Begin with a concept such as democracy, education, happiness, courtesy, brotherliness, worship. Formulate a theme that crystalizes your credo. Develop the speech by means of the most appropriate pattern of the four listed in this chapter.

4. Make a cutting of an entertaining speech or piece of writing by Mark Twain, Artemus Ward, Robert Benchley, Will Rogers, Stephen Leacock, James Thurber, E. B. White, or someone else whose works you enjoy and would like to share. Prepare an introduction of your own.

5. Work up an entertaining talk based on a personal experience or an imaginative commentary on human behavior. Before you give it, check over the keys to entertaining talk and the suggestions on humor given in this chapter. Use as many of them as you can.

22. Reading Aloud

Skill in reading aloud is of inestimable value to you as a speaker whenever you read from a manuscript, but this chapter also discusses oral reading as a form of communication in its own right. Listening to effective oral reading enables an audience to extract more of an author's meaning and feeling than they would get by reading the same work silently.

ORAL READING AND COMMUNICATION

The purpose of reading aloud, as it is of speaking, is to communicate with your listeners. This is true whether you read from a novel, a news story, a play, a market report, or a sonnet.

The oral reader has a dual obligation—to his audience *and* to his material. When you read silently, you are the only person who is "listening." You skim, and you slow down. If the meaning of a passage escapes you, you go back and read it again. You pick up the meaning of a new word or phrase from its context. As you read along, you adjust yourself to the writer's sentence structure and punctuation. But when you read aloud, your audience must depend entirely on you to convey the meaning. Hence, reading aloud is a more complex act than reading silently. As a reader, you must make the written word immediately intelligible, meaningful, and vital. It is through sensitive interpretation that you discharge your obligation to your material and to your audience.

All of this may strike you as obvious. But how many readers show *by their reading* any real competence to interpret the written word? The plain and painful fact is that good readers are rare. Absurd as it may seem, some people read lyric poetry in much the same way that they read the minutes of the last meeting of their club. Even remarkably fine speakers frequently lose their audience when they begin to read. They fence themselves off with wooden words. At the other extreme are the people who look on every opportunity to read as a chance to give a dramatic performance. They're out to make a show of it, and they go about it in the spirit of a prima donna. Listeners may be either amused or embarrassed by such histrionics, but they respond not at all to the writer's message.

Good reading, like good speaking, requires special preparation before you face your audience.

ANALYZING YOUR MATERIAL

FAMILIARIZE YOURSELF WITH THE INTELLECTUAL CONTENT

Successive private readings of a selection may reveal new meanings. If it is your own composition, you may be surprised to discover as you read it aloud that it conveys meanings you hadn't intended. If the selection was written by someone else, first read it for the general sense. As you do so, look up unfamiliar words and allusions. And while you are at it, learn to pronounce the words you're not sure of.

In subsequent readings look for answers to these questions: What is the writer's purpose? What is the central idea or theme that holds the work together? What are the subsidiary ideas? Is the thought immediately apparent, or is it intricate and elusive? If you plan to read only a portion, know how it fits into the whole work. Answers may be easy to come by, or you may have to dig for them. When necessary, consult outside sources such as reviews, critical commentaries, and references books.

You will acquire a deeper understanding and appreciation of your selection if you know something about its background. By way of illustration, consider two quite different types of material. The first is *J.B.,* a play by Archibald MacLeish. If you are guided solely by the contemporary circus setting of the play, you will miss the profound and timeless problem with which the poet deals. When you compare this play with the Book of Job, from which MacLeish drew his inspiration, you will appreciate more fully man's search for an answer to the meaning of his afflictions. An awareness of this background will heighten your respect for a modern treatment of an ancient theme, and will enable you to bring to your reading greater breadth and depth of knowledge. In short, understanding establishes both the desire and the right to communicate the writer's message.

Thomas Jefferson's First Inaugural Address offers a second illustration. Take this paragraph:

> During the throes and convulsions of the ancient world, during the agonizing spasms of infuriated man, seeking through blood and slaughter his long-lost liberty, it was not wonderful that the agitation of the billows should reach even this distant and peaceful shore; that this should be more felt and feared by some and less by others, and should divide opinion as to measures of

> safety. But every difference of opinion is not a difference of principle. We have called by different names brethren of the same principle. We are all Republicans, we are all Federalists. If there be any among us who would wish to dissolve this Union or to change its republican form, let them stand undisturbed as monuments of the safety with which error of opinion may be tolerated where reason is left free to combat it.

True, the general sense of Jefferson's remarks is not hard to figure out. His call for amity and his stand for civil liberty are familiar. But it is precisely because readers are too often content with such off-the-top-of-the-head reactions that their reading adds nothing to the listener's understanding or appreciation.

As a reader, you are somebody else's representative by your own choice. It would be a desecration to accept and read Jefferson's lines as if all he had done was to strike off shopworn platitudes, pious and empty generalizations wholly detached from the age in which they were written. Look at the passage again. It is filled with oblique references to past events and unsettling ideas. It carries intimations of the French Revolution and its impact on American politics, of bitter domestic struggles over the Alien and Sedition Laws, of the abusive political campaign of 1800, of Jefferson's persistent work in behalf of civil rights. Here also is a distillation of Jefferson's faith in the free mind. No one can expect to convey the inner meaning of the speech until he is steeped in the circumstances of its origin. And while we're on the point, note that the eighteenth-century expression "it was not wonderful" should be understood as "it was not remarkable" or "it is to be expected that."

DISCOVER THE PREVAILING MOOD OF THE WORK

As you pursue your analysis, you will discover that some materials have little or no emotional content and that others pulsate with feeling. We want factual reports to be presented with lucidity, precision, and just enough highlighting to bring out the essentials. It is a mistake to inject emotion into materials that were free from emotion when they were written. But aside from strictly factual reports, in most prose compositions the writer's emotions are in some way involved. Often he makes a deliberate effort to involve your emotions too.

First of all, then, discover the *nature* and *intensity* of the writer's feelings. It would be hard to miss the fervor of Patrick Henry's peroration in his famous speech on the eve of the Revolutionary War:

> It is in vain, sir to extenuate the matter. Gentlemen may cry, Peace, Peace —but there is no peace. The war is actually begun! The next gale that sweeps from the north will bring to our ears the clash of resounding arms! Our brethren are already in the field! Why stand we here idle? What is it that

gentlemen wish? What would they have? Is life so dear, or peace so sweet, as to be purchased at the price of chains and slavery? Forbid it, Almighty God! I know not what course others may take; but as for me, give me liberty or give me death!

Henry's appeal is directed to elemental emotions. His vivid words and jabbing sentences excite strong, sensory responses. Put the speech in its historical context and you will sense how inflammatory it was when it was delivered. This doesn't mean that you should read the passage as if it were a pyrotechnic display; neither should you read it as if you were reciting the multiplication table. Discover the authentic emotion and then suggest it to your listeners.

Now let's look at a passage from Lincoln's Second Inaugural Address:

With malice toward none, with charity for all; with firmness in the right, as God gives us to see the right, let us strive on to finish the work we are in; to bind up the nation's wounds; to care for him who shall have borne the battle, and for his widow, and his orphan—to do all which may achieve a just and lasting peace, among ourselves and with all nations.

Both Henry's and Lincoln's words have an emotional tone. But that is where the similarity ends. Henry was animated by and tried to arouse a combative spirit; Lincoln was moved by and sought to move others to compassion. Your appreciation of the mood of Lincoln's speech will be strengthened if you understand the moment in history at which he spoke. Here was a soul-tortured president presiding over the destiny of the Union during the only civil war that has ever afflicted it. The agony of Lincoln and his age is an essential fact in the mood of his speech.

Poetry vividly illustrates variety in kind and intensity of mood. A poem may express rapture, whimsey, melancholy; it may be pensive, contemplative, ecstatic, despairing, triumphant. You will develop and refine your perception by selecting poems for reading that exhibit these differences. A few selections will suggest what we mean. You will recognize at once the whimsey in these stanzas from Lewis Carroll's "Father William."

"You are old, Father William," the young man said,
    "And your hair has become very white;
And yet you incessantly stand on your head—
    Do you think, at your age, it is right?"

"In my youth," Father William replied to his son,
    "I feared it might injure the brain;
But, now that I'm perfectly sure I have none,
    Why, I do it again and again."

"You are old," said the youth, "as I mentioned before,
    And have grown most uncommonly fat;

Yet you turned a back-somersault in at the door—
  Pray, what is the reason of that?"

"In my youth," said the sage, as he shook his gray locks,
  "I kept all my limbs very supple
By the use of this ointment—one shilling the box—
  Allow me to sell you a couple?"

"You are old," said the youth, "and your jaws are too weak
  For anything tougher than suet;
Yet you finished the goose, with the bones and the beak—
  Pray, how did you manage to do it?"

"In my youth," said his father, "I took to the law
  And argued each case with my wife;
And the muscular strength which it gave to my jaw,
  Has lasted the rest of my life."

Move now to John Keats' poem "On the Grasshopper and the Cricket."
Here is a contemplative comment on the ceaseless rhythm of nature's
music.

The poetry of earth is never dead:
When all the birds are faint with the hot sun,
And hide in cooling trees, a voice will run
From hedge to hedge about the new-mown mead;
That is the Grasshopper's—he takes the lead
In summer luxury,—he has never done
With his delights; for when tired out with fun
He rests at ease beneath some pleasant weed.
The poetry of earth is ceasing never:
On a lone winter evening, when the frost
Has wrought a silence, from the stove there shrills
The Cricket's song, in warmth increasing ever,
And seems to one in drowsiness half lost,
The Grasshopper's among some grassy hills.

Now contrast the poems by Carroll and Keats with the last stanza of
Matthew Arnold's "Dover Beach." Here you confront complex emotions
—darkness and melancholy leavened by the affirmation of an enduring
value.

Ah, love, let us be true
To one another! for the world, which seems
To lie before us like a land of dreams,
So various, so beautiful, so new,
Hath really neither joy, nor love, nor light,
Nor certitude, nor peace, nor help for pain;
And we are here as on a darkling plain
Swept with confused alarms of struggle and flight,
Where ignorant armies clash by night.

Finally, we perceive stark, unrelieved despair in these lines from Shakespeare's *Macbeth.*

Tomorrow, and tomorrow, and tomorrow,
Creeps in this petty pace from day to day
To the last syllable of recorded time,
And all our yesterdays have lighted fools
The way to dusty death. Out, out, brief candle!
Life's but a walking shadow, a poor player
That struts and frets his hour upon the stage
And then is heard no more; it is a tale
Told by an idiot, full of sound and fury,
Signifying nothing.

Sometimes the authentic mood of a poem is not easy to discover. It may be half-concealed and elusive. It may lurk in a word or a metaphor, in the music and rhythm of the language. Should you find that the essential feeling eludes you, either consult somebody who can help you or choose something else that is within the range of your understanding.

KNOW THE STRUCTURE OF YOUR SELECTION

Meaning and mood will emerge more clearly if you analyze the design of a work. Lincoln's Gettysburg Address offers a classic example. On this occasion, Lincoln wanted to do two things: to honor the heroic sons, husbands, and fathers who had been killed, and to state the case for democracy. In order to blend these two purposes into one unifying theme, he developed his haunting metaphor of birth, death, and rebirth—in the life of man and in the life of a nation. Thus Lincoln not only suggested the historical parallels between the life of a man and a nation, but he projected his faith in eternal democracy by linking it with man's aspirations for eternal life.

We gain a sharper perception of a writer's or speaker's purpose and meaning by exploring the structural artistry of his work. Is the work composed of a chain of arguments, or is it discursively topical as in a familiar essay? Is it didactic exposition, or does it unfold through a succession of poetical metaphors? Does the work move on one plane, or does it build to a climax? Your interpretation of thought and mood may be greatly influenced by questions you ask about the structure of a work.

READ EXPERIMENTALLY BEFORE YOU READ TO AN AUDIENCE

Having analyzed the thought, mood, and structure of a work, test the results of your study by reading the work aloud to yourself. Listen critically to your reading, and, if possible, make a tape recording or get the reactions of a friend. You may discover a great gulf between the way you want to read and the way it actually comes off.

First read through your selection without stopping, to catch the swing of the author's style and to locate trouble spots. A sentence that gives no trouble to the eye may prove sticky on the tongue: "Complex statistical statements excite us less than sensitively selected examples." Other things come to light—long, winding sentences that need to be punctuated by inflections; a patch of choppy phrases that needs to be smoothed out orally; a switch in the rhythm to which you must adapt.

Work on the specific problems you turn up. Slow down as you move through tongue-tangling sentences, and sharpen your enunciation. Pay attention to the way you group words. Stammering, illogical groupings break the thought and drive listeners to distraction. For example, "It has / been said / that / the Russians / have / given to science / some of / the aura that / they have denied / to religion." A more natural grouping would be, "It has been said / that the Russians have given to science / some of the aura that they have denied to religion." In addition to natural grouping, spot the sentences and passages that need to be highlighted, and experiment with several ways of giving them prominence. An increase in volume of voice is not the only way to gain emphasis. A change in rate or pitch, or a pause, may be a better way.

Reading smoothly, of course, is not enough. As you experiment, concentrate on communicating faithfully the facts, ideas, and images of your material. Factual material calls for clarity, accuracy, and objectivity. Be especially careful to avoid injecting personal attitudes into reportorial reading. "The governor suggested that the budget for the next fiscal year will require a slight and temporary increase in the sales tax" is a simple, straightforward statement. But if phrases such as "the governor" and "slight and temporary increases" are doctored with inflections, the meaning is colored by the reader's attitudes of admiration or derision.

Give ideas the stature they deserve. Suppose you were to read these lines from John Milton's *Areopagitica:* "Though all the winds of doctrine were let loose to play upon the earth, so Truth be in the field, we do ingloriously, by licensing and prohibiting, to misdoubt her strength. Let her and Falsehood grapple: Who ever knew Truth put to the worse in a free and open encounter?" Here is a ringing declaration of faith, not a mundane statement of fact. When sentiment and ideas are majestic, your reading should endow them with impressiveness. Conversely, avoid giving an idea an importance greater than it warrants. It would sound pretty silly if Joe were to announce his plans to walk to the corner grocery store as if he were embarking on an expedition into outer space.

The imagery of a work will be more vivid if you re-create sensory experiences that are similar to those indicated by the writer. You may not have had exactly the experience he describes, but you can approximate it by drawing on your memory and imagination. Let your mind's eye see "a crowd, a host, of golden daffodils . . . tossing their heads in sprightly dance," about which Wordsworth writes. Let yourself see, touch, and smell "the strong crust of friendly bread" about which Rupert Brooke writes. And "the cool kindliness of sheets," "live hair that is shining and free," "the musty reek that lingers about dead leaves." Consider the extreme distress that Coleridge describes in these lines:

> And every tongue, through utter drought,
> Was wither'd at the root;
> We could not speak, no more than if
> We had been choked with soot.

It's unlikely that you have ever had such a desperately parched feeling, but you do know what it's like to be thirsty. Recall the circumstance, and re-create accurately the specific sensations you felt at the time. Heightening your own empathic responses to a writer's imagery enables you to read with a vividness that is likely to stimulate listeners to re-create comparable sensory experiences of their own.

SOME PRACTICAL CONSIDERATIONS

PREPARING COPY

Even under ideal conditions it is hard to read small print set in lines tightly squeezed together. The problem is compounded when you read to an audience. Whenever the printed page is unsatisfactory, take the time to type up the material for the occasion. Typed copy, double spaced, is preferable to copy that you write out in longhand.

ESTABLISHING A CONTEXT FOR YOUR READING

When the material you are reading is just a small part of your whole speech, work it in through easy transitions. But when the reading is the main business at hand, work up a short extemporaneous introduction that identifies your selection and its author, stimulates interest in the selection, and establishes a congenial mood for your reading. You may or may not need to develop a conclusion of your own. Much depends on the material, your purpose in reading, and the circumstances.

INTERPOLATING COMMENTS

If you are reading instructions or obscure technical material, stop and clarify the important points as you go along. Sometimes you may want to interrupt your reading momentarily to underscore your author's point in your own words. In short, feel free to interpolate your own comments whenever they will add significantly to your audience's interest, understanding, and appreciation. Refrain, however, from intruding excessively with comments of your own. You can ruin the fine edge of a poem, story, or a particularly well-written article with a disruptive commentary.

HANDLING YOUR MATERIALS WHILE READING

If you plan to read here and there in an article or book, always mark your places beforehand. You will be embarrassed and your audience will grow anxious if you have to fumble around while trying to find your place. These awkward moments dissipate any success you may have won up to that point.

The clumsy handling of a book, magazine, or manuscript may be enought to spoil an otherwise effective reading. The ideal is to manipulate these materials so that your listeners are hardly aware of them. If you are using a speaker's stand, you may want to place your materials there and leave them there. If you like more freedom and mobility, then hold your magazine or book in one hand. Hold it high enough so that you can read it easily, and a bit to one side so that you can see your audience readily. Avoid holding it up so high that it covers your face, or so low that your body looks like a question mark. Never let the book, magazine, or whatever you are using block your line of vision. If you are well prepared, you should be able to look directly at your audience most of the time.

QUESTIONS FOR DISCUSSION

1. Chapters 5 and 14 can profitably be studied together with this chapter. Discuss the following questions relating to this suggestion:
    a. What is the role of voice and diction in reading aloud either your own or another's composition?
    b. What reciprocal values for the effective use of voice and diction can be gained by reading aloud?
    c. What gains in oral language and style can be expected by composing speech in writing and reading aloud?
    d. What values do you see in oral reading other than potential improvement in voice and diction and oral composition?
2. Discuss the relationships among public speaking, the oral interpretation of literature, and acting. How do they differ as modes of communication? Does competence in one contribute to competence in the others?

EXERCISES

1. Make a brief report on the content of an article or a book you have read recently. Read aloud selected pasages that point up the writer's ideas in a way that will bring them home to your listeners.

2. Take a somewhat technical piece of writing that you understand and think you can explain to your audience. Skillfully weave in enough interpolations to make it clear.

3. Write out a speech or report of your own. Maintain your best oral style in your writing. Read it aloud to the class. Be as communicative as you can. See if you can make the audience forget you are reading from a manuscript.

4. Choose one of the sample speeches that appear at the end of this book for reading aloud to the class. Analyze it and practice reading it beforehand.

5. Poetry that deals in values people live by offers fine opportunities to combine reading and speaking. Robert Frost's "Mending Wall" is a good example. Prepare your own introduction to such a poem. Give your introduction extemporaneously and then read the poem.

6. Choose a play, speech, poem, or story that has been read aloud by someone else and has been recorded. Familiarize yourself with the work before you listen to it. Then listen several times to the recording. Evaluate the skill of the reader. Did your reactions to the way the work was read change after successive listening experiences? Could you suggest ways in which the reading might be improved?

23. Speaking in Public

We have been talking about the principles and methods of public speaking all through this book. But now we shall deal with some of the special forms and the conventional procedures and amenities associated with them. This information will help you apply what you already know about public speaking in situations that call for special adaptations—public deliberation, public policy making, and speeches for special occasions.

PUBLIC DELIBERATION

Dealing with public questions in a way that will induce learning and understanding is one of the most important functions of public speech. Inquiry, reporting, and advocacy serve this function. Here are some adaptations of these basic methods that are useful in public deliberation.

PANEL DISCUSSION

This is an ingenious device for conducting group discussion in the hearing of an audience. We are all familiar with the unique values of give-and-take discussion in small, intimate, face-to-face groups. Panel discussion attempts to achieve these same values for larger groups.

The members of the panel, usually four to eight people, sit in a semicircle facing the audience, preferably around a table on a raised platform. The panel leader opens the discussion and acts as chairman. He tells the audience what the panel is going to discuss, introduces the members, and starts the discussion by asking a question or two.

The panel discusses the subject in conversation among themselves much as they would in private discussion, but they must never forget that they are talking for the benefit of the audience. They must speak clearly and loudly enough to be heard easily, and they must keep the discussion moving along at a brisk pace. The steps in reflective thinking explained in Chapter 18 provide a good general pattern for the discussion.

This kind of public conversation requires speakers who are both articulate and well informed. At its best, it is a lively interchange among knowledgeable people who hold different points of view and are prepared to explore their differences cooperatively.

THE SYMPOSIUM

A symposium is usually made up of three to five persons who deliver short speeches on a problem in front of an audience. Its chief difference from the panel is that it uses public speeches rather than group discussion. And it differs from public debate in that it uses the methods of inquiry and reporting rather than the methods of advocacy. The purpose of a symposium is to instruct and to increase understanding, not to persuade.

A symposium opens up a problem and gives it a thorough airing. The best way to do this is to have each speaker explain his point of view on the problem as a whole. Another way—though usually less effective—is to assign a different phase of the problem to each speaker. The first speaker defines and lays out the problem, the second analyzes it, and the others suggest various solutions.

The leader of the symposium simply acts as chairman. He introduces the speakers, makes a few opening remarks, fills in between successive speeches, winds things up after the last speaker has finished, and takes charge of the question-and-answer period.

DEBATE

Debate is a familiar method of public deliberation in which speakers oppose each other on propositions of public interest. The debater uses the methods of advocacy. Admittedly partisan, he tries to win support for his position. Listeners benefit from the chance to hear different points of view advanced and defended—an experience that helps them to extend their own knowledge and thinking on the question being debated. In addition to these educational values, a good debate often provides stimulating entertainment.

Ordinarily, the opposing debaters speak from the same platform on the same occasion, and the debate is conducted according to procedures agreed upon in advance. Often, however, there are public debates in which the opposing speakers never meet each other face to face. In a sense, a national political campaign is a running debate that stretches out over several weeks or months. The candidates take sharp issue on public questions and pursue their interests in speech after speech, reply and counter-reply, before audiences all over the nation.

The essentials of a good debate are a carefully worded proposition or resolution, one or more speakers who support this proposition (the affirmative), one or more speakers who oppose it (the negative), and arrangements that permit opposing speakers to develop their cases and reply to each other. In a properly planned debate, the proposition is phrased so that the affirmative has the burden of proof (see p. 207) and has the opportunity to open and close the debate. Here are some suggestions for arranging debates.

THE TWO-SPEAKER DEBATE

Affirmative constructive speech	10 minutes
Negative rejoinder (reply and constructive case)	14 minutes
Affirmative rebuttal	4 minutes

THE TEAM DEBATE

Constructive Speeches		Rebuttal Speeches	
First affirmative	10 minutes	First negative	5 minutes
First negative	10 minutes	First affirmative	5 minutes
Second affirmative	10 minutes	Second negative	5 minutes
Second negative	10 minutes	Second affirmative	5 minutes

THE CROSS-QUESTION DEBATE

The first affirmative presents the entire affirmative case	20 minutes
The first negative questions the first affirmative	10 minutes
The second negative presents the entire negative case	20 minutes
The second affirmative questions the second negative	10 minutes
The first negative presents the negative rebuttal	10 minutes
The second affirmative presents the affirmative rebuttal	10 minutes

In a good debate, no matter what arrangements are prescribed, the debaters hold close to the issues and make adaptations and replies to the arguments of their opponents throughout the debate. This requires a thorough knowledge of the ins and outs of the subject, analytical and tactical skills, and, above all, competence in extemporaneous public speaking.

THE OPEN FORUM

Every panel discussion, debate, and symposium requires an audience. Ideally, the members of the audience should be more than a group of passive onlookers. They should be brought in as active participants. The best way to let the listeners have their say is to arrange for an open forum after the regular program. This is a question-and-answer period conducted by the discussion leader or chairman.

One way to conduct on open forum is to have members of the audience write questions on slips of paper and send them up to the chairman. During a brief recess, the chairman can sift through the questions and arrange them in logical order. Written questions cut short the cranks and the frustrated orators who have their own little speeches all prepared.

But a better way is to invite questions from the floor. This makes for livelier, more spontaneous discussion. One question suggests another, and the audience has a chance to hear each question as it is presented. The chairman should keep the proceedings as informal as possible and should have the questions put directly to speakers on the platform. He should intervene only to clear up confusion or misunderstanding, or to decide which member of the audience has the floor when several speak at once.

Most audiences take a lively interest in the question-and-answer period. But if the leader suspects that an audience may be slow to respond, he may sum up the discussion in a way that spotlights vital and controversial issues. He may ask a few questions of his own that will suggest others to the audience. Or he may put the first question to one of the speakers. But he must never hint that he expects to have a hard time in getting questions from the audience. Once the forum is under way, the leader should be content to repeat questions that are inaudible, help clarify ambiguous questions, and keep each question and answer within reasonable time limits.

PUBLIC POLICY MAKING

Policy making goes beyond deliberation for educational purposes. Any policy-making body must express the will of the group in the form of specific decisions. It must come up with a firm conclusion on which other people can act. The policy-making groups with which you are most familiar are committees, boards, councils, and legislative bodies. Actually, any organized group or public assembly can adopt resolutions and take whatever actions its needs and interests may dictate. Many of these groups have their own procedural rules. Here are some tips on committee procedure and parliamentary debate that apply to most of the situations you are likely to face.

COMMITTEE PROCEDURE

Large legislative assemblies seldom talk through problems in full session, for too many participants make the discussion unwieldy. Instead, legislatures usually refer problems to committees for investigation and recommendation.

In the early stages of its work, at least, it is wise for a committee to proceed as a discussion group. If the discussion leads to a solution on which the members agree, their job is done; all they have to do is report their findings to the larger group. Very often this is exactly what takes place in a committee, especially where the members are accustomed to cooperative procedures and united in their desire to find the best answer to the problem.

If disagreement develops and persists, however, then the chairman of the committee should call for motions and conduct debate on these motions until a majority decision is reached (see below).

A committee uses formal debate only as a last resort after making every attempt to keep the discussion informal and cooperative. If the chairman calls for formal motions at the very outset, he runs the danger of crystallizing differences of opinion that might have been resolved in the opening discussion. An even greater danger is that the group may fail to analyze the problem carefully, because it has been hurried into a decision before developing the information and understanding it needs.

PARLIAMENTARY DEBATE

Parliamentary debate is the most useful method of determining policy in any large assembly. Recommendations for consideration may come from committees or be initiated by any member of the assembly. In either case, these recommendations are presented as motions for debate and action. Often, agenda are worked out in advance to determine the order of business.

Most policy-determining groups use the standard rules of parliamentary procedure to govern debate. You are already familiar with some of these rules. They are used in class meetings, clubs, fraternities, and wherever business is conducted in public meetings. If you are hazy about these rules, it will be worth your while to get them firmly in mind. There are many excellent manuals on parliamentary law, but the brief résumé below will suffice for most occasions.

The *principal motion* is used to introduce a proposal when there is no other motion before the assembly. The maker of the motion states his proposal and may, if he chooses, explain it. The motion itself should be a clear, unambiguous proposal that the secretary can record in his minutes. If the motion is seconded, it is then thrown open to debate. During debate, *subsidiary motions* may be applied to the principal motion. For example, someone may move that the principal motion be amended; then the motion to amend becomes the subject of the debate. If this amendment is carried, then the principal motion as amended is before the house. Merely passing an amendment does not mean that the principal motion has been passed.

Each of the six *subsidiary motions* in the accompanying table takes precedence over those above it and yields to those below. Of the subsidiary motions, "the previous question" is puzzling to some people. Its purpose is to stop debate. In most assemblies, all you have to do is call for the question if you want to halt debate and get a vote on the resolution before the house. But if somebody objects to this method of stopping debate, you may then offer a formal motion to have the previous question brought to a vote. If your motion is seconded and carried by a two-thirds vote, the chairman must then put the question itself to a vote.

TABLE OF PARLIAMENTARY MOTIONS

Motions	Need a Second?	Amend-able?	Debatable	Vote Required	May Interrupt a Speaker
I. Principal Motion					
1. Any main question or any independent matter of business before the meeting	yes	yes	yes	maj.	no
II. Subsidiary Motions					
2. To amend	yes	yes	yes	maj.	no
3. To postpone indefinitely	yes	no	yes	maj.	no
4. To refer to a committee	yes	yes	yes	maj.	no
5. To postpone to a certain time	yes	yes	yes	maj.	no
6. Previous question	yes	no	no	2/3	no
7. To lay on (or take from) the table	yes	no	no	maj.	no
III. Incidental Motions					
8. To suspend a rule	yes	no	no	2/3	no
9. To withdraw a motion	yes	no	no	maj.	no
10. Question of consideration	no	no	no	2/3	yes
11. A point of order	no	no	no	Chair*	yes
12. Appeal from decision of chair	yes	no	no	maj.	yes
IV. Privileged Motions					
13. To make a matter of business a "special order" for a given time	no	no	no	2/3	yes
14. Questions of rights and privileges	no	no	no	Chair*	yes
15. To adjourn (unqualified)	yes	no	no	maj.	no
16. To fix time for next meeting	yes	yes	no	maj.	no

*Requires only decision of Chair; no vote unless appealed.

Source: Quoted with some changes from Gregg's *Handbook of Parliamentary Law* (Boston: Ginn and Company, 1910) in J. M. O'Neill, ed., *Foundations of Speech* (Englewood Cliffs, N.J.: Prentice-Hall, Inc., 1941), p. 395.

Incidental motions arise out of other motions. Their purpose is to make it easier for these motions to be considered. The order in which they are listed in the table is not significant.

Privileged motions have to do with the general conduct of the meeting. They arise independently of other motions and take precedence over them. However, any incidental motion or subsidiary motion that is properly applied to the privileged motion itself takes precedence over the privileged motion to which it is applied.

For speed and convenience in using the table of motions, we have listed below the specific purpose or object of each motion in the table.

OBJECTS OF MOTIONS[1]

1. Main motion—to bring original business before the assembly.
2. To amend—to modify a question that is before the assembly.
3. To postpone indefinitely—(a) to dispose of a question for the session without voting on it directly; (b) used by the opponents of a question to determine their strength.
4. To refer to a committee—to secure the advantage of action by a smaller group, or of greater freedom in debate in dealing with a question.
5. To postpone to a certain time—to defer action on a question to some future time.
6. Previous question—to suppress debate and bring the assembly to a vote.
7. To lay on the table—(a) to postpone a subject so that it may be taken up at another time during the same session; (b) to stop debate and suppress a question for the session, provided a majority cannot be secured to take the question again from the table.
8. To suspend a rule—to make temporarily possible an action contrary to the standing rules or rules of order of an organization.
9. To withdraw a motion—to expedite business in case of a changed opinion by the maker of the motion.
10. Question of consideration—an objection to the consideration of a question to enable the assembly to avoid irrelevant, unprofitable, or contentious questions.
11. A point of order—to correct a breach of order or an error in procedure.
12. Appeal from decision of chair—(a) to invoke a rule that the chairman has ignored or misinterpreted; (b) to appeal to the assembly to overrule the chairman on any rule where an opinion or a judgment may be exercised.
13. Special order—to set a specific time to consider a certain matter of business when all other things will be set aside.
14. Questions of rights and privileges—to secure to the assembly or any of its members some right with respect to safety, comfort, dignity, reputation, or freedom from disturbance.

[1]From J. M. O'Neill, ed., *Foundations of Speech* (Englewood Cliffs, N.J.: Prentice-Hall, Inc., 1941).

15. To adjourn—to bring a meeting to a close.
16. To fix time for next meeting—to fix a time or place for reassembling.

Debate for the purpose of determining policy follows the methods of advocacy. Even though it follows the formal rules that we have outlined here, it is still debate. If you make a motion, you must state it clearly and assume the responsibility for defending it. Any motion is vulnerable unless you can present a convincing defense of it when the opposition raises objections. Opponents of the motion will defeat it if they can attack it successfully on one or more vital counts.

SPEECHES FOR SPECIAL OCCASIONS

Some speeches are designed primarily to recognize special occasions and to strengthen our ties with our fellow men. Often you are under something of an artistic obligation in handling these courtesies. Poise, graciousness, and appropriateness in style and manner are especially important on such occasions. The methods of evocation are appropriate to speeches for these occasions.

SPEECHES OF INTRODUCTION

When you introduce a speaker to an audience, your job is to establish good speaking relationships between him and his listeners. Think of yourself as a go-between, a situation-maker, not as a principal in the show.

Find out all you can beforehand about the person you are introducing. If possible, talk with him and with people who know him. Track down some reliable biographical sketches, but don't try to use everything you gather together. Don't make your introduction sound like a paragraph from *Who's Who*. If the audience doesn't know much about the speaker, choose information that will identify him, establish his qualifications to speak, and make him liked as a person. If you can, let the audience see for themselves what kind of a person he is by telling an anecdote that puts him in a favorable light. If he is already well known, keep your introduction short and concentrate on the warm sentiments the audience feels toward him.

Above all, be accurate. You may have heard introductions in which the speaker's name was mispronounced or completely garbled. Not every speaker can transform a blunder into a pleasantry, as Rabbi Stephen Wise did when he was introduced as Rabbi Mann. "These days," he retorted, "it's a wise man who knows his own name."

Avoid a long speech. Remember, the audience came to hear the main speaker, not you.

SPEECHES OF WELCOME AND FAREWELL

You are a member of an organization or a community that is playing host to visitors, and you are selected to represent the host group. Make your greetings cordial and try to use a little originality. Most speeches on these occasions are dismally trite and are delivered in an inflated or perfunctory manner. Be direct, sincere, and brisk.

Make it clear that you really know whom you are welcoming, what they stand for, and what they have contributed. If the visitors represent a group dedicated to an ideal or to a program of public service, give your talk an inspirational note. Make your visitors feel at home. Show your hospitality by pointing out the services and facilities at their disposal, and the attractions and special events that will add to their pleasure. End by wishing your guests a pleasant and profitable stay.

Speeches of farewell are given at dinners or other ceremonies honoring someone who is leaving the group. When you make such a speech, feel free to reminisce about the past, express the esteem in which the departing person is held, and extend the group's good wishes.

What if you are the person who is departing? Here you have a chance to show publicly your affection and respect for the friends you are leaving, and to express appreciation for the pleasant associations you have had with them. If you have a personal philosophy that you want to share, this is a perfect occasion to put it into words. In short, show that you have responded warmly to your friends' sentiment.

SPEECHES OF COMMEMORATION

Every society has certain anniversaries that it commemorates with special speeches. For example, we celebrate the Fourth of July, Memorial Day, United Nations Day, and the birthdays of distinguished men and women. Ordinarily, you will key a speech of commemoration to the immediate occasion, unless it is understood that you are free to use the occasion as a springboard to some related subject. If you are dedicating a park, talk about the work of the people who made it possible, about its values and uses for the community. If you are commemorating United Nations Day, build your talk around the history, purposes, work, and accomplishments of the organization. If you are offering a tribute, invite your listeners to look again at the life and career of the person whom you are praising.

But don't make your speech of commemoration a bloodless catalogue of facts. Go about it in an inspirational manner. Stir your listeners to contemplation and help them to look at the event, deed, or life as a symbol.

SPEECHES OF PRESENTATION AND ACCEPTANCE

These talks reflect the prevailing mood of the occasion. They put into words what everyone is feeling. A football banquet at which varsity letters are awarded invites lightness and gaiety. When the senior class presents a gift to the college, dignity is the order of the day. Occasions of this sort are often charged with sentiment. But if you are making a speech of presentation, you must keep a nice balance between what you are feeling and what good taste permits. Suggest the appropriate sentiment, but don't parade it.

Bring out the reasons that have prompted the gift or award. For example, assume that you and your associates are honoring the school physician for long and faithful service. First, suggest the group's feelings toward him. Then supply the reasons for these feelings—reasons that grow out of his years of service to the group. You might climax your talk with a short citation, then present the gift or award.

A speech of acceptance should measure up to what is expected by those who are making the gift. A simple "thank you" is enough when numerous awards are handed out at one time, as at an honors convocation. If you are accepting an award in behalf of an organization, express your appreciation for the entire group and say why the award will be meaningful to all the other members. Single out the individuals who contributed most toward winning the award. If a presentation is being made to you personally, your acceptance should be a simple, sincere statement of gratitude. Speak of the gift as a symbol of mutual esteem and affection.

AFTER-DINNER SPEECHES

Many after-dinner speeches are serious talks on serious subjects. Each day countless reports, political speeches, and other forms of serious speaking take place at mealtime. But most people associate the term *after-dinner speaking* with entertainment, and that is the sense in which we shall use it here.

Everything we said in Chapter 21 about speaking to entertain applies to after-dinner speeches. Look for a theme that lends itself to the light touch and that will make it easy for you to hold attention agreeably for a specified time. Your talk need not be predominantly humorous, but it should offer some chances for humor. Make it sprightly throughout. Concentrate on making what you have to say interesting in its own right, and let the humor show itself naturally from time to time.

QUESTIONS FOR DISCUSSION

1. Many of the readers of this book will be familiar with school debates and intercollegiate debates. We raise the question here: What are the values of such debate? If we may answer our own question, *the principal value lies in teaching students how to debate!* Competence in debate is an

enormously useful skill, because debate—legislative or parliamentary debate—is a principal policy-determining method in our society. Problems of all sorts are a given datum in human experience. They arise in any group —family, club, or elected representative assemblies. When these problems present themselves as questions of value and policy on which disagreement persists, the most viable procedure, short of orders, commands and other authoritarian methods, is *debate*. In formal situations you make motions, debate these motions, and yield to majority votes. In other situations you do the same thing less formally.

Debate is inherently competitive advocacy and, like other competitions, is open to abuse. Properly conducted training in debate will teach students how to minimize these abuses. In any case, it is completely fatuous to contend that we can conduct our affairs in a democratic society without recourse to debate when less competitive methods fail to yield a working consensus.

    a. Discuss this case for debate. Do you agree or disagree?

    b. What other values do you see in debate?

    c. What are the principal abuses and limitations?

2. Discuss the following statements:

One way of describing democracy is to call it a system that provides for the management of public business by public discussion.[2]

The essential need is the improvement of the methods and conditions of debate, discussion, and persuasion.[3]

EXERCISES

1. Organize the class in small groups. Some groups will plan panel discussions; others will plan symposiums. A group may choose to discuss a new book, a political question, the implications of a scientific discovery, a philosophical problem, and so forth. Devote one class period to each panel or symposium. Reserve time for questions from the class and for criticism.

2. Plan a series of debates in which each type of debate is represented. Select propositions that can be debated without extraordinary preparation. Don't overlook the possibility of campus problems.

3. Have the class select several controversial problems, and let several students prepare speeches of advocacy on each of them. Elect a chairman

[2]Lyman Boyson, "Discussion in the Democratic Process," (unpublished lecture, Symposium in Public Speaking, Northwestern University, 1938), p. 1.
[3]John Dewey, *The Public and Its Problems* (New York: Henry Holt and Company, 1927), p. 208.

for each period, and reserve half the period for an open forum following the speeches. Have a short critique on the prepared speeches and the open forum.

4. Devote two or more class periods to parliamentary debate. Organize the meeting and elect officers. Members of the class should come prepared to offer motions, experiment with the table of motions, and debate those that admit of debate. In the first period, appoint committees with responsibility for reporting at the next meeting. Committee reports offer opportunities for further parliamentary action.

5. Plan short talks that introduce people from many stations and walks of life. Evaluate the talks in terms of the propriety with which the people are introduced.

6. Prepare a tribute to some person. Choose someone from one of the following fields who is already well known to the class and whom you admire.

Politics	Science	Social work
Literature	Entertainment	Education
Art	Industry	Religion
Medicine	Agriculture	Communications
Engineering	Law	Sports

24. Microphone and Camera

We live in an age of electronics—of public-address systems, radio microphones, and television cameras. Doubtless, you will be called upon to use one of these devices at one time or another. So it is worth your while to learn how to get the best results from them. Good speech remains good speech whether or not you are speaking before a microphone or camera. *But there are important differences.* This chapter will tell you about the adaptations you need to make in your regular speech habits if you are to speak before the microphone and the camera with assurance and competence.

THE PUBLIC-ADDRESS SYSTEM

Amplification of your voice is often helpful, and when you are speaking in large auditoriums or out-of-doors it may be essential. On such occasions a public-address system in good working order with an experienced operator at the controls is often the only means of getting through to your audience.

But don't use a public-address system if you can make yourself heard easily without it. Without a microphone you are freer to move around the platform, and you avoid erecting a physical barrier between yourself and your audience. If you can speak without strain and be heard without strain, you will establish closer rapport with your audience without an amplifying system.

The principal advantage of a public-address system, apart from simple audibility, is that it enables you to talk to a large audience more intimately than you could without it. It lets you speak with exactly the same volume and inflections you would use in talking to a small group. In fact, you will get very poor results if you depart from the conversational level of speaking. Don't forget that you are using the system and begin to shout into the microphone as if you were trying to project your voice to

potential? The intellectuals who can draw upon their rational disinterested approach and their fund of learning to help reshape our political life can make a tremendous contribution to their society while gaining new respect for their own group.

I do not say that our political and public life should be turned over to experts who ignore public opinion. Nor would I adopt from the Belgian Constitution of 1893 the provision giving three votes instead of one to college graduates; or give Harvard a seat in the Congress as William and Mary was once represented in the Virginia House of Burgesses.

But, I would urge that our political parties and our universities recognize the need for greater cooperation and understanding between politicians and intellectuals. We do not need scholars or politicians like Lord John Russell, of whom Queen Victoria remarked, he would be a better man if he knew a third subject—but he was interested in nothing but the Constitution of 1688 and himself. What we need are men who can ride easily over broad fields of knowledge and recognize the mutual dependence of our two worlds.

"Don't teach my boy poetry," an English mother recently wrote the Provost of Harrow. "Don't teach my boy poetry; he is going to stand for Parliament." Well, perhaps she was right—but if more politicians knew poetry, and more poets knew politics, I am convinced the world would be a little better place to live on this Commencement Day of 1956.

A SPEECH OF EVOCATION: "A NEW DEAL FOR DAD"[4]

ADLAI E. STEVENSON

I have come here today not so much to accept an award as to strike a much needed blow for fatherhood in America.

There was a time when father amounted to something in the United States. He was held with some esteem in the community; he had some authority in his own household; his views were sometimes taken seriously by his children; and even his wife paid heed to him from time to time.

In recent years, however, especially since World War II, father has come upon sorry times. He is the butt of the comic strips; he is the boob of the radio and TV serials; and the favorite stooge of all our professional comedians.

In short, life with father seems to have degenerated into a continuous sequence of disrespect or tolerance at best. It appears that the poor fellow is unable to hang a picture or hit a nail without some mishap; no radio or

[4]Remarks to the National Father's Day Committee, New York City, May 25, 1961. Text taken from Adlai E. Stevenson, *Looking Outward,* ed. Robert L. Schiffer and Selma Schiffer (New York: Harper & Row, Publishers, 1963), pp. 273–76. Reprinted by permission.

clock will ever work again after he fixes it; he can't boil water or even barbecue a steak, at least not without burning it.

Every time the so-called head of the household attempts to assert himself or express his opinions, the whole family is convulsed with indulgent if not scornful laughter.

Personally, I think all this has gone far enough, and father certainly needs his Day! So all of us fathers should be grateful to you for contriving this brief hour of recognition. I am honored that you have chosen me, a father and a grandfather.

I do not think we would want father restored to his nineteenth-century role of absolute monarch, but, even though we don't want him to be the autocrat of the breakfast table, I think we might consider giving him at least a polite seat at the table.

After forty or fifty years of life, after hard experience in the world of affairs, after education both in college and in the school of hard knocks, and after sweating away at earning a living for the whole family, it is conceivable that father could have learned a thing or two, and the rest of the family could listen to him with profit once in a while for the honor of raising a plaintive voice on behalf of so many. We might even have some better-behaved children if they did listen to him now and then. But of course I except my own children. I have to—or I might not survive Father's Day!

In all candor, I cannot say that I know for sure just how seriously my own children listen to me, but, God bless them, they at least pretend they do.

So all things considered, I have this suggestion to offer: Instead of a Father's Day, maybe we should try a Father's Year for a change. In any case, whatever we call it, let's have a New Deal for Dad!

Now it has been said the paternity is a career imposed on you one fine morning without any inquiry as to your fitness for it. That is why there are so many fathers who have children but so few children who have fathers.

Is there truth or cynicism in this remark? A bit of both, I imagine, but far too much of the former for my taste.

It is an all too visible truth that fatherhood is no longer the sacred duty it was once held to be. There are, today, far too many absentee fathers, fathers in name only. Paradoxically, and this is an insight into the nature of contemporary society, they are, in many cases, men whose ability, sense of responsibility and moral integrity outside the home are of the first order.

Apologists for these errant progenitors (in most instances, offenders themselves) have called up a multitude of rationalizations in their defense —two world wars in less than half a century, the pressures of modern urban life, business before pleasure, country before self and other tired old saws.

What nonsense. There is absolutely no excuse for a parent to abdicate his most important duty—the proper raising of his children. No father should be allowed to get away with the cowardly logic which concludes that his only job in the family is to pay for the bacon.

His role is much more grandiose than that. If it is to be properly fulfilled, he should be, in his realm, a man of many faces—an artist, a philosopher, a statesman and, above all, a prolific dispenser of good sense and justice.

But it is vitally important, especially in the early years, that his children see in father a working model of the social order in which, not so many years hence, they will be expected to play a dynamic part.

How can we, the parents, hope to secure a just and rational society if we neglect the development of those very instruments, our children, most necessary for its implementation? What good does it do to conceive grand moral, social or political plans for a better world if the children who will have to live them out fail to see their importance?

I know there are utopians who believe that human progress is inevitable, a divine trajectory irreversible in its upward motion. Let me just point out to them that in the last few thousand years we have blazed what I consider to be a trail of questionable glory—from Abraham and Isaac to Dennis the Menace.

I fear that no logic, no optimism can controvert the irrefutable equation that a father brings to his son what his son brings to the world. For sure, leaders in Soviet Union believe this. In Russia, children are barely out of diapers before the full attention of the stage is focused squarely upon them. They are prodded, led and coaxed through the intricate social, moral and political byways of the system into which they were born. By the time they reach maturity their values are crystallized and they know their duties as responsible Soviet citizens.

In a democracy—in America—the state does not presume to be the father of the man. That responsibility is left to our schools, our churches and, most of all, to our parents.

On the contrary, to our way of thinking, it is the individual who is destined to become the father of the state. And to succeed in his parenthood, he must himself be well trained.

In a very real sense, a father's relations with his children should be a microcosmic reflection of their relations with the society in which they live. Through his actions a father must teach his children the intrinsic meaning of the democratic concept—freedom with restraint and the nature of integrity.

Several years ago, at a "Father-and-Son Team of the Year" ceremony held by the National Father's Day Committee, the father was the first to speak and said:

> I claim no credit for my son being what he is ... people make their own intellectual and moral characters. If he was helped in making his by me ... it was he who decided to accept the help. The decision in such matters is finally with ourselves. To say that responsibility begins at home should mean, I think, that it begins—and ends, too—in the individual. Sooner or later he must help himself. There are no alibis.

The son then spoke of his father:

> He has been able to move me, to laughter and to tears, for as long as I can remember, both in public and in private—and that's of the greatest importance. For my father has been to me both a public and a private man.
>
> But my experience has reminded me of something that he taught me —not consciously, I'm sure, but as an example. For the extraordinary thing about my father is that his public face and his private face have been the same. He has been the same man to the world as he has been to his family. And that is harder than it sounds.
>
> It is the very definition of integrity, I suppose.

In modern society everyone faces in some degree the problem of making his public face the same as his private face.

How far any individual succeeds in this effort—which is indeed harder than it sounds—may be taken as a rough measure of "public ethics" for our time and place. Thus in an era of growing artificiality of tinsel and packaging and makeup, and "falsies" of mind and body, the highest compliment that can be paid to a public man is paradoxically that he is made of the same stuff all the way through, inside and out. The more public responsibility he carries, the more important it is to have a private face that can without embarrassment be displayed in public.

I hope no one asks my sons how I've performed in that respect.

Index